AF541432

THE LAST COLONY

Muzaffarabad-Gilgit-Baltistan

Editors
P. Stobdan
D. Suba Chandran

India Research Press
with
Centre for Strategic and Regional Studies
University of Jammu

THE LAST COLONY
P. Stobdan and D. Suba Chandran

India Research Press
Flat No. 6, Khan Market, New Delhi - 110 003
Ph.: 24694610; Fax : 24618637
www.indiaresearchpress.com
contact@indiaresearchpress.com; bahrisons@vsnl.com

2008

ISBN-13 digit : 978-81-8386-067-3
ISBN-10 digit : 81-8386-067-2

Cataloguing in Publication Data
P. Stobdan and D. Suba Chandran
The Last Colony

1. Jammu & Kashmir/J&K 2. Kashmir 3. Pakistan occupied Kashmir/PoK
4. Azad Kashmir 5. Pakistan 6. Gilgit & Baltistan 7. India 8. South Asia
9. Indo – Pak 10. Northern Areas
I. Title II. Author

Printed for *India Research Press* at Focus Impressions, New Delhi.

Contents

Foreword *v*

Introduction *ix*

About the Contributors *xiii*

About the CSRS *xvi*

CHAPTER 1
"Northern Areas": With Special Focus on Baltistan 3
P. Stobdan

CHAPTER 2
Jihadi Groups in PoK: Post-Earthquake Dynamics 39
Kanchan Lakshman

CHAPTER 3
Sectarian Violence in the Northern Areas 55
D. Suba Chandran

CHAPTER 4
Diamer-Basha and Mangla Dams: 87
The Emerging Water Conflict in PoK
Seema Sridhar

CHAPTER 5
Chinese Strategic Interests in PoK 125
Jabin T. Jacob

CHAPTER 6
Global Perspectives on PoK 159
A Critique of Human Rights Watch and
European Union Reports
Mathew Joseph C.

CHAPTER 7
Northern Areas: Myths, Politics and Facts 177
A Critique of ICG Report
D. Suba Chandran

CHAPTER 8
Political Development in PoK: A Chronology Since October 2005 — 203
Priyashree Andley

Index — 239

Foreword

We are at the cross roads of history. On the one hand, the international system is increasingly getting integrated through the process of globalization, and, on the other, there is a conflict of values and interests that seem to be driving the world apart. What will the future of the world look like? Will the international system emerge more stable and harmonious or will we descend into violent turmoil?

South Asia is no exception to this mega trend. . While some cities and sub regions are totally connected with the global network, some sub regions are yet to even enjoy the basic fruits of development and democracy. Under-development of a particular sub region has the potential to pull down the growth of its neighboring regions – politically, economically and culturally. While it is the duty of the State to ensure that the institutions in any region perform and deliver, the neighbors cannot remain silent spectators.

In Jammu and Kashmir, especially, the regions under Pakistan's control – Mirpur, Muzaffarabad and Gilgit are a paradox today. They have much in common with the rest of J&K. Mirpur and Muzaffarbad are linked to Jammu, Rajouri and Poonch districts – historically, culturally and emotionally. So is Gilgit and Skardu with Kargil and the rest of Ladakh. Unfortunately, in the last sixty years, these two sub regions of J&K, one with in India and the other occupied by Pakistan have grown politically with different outlooks.

Despite the democratic deficit in between and the militant upheaval since the 1980s, governmental institutions, political governance and secular fabric of J&K under India has remained positive and is progressing at a faster pace. Popular expression – political and separatist is allowed and even encouraged. The number of news papers published from Jammu and Srinagar, TV channels, including the private ones, and processions in the streets would highlight the level of popular expression at the ground level on the Indian side. In the long term, such expressions provide critical inputs to the governments, national and international communities to what is happening inside. Positive developments such as democratic elections, economic boom, tourist inflow and peace processes are welcomed, while negative developments such as violence and human right violations are condemned.

This process of internal and external assessments provides vital inputs to the State to reorient its policies and programmes. Unfortunately, we know little about those parts of J&K under Pakistan's control. How many news papers are published from Muzafarabad and Gilgit? How many news channels – private and State telecast their events from these two major cities? Are the anti-State expressions allowed to be expressed democratically or otherwise? Does Islamabad understand what is actually happening at the ground level in these regions. Is there an understanding or awareness of events in India, particularly in Jammu, Kashmir and Ladakh regions.

It is imperative for all the sub regions of J&K to know each other. Today, there are two bus services between Poonch and Rawlakot, and Srinagar and Muzaffarabad. Opening the LoC to allow people belonging to the divided families is a good beginning. Now people on both sides of the LoC could get first hand information about each other. But this interaction needs to be enlarged. Movement of people in general, instead of only divided families, should be allowed to cross. This movement should also be enlarged to include Jammu and Kargil districts. Movement of goods and tourists should follow. For more the interactions more will be the understanding of each other.

The academic community on both sides of the LoC has an important role to play in understanding each other. Institutions of higher education, especially the colleges and universities on both sides of the LoC could play a lead role on this most important issue. Exchange of students and scholars and exclusive departments and centers to study each other is the need of hour. Investments on such exchanges and studies, would help the two regions to understand each other and appreciate each others problems, besides bringing them together.

University of Jammu has been pioneering these efforts. It has hosted people from across the LoC for discussions, arranged internal conferences and has been publishing a magazine *Across LoC.* It is expected, in the near future, the University will also be able to invite students from across the LoC. This book is a part of that endeavor.

Amitabh Mattoo
VC"s Lodge
University of Jammu
November 2007

Introduction

There has been an increased international focus on Pakistan-occupied Kashmir (PoK) in recent years, especially after the October 2005 earthquake. A spectrum of credible international reports have appeared since then highlighting the plight of people inside PoK, which includes what Pakistan, calls "Azad Jammu and Kashmir" and "Northern Areas". The International Crisis Group (ICG), an independent research organisation based in Brussels, published a report titled *Discord in Pakistan's Northern Areas* in March 2007. Earlier in 2006, the Human Rights Watch (HRW) published a report titled *"With Friends Like These..." Human Rights Violations in Azad Kashmir.* Again in 2006, Baroness Emma Nicholson authored a report titled *Kashmir –Present Situation and Future Prospects*; the draft report was submitted to the European Union Parliament, which passed the same in May 2007, with an overwhelming majority.

Three developments have set off the sudden interest towards the region primarily comprising – Muzaffarabad, Gilgit and Baltistan. First, the devastating earthquake of October 2005, perhaps for the first time brought the international community, especially the donor agencies and NGOs into PoK for relief operations. They witnessed the lack of basic fundamental rights, absence of local participation in the administration and the over imposing role by Pakistan's military and its bureaucracy on the people. Besides, during the relief and rehabilitation programme they also witnessed the overwhelming control by the jihadi groups, especially of Muzaffarabad region.

Second, post 9/11, the spurt in *jihadi* activities inside Pakistan also coincided with the increased international anxiety over what is happening not only inside Pakistan, but also in its neighbourhood. Heightened activities on both sides of the Durand Line and the Line of Control came under sharp international scrutiny, as such to view the issues in the right perspective. The successful conduct of transparent elections in Jammu and Kashmir in 2002 and the subsequent changes in the State has broadened the international understanding of the ground situation. A comparison between the two parts of Kashmir in a holistic manner, therefore, became inevitable, as one could see in Emma Nicholson's report.

Third, sectarian violence in Gilgit and Baltistan in recent years has assumed disastrous proportions, with the State in Pakistan openly siding with one section. The perennial outburst of sectarian strife has exposed and alienated the population in Gilgit and Baltistan, besides absence of any basic rights from administration to justice. Emma Nicholson described the Northern Areas as "black holes".

It is imperative that India takes note of this changed atmosphere at the local and international levels. Muzaffarabad, Gilgit and Baltistan are legally a part of India and are of strategic importance to peace and security of the entire region. Available literature, published by the scholars in Pakistan has highlighted the *jihadi* infrastructure, training and influence in Muzaffarabad region. While there have been reports indicating that the infiltration has declined in recent years, the military and strategic community is not fully convinced that the jihadi infrastructure in this region is totally dismantled.

On the contrary, recent reports indicate the growth of a new phenomenon in this area – the growing influence of fundamentalist forces of Taliban variety. This issue came to the fore when the United Nations closed its operations and offices in Bagh district, as there were numerous attacks on its officials by fundamentalist forces. The UN announced: *In view of the current situation and the prevailing tension, the UN in Pakistan has decided to suspend work with immediate effect.* The threats are being issued by and through the Awami Action Forum (AAF), a local group; available open sources do not indicate, whether this AAF constitutes the local population or is imported from elsewhere with an element of local support. Officials belonging to the United Nations working in this area, however, have confirmed that there is an element of local support to the AAF by a few extremist religious leaders and even members of an opposition party. Their objective is to stop development projects in those areas that are hit by the earthquake.

There are larger implications of this growing radical influence in PoK. The immediate implication will be on the rehabilitation and reconstruction process. As mentioned earlier, such attacks, threats and closure of NGO activities will not only affect the ongoing projects, but also future ones.

Second, and in fact, the most important aspect of this episode is the long-term one in terms of local participation in community development projects. Like the rest of South Asia, there is so much of "State" in every aspect of development projects; as a result there is over dependence on the State as the provider of everything from roads to schools to water. In PoK, where democracy has been a charade, local participation has been worse or nil. The presence of NGOs – national and international is likely to change this situation in terms of allowing the locals to take part actively in the developmental projects rather than just being at the receiving end. Though in a limited sense, this is a process of empowerment, especially in rural areas. The exit of NGOs will stop this process. Perhaps, this is the primary idea behind the vested interests supporting the AAF.

Third, if the AAF succeeds in keeping the national and international NGOs forever, what will it mean for the society as a whole? Clearly, it will be seen as a success by the fundamentalist forces. Like Lal Masjid in Islamabad, there will be new additions in their orders; fatwas will expand the focus. The Kashmir society, cutting across the LoC has been the most liberal and moderate of all Muslim societies in South Asia. Now, there is a danger of creeping radicalisation on both sides of the LoC. If the AAF is taking care of moral policing in PoK, in Kashmir Valley, one witnessed the Dukhtaran-e-Millat going on an offensive during the last one year.

It is imperative to understand and analyse the changing dynamics across the LoC. This book is a part of the research activities being carried out on this impinging issue by the Centre for Strategic and Regional Studies (CSRS) with sponsorship of the Ministry of External Affairs, Government of India. This book may not be a comprehensive effort to explain all aspects of what is happening in PoK, but a beginning to understand some key issues and events. It is hoped, this book will raise further questions and debates. The CSRS also plans to make this a continuous process, in terms of bringing out further publications on the subject, by updating this and adding new subjects of interest.

P. Stobdan
D. Suba Chandran

Jammu
November, 2007

About the Contributors

Prof. PHUNCHOK STOBDAN is the Director, Centre for Strategic and Regional Studies (CSRS), University of Jammu. Earlier, he served as Director of Indian Cultural Centre and First Secretary, Embassy of India, Almaty (1999-2002) and was instrumental in broadening India's strategic and cultural interests in Central Asia. He has also served in the National Security Council Secretariat (NSCS), Government of India (2004-2005) and was a Senior Fellow, Institute for Defence Studies and Analyses (IDSA) New Delhi (2005-2006). He has written extensively on strategic affairs, both in India and abroad, and has authored over 150 papers including four books. He has represented India at various international conferences and bilateral dialogues, and contributed several policy inputs on key foreign/security issues to the government. He can be contacted at pstobdan@gmail.com.

Dr. MATHEW JOSEPH C. is Senior Lecturer at the Department of Strategic and Regional Studies, University of Jammu, Jammu and Kashmir. His research concerns include the issues related to the society and politics in Pakistan and Himalayan countries, especially Bhutan. He is currently engaged in a project on the impact of Islamisation on the state and civil society in Pakistan. He can be contacted at mathewjosephc@gmail.com.

Dr. D. SUBA CHANDRAN is Assistant Director at the Institute of Peace and Conflict Studies (IPCS), New Delhi and is currently a Visiting Fellow at the CSRS, University of Jammu. His primary area of research includes Pakistan's internal security, in particular Balochistan and FATA; and J&K. Since January 2007, he is undertaking field research in Kashmir on a study titled – *People, State and Violence: Conflict Transformation in Jammu and Kashmir.* He also edits an annual titled *Armed Conflicts and Peace Processes in South Asia.* He can be contacted at subachandran@gmail.com.

Dr. KANCHAN LAKSHMAN is a Research Fellow at the Institute for Conflict Management (ICM), New Delhi and Assistant Editor for the Institute's quarterly journal *Faultlines: Writings on Conflict and Resolution*. The primary focus of his research and documentation activities has been the terrorism in Jammu and Kashmir and in Pakistan. He has published extensively on issues related to terrorism and political violence in South Asia. He can be contacted at kanchanl@satp.org.

Mr. JABIN T. JACOB is a Research Fellow at the Institute of Peace and Conflict Studies (IPCS), New Delhi. He is pursuing his PhD from the School of International Studies, Jawaharlal Nehru University, New Delhi on centre-province and inter-province relations in China and from 2004-2006, was in the Mandarin Studies Programme at National Chengchi University, Taipei, Taiwan. His research interests include issues of East Asian political economy and Chinese relations with India, the US and Japan. He is currently engaged in a project on framing new perspectives for examining Sino-Indian relations. He can be contacted at jabin@ipcs.org.

Ms. SEEMA SRIDHAR is a research scholar at the School of International Studies, Jawaharlal Nehru University, New Delhi. Her research interests include Indo-Pak relations, in particular the bilateral water disputes and the peace process, Kashmir, Conflict resolution and peace-building. She is currently working on a study, "Autonomy as a Tool of Conflict Management: Conditions for J&K" to be published in an edited volume; a research paper on "Terrorism in Pakistan, post-9/11" for an edited book; and a paper titled "Global and Regional Hegemony: Dilemmas in Indian Foreign Policy". She writes regular columns for India News and Feature Alliance (INFA). She can be contacted at seema_seems@yahoo.com

Ms. PRIYASHREE ANDLEY is a Research Officer at the Institute of Peace and Conflict Studies (IPCS), New Delhi. Her research interests include Jammu and Kashmir, Pakistan and Conflict Resolution. She is currently working on two studies: the first on the Gujjars, an ethnic minority with tribal status in J&K; and the second on the role of Village Defence Committees (VDCs) in Jammu as a model for involving civilians in counterinsurgency operations. She writes a regular column – *Perspectives from New Delhi* on issues relating to J&K in a monthly magazine – *Epilogue*, published from J&K. She can be contacted at p.andley@gmail.com

About The Centre For Strategic And Regional Studies

The Centre for Strategic and Regional Studies (CSRS) at the University of Jammu (Jammu & Kashmir) has been conceived and established to undertake focused research on strategic issues, national security and geo-strategic developments in regions contiguous to India.

To achieve an effective synergy in its activities the CSRS has endeavoured to draw upon the expertise available in the well-developed social sciences faculties of economics, political science, history and sociology of the University of Jammu. Besides, a full-fledged visiting lecturers' programme and networking with other similar Centres/Institutes within the country and abroad ensures that CSRS stays abreast of the rapidly-transforming developments in the chosen niches of research on security issues. It organises national seminars periodically on various security issues related, besides regular seminars/discussions on current events. Recently, along with the Northern Command of the Indian Army, the CSRS organised a two-day conference on *Jammu and Kashmir and the Region.*

The Centre publishes a regular refereed biannual journal - *Security and Society;* the articles are written by scholars, retired bureaucrats and military personnel both from inside and outside the country. Besides, the CSRS has also produced books. Some of the recent publications include: *Pakistan in a New Strategic Environment* (New Delhi: Knowledge World) and *Central Asia: Current Challenges and Future Prospects* (New Delhi: Knowledge World).

The Centre also publishes *PoK Focus,* an electronic fortnightly comprising analysis, documents and news reports relating to Muzaffarabad, Gilgit and Baltistan.

CHAPTER 1

"Northern Areas" With Special Focus On Baltistan

Prof. P. Stobdan[1]

The so-called "Northern Areas" is the former Gilgit Agency, Gilgit Wazarat, Astor Wazarat and Skardu Tehsil of Ladakh Wazarat of the Jammu & Kashmir State. This region is spread over 72,496 square kilometres with a population of 5, 74,543 (in 1991).[2] Ever since Pakistan occupied these areas, it fiddled with the historical and political aspects of the units of the State in order to create confusion and then annex the area into its own. Pakistan, through various laws, deliberately left the status of the area somewhat amorphous. On the one hand, the region was separated from the so-called "Azad Kashmir" to be ruled directly by Islamabad; on the other hand, it linked the accession of the region to the plebiscite to be held in Kashmir in future. "Northern Areas" therefore, remained in political incognito – its status still being undefined and possibly could be called the only secret colony on the earth. As a result, the people belonging to the area, claimed by India, are still restless, yearning for someone to own them.

---

1 Prof P. Stobdan is the Director, Centre for Strategic and Regional Studies (CSRS), University of Jammu, Jammu.

2 *Pakistan 1991: An Official Handbook*, Directorate General of Films and Publications, Ministry of Information and Broadcasting, Government of Pakistan, Islamabad, 1991.

Until the Jammu & Kashmir interim constitution was promulgated in 1974, the so-called Karachi Agreement of 1949, signed between the Pakistan Government and President of Muslim Conference, guided the relations between Pakistan and occupied territories. Under this agreement, the matters such as defence, foreign affairs (including UN negotiations) and administration of the "Northern Areas" were left with the Pakistan Government. Among other reasons there was also the relative inaccessibility of the "Northern Areas". This agreement was supposed to have been a temporary agreement, in view of the fact that a plebiscite would soon take place.

This was done with the understanding that Pakistan would administer the "Northern Areas" as a delegation of the authority vested in the Jammu & Kashmir Government. On several occasions, Pakistan could not but mention that these territories are part of the State of Jammu & Kashmir. In the first instance, the commission issued to the JCOs of the Gilgit Scout (later converted to the Northern Light Infantry) was in the make of President of "Azad Jammu & Kashmir" (AJK) rather than the President of Pakistan. Secondly, Pakistan is committed to its stand at the UN, that the "Northern Areas" are part of the plebiscite areas. Thirdly, Pakistan agreed in the Sino-Pakistan Frontier Agreement of 1963 that the sovereignty of this area did not rest with Pakistan, and once the Kashmir dispute is resolved the boundary treaty could be renegotiated.

The "Northern Areas" was initially administered under the Frontier Crimes Regulation (FCR), along the code of laws operated in the Federally Administered Tribal Areas (FATA). However, the Gilgit Agency was later separated from the NWFP in 1950 to be a part of the Ministry of Kashmir Affairs. Under this arrangement the Political Resident for Gilgit and

Baltistan looked after the administration. In 1952, the Joint Secretary of Kashmir Affairs Division was entrusted with the administrative in charge. Later in 1967, a separate post of Resident was created with its headquarters at Gilgit. He functioned as the head of the administration, High Court, Commissioner under FCR and Revenue Commissioner. The Resident also exercised legislative power. The Resident was supported by two political Agents, one each for Gilgit and Baltistan.

In 1974, Zulfikar Ali Bhutto, to improve matters, abolished the FCR and changed it into Federally Administered "Northern Areas" (FANA) by dividing the region into five districts, entailing a host of new problems.

Notwithstanding Pakistan's claim that the people of "Northern Areas" threw off the yoke of the Dogra Raj of Kashmir and voluntarily joined Pakistan in 1947, the factual position on the ground suggested a completely different picture. Many of the local *Rajas* and tribal rulers assumed full control over their people and had no intention of joining with Pakistan. The tribal areas of Darel and Tangir resisted joining Pakistan until 1951. The *Mirs* of both Hunza and Nagar States retained autonomy and their *Jirgas* and *Panchayats* governed the areas until 1972. The four districts of Gilgit Agency– Punial, Koh-i-Ghizer, Ishkoman and Yasin were administered through *Rajas* with the status of Governors. In 1972, the Pakistan Government abolished the *Jagirdari* system, institutions of *Rajas* like the *Mir* of Nagar and the Agency system. The Gilgit Agency was converted into Gilgit and Baltistan districts to be administered by Deputy Commissioners. Soon Gilgit was divided into two districts to make Diamer district that included the sub-divisions of Astor, Chilas and Darel/Tangir. By 1974, Zulfikar Ali

Bhutto visited the region and announced fundamental reforms, which included the forceful abolition of Hunza State. One more district Ghanche was created out of Baltistan district and another district Ghizr was added to Gilgit region. The *Mir* of Hunza strongly opposed the Sino-Pakistan agreement under which some portion of Hunza was ceded to Beijing in 1963.

I

"Northern Areas"

There is no doubt that the people of the "Northern Areas" have strongly resisted their absorption into Pakistan, or they have preferred to join the AJK, which in any case is not the sole successor of the State of Jammu & Kashmir. The legal developments which took place in Pakistan also suggest that the "Northern Areas" could not be incorporated into Pakistan's constitution (Article 1) nor the so-called AJK Interim Constitution promulgated in 1974 defined these areas as under its administrative control.

The region has been subjected to various atrocities and discrimination under the Pakistani rule through the Resident Commissioner, an outsider equivalent to a colonial Governor. Interestingly, both Pakistan and AJK made attempts to absorb the "Northern Areas" into their respective jurisdiction. There have been debates in Pakistan over "Northern Areas" becoming the fifth province of the Federation. The accession would have been possible through an Act of Parliament or by constitutional amendment. However, Islamabad was confronted, apart from AJK's objection, with three major obstacles in the act of incorporation. Firstly, it requires the consent of other provinces to create the province of "Northern Areas" by creating National Assembly Seats and Senators. Secondly, Islamabad is faced with the problem created by its own stand on Kashmir. Absorption of the "Northern Areas" would mean Pakistan acknowledging India's right to hold the territories of Jammu & Kashmir. Thirdly, of course, the people of Gilgit and Baltistan seek a separate identity to themselves.

District	**Capital**
Gilgit	Gilgit
Diamer	Chilas
Ghizer	Gahkuch
Baltistan	Skardu
Ghanchee	Khaplu

Pakistanis also, at various points of time, have shown enthusiasm about absorption of the area as part of the deal brokered by the US for the final solution of the Kashmir problem.

In 1993, the "Azad Jammu and Kashmir" High Court had declared that the "Northern Areas" (Gligit, Baltistan, etc) are legally part of Kashmir and should be reverted to the AJK.[3] The AJK's stand is the same as that of India. It claims that the Dogra Maharaja ruled the "Northern Areas". The British had extracted the region from the Dogras on lease but never actually removed it from the ownership of the Maharaja. The lease had reverted after the British left. The AJK claimed that it has has all the legal rights to reclaim the "Northern Areas".

The four decades of separation have however created certain technical problems, which may go against the reunion of "Northern Areas" in the AJK. Firstly, it is privately felt by the AJK's leading politicians that inclusion of the "Northern Area" would mean increasing the number of seats in the Legislative Assembly by at least a quarter, which will upset the political balance in the AJK. Secondly, its merger will create administrative problems; particularly due to the inaccessibility of the region may lead to sectarian clashes. Already, the

---

3 "Pak Says Gilgit, Baltistan Are Not Part of Its Territory", *Rediff* net, 1977.

sectarian conflicts have become the core political issue and cause of the secessionist movement in Baltistan.

The Pakistanis also talk of various options regarding the status of the "Northern Areas". One option is of granting it a Legislature with a Chief Minister, as well as, a High Court of its own to the region. Whereas, it could have a common President and a Supreme Court with the AJK, combined with representation for the "Northern Areas" on the AJK Council (which functions both as an Upper House for the AJK legislature, as well as an interface for the Pakistan and AJK). Such a mechanism according to the Pakistan would be qualifying the status of the "Northern Areas" as a part of AJK until the UN plebiscite.

Currently, the "Northern Areas" is directly run by the Ministry of Kashmir Affairs, which itself has developed a vested interest that resists any change. However, owing to mounting pressure, Islamabad had decided to form the "Northern Areas" Council, which is still headed by the Pakistani Minister for Kashmir and "Northern Areas". Islamabad's move has been perceived by people as a camouflage for its questionable intentions. They claim that subsequent governments in Islamabad sent senior officials from the North West Frontier Province (NWFP) to senior administrative posts in Gilgit and Baltistan to prepare the ground for the final act of its incorporation in Pakistan's NWFP. Even after 45 years of Pakistani double talk over the status of the "Northern Areas", it can not even support the independence of Jammu & Kashmir, for fear of losing the "Northern Areas".

II

Social and Religious Tensions

The question of "Northern Areas" is a complex one. Firstly, the people are of a different ethnic group with diverse sub-ethnic communities practising different sects of Islam. The major social divisions are along caste lines – Yashkun, Shin, Ronu, Kremin and Dom. Yashkuns form an overwhelming majority of people follow either Molai or Shia sects, and only a few are Sunni. Even though the AJK talk of sharing commonalities with the people of the "Northern Areas", the same is not reciprocated by the latter. The only commonality among the Kashmiris, Gilgitis and Baltis is that they were all ruled by the Dogras.

During the rule of General Zia several Islamic organisations like the Tehrik Nifas Figh Jafaria have emerged to protect the interests of the Shia minority in Pakistan. This in turn led to the formation of the Anjuman Sipah Sahaba (ASSP) to voice the sectarian rhetoric of the majority of Sunnis. Besides, there are numerous numbers of other sectarian organisations, which have come up during Zia's regime. In Gilgit and Baltistan too, Pakistan always tried to divide the people along sectarian lines. During Zia's martial law period, not only did Molasim gain popularity but Shariat law was also introduced, in the name of Islam. The region has been witnessing large-scale sectarian clashes since 1982, following the assassination of the leaders of the two different commentates. In 1996, the Pakistani Army fired upon Shias protesting against settlements of outsiders in the region. In 1988, the police burned the Shia protestors alive.

While the region's population is divided – Sunnis for integration with PoK and Shias for upholding the regional identity – there is little for Pakistan to achieve for itself in Gilgit and Baltistan.

In recent years resentment among the people against the Pakistani authorities has risen. Till the 1990s, the political demands in Gilgit and Baltistan were largely focused on demanding civil rights, right to vote, and other constitutional status within Pakistan, but the demand is growing for "self-rule" and complete independence from Pakistan, as granted to them under the UN resolution passed on August 13, 1948. The genesis of the ongoing problem started during Zia's rule when a plethora of youth organisations sprung up in the region. The formation of the Karakoram Students Organisation (KSO), and the Baltistan Students Federation (BSF) were catalysts for political change in the region. These organisations later led to the setting up of the "Unemployment Action Committee" in Gilgit and spearheaded a movement against Punjabi youth and other outsiders getting administrative jobs in the region. The movement further led to the formation of the Balwaristan National Front (BNF), which proclaimed that Gilgit and Baltistan were a subjugated nation whose proper name was Balwaristan "land of heights". A complete nationalist ideology is evolving around the concept of Balwaristan, a nation firmly grounded in a common history, geography and culture, which stretch from Chitral in the west to Ladakh in the east. Among its founders is Nawaz Khan Naji, who has been articulating the concept and the creation of Balwaristan to include the entire area of Gilgit and Baltistan and Ladakh region.[4] A chain of mountain peaks and an Ibex, which is the national symbol, signifies the importance of creating a nation

[4] Martin Sokefeld, "Balwaristan: High Country", *Himal,* May 11, 1998, pp. 28-31. Sanjay Suri, "The Forgotten Kashmir" *Outlook,* September 22, 1997.

to include the people and areas that cross both sides of the Line of Control. The national ideology of Balwaristan has already reinstated the historical legendary hero of the region, Gohar Aman of Yasin, who was earlier rejected as a cruel person. His name is now being glorified and being treated as a symbol of freedom struggle among the Balwar people.

The people of Gilgit and Baltistan no longer want to be on the fringe of the Pakistani nation state. Following the BNF emergence, other groups have also taken up their cause for complete cessation from Pakistan. The Karakoram National Movement called for the "Karakoram" nation, while the Boloristan Democratic Front called for the creation of "Boloristan" based on the ancient legacy of Bolor kingdom. Whereas the Mutahida Qaumi Party of Gilgit and Baltistan wants the region to be named as "Gilgit-Baltistan".[5] Anti-Pakistani feeling is increasing amidst the growing urge for the preservation of their distinct ethnic identity. Irrespective of religious, sectarian and party affiliations, various regional organisations form a common alliance under the umbrella of the Gilgit-Baltistan National Conference (GBNC). The 1993 conference resulted in a "Northern Areas" United Front, which continue to champion the cause of the region's separation from Pakistan. Many BNF and other PoK leaders blame India for not realising its claim over the area with action. According to them, India having accepted the accession, should have taken the responsibility of liberating Gilgit and Baltistan from the Pakistani clutches.

It is now described everywhere that Baltistan is a better known area than Pakistan itself in the western world. The

---

[5] P.S. Suryanarayan, "Gilgit-Baltistan rebels seek self-rule", *The Hindu*, August 27, 1996.

western visitors find complete fascination for Baltistan's unique characteristic. More than 75 foreign tourists coming to Pakistan make their destination Baltistan, contributing an enormous amount of foreign exchange for Pakistan. Yet Pakistan does not allocate sufficient funds for the region's development, a complaint usually expressed by the people. Besides, most of the river water originating from Gilgit and Baltistan Areas is the main source of irrigation in the plains of Punjab and Sindh. The Pakistan Government pays royalty for the Indus water to the North-West Frontier Province (NWFP) and not to Gilgit and Baltistan. Similarly, the BNF and others allege that the Pakistani government exploits the mineral and forest resources of the region. Resentment is also growing both in "Azad Kashmir" and in Gilgit and Baltistan over the settlements of Pathans from NWFP, Punjabis and even Afghan refugees from Afghanistan.[6] In recent years protests and demonstration against the Pakistani rule have increased. November 1 is no longer celebrated as "Freedom Day" but as "Martyrs Day". Since 1996, including the 50th anniversary of Independence Day is being celebrated as a "Black Day" in Gilgit and Baltistan. In many cities including Skardu, police opened fire on demonstrations against Pakistani domination. In 1996, there was a massive unrest over recruitment to the Chitral scouts, in which the recruitment drive was tilted in favour of candidates from NWFP. In 1997, students were forced to go to Rawalpindi and Islamabad to appear in their BA examination because an invigilator was beaten in Gilgit. As a result, many students could not appear in the exam.[7] The anti-Pakistani demonstration is becoming more intense and frequent after the landmark judgement of the High Court that the "Northern Areas" belonged to the State of Jammu and Kashmir. In recent

---

[6] Sanjay Suri, "The Forgotten Kashmir" *Outlook*, September 22, 1997.

[7] *Times of India*, April 27, 1999.

years, Pakistani authorities have been saying that the development funds for Gilgit and Baltistan are being spent for the liberation of Kashmir from India. Now the Gilgit-Baltistan United demands include the withdrawal of Pakistani troops from Gilgit and Baltistan and seek merger with Ladakh and Kargil. Against these developments, the federal minister for Kashmir Affairs and "Northern Areas" has lately come up with a statement that "a reform package granting fundamental constitutional powers to representatives of the "Northern Areas" was now in its final stage and would be soon sent to the federal cabinet."[8] However, it is highly unlikely that this late measure will quell the unrest and, in fact, this will only unfold the beginning of a new voice in the region.

Major Fault Lines

Gilgit and Baltistan had a rich historical legacy with its own pagan past and enshrined several famous kingdoms and a plethora of pre-Islamic beliefs and customs until they embraced Islam. However, the cultural landscape of the region has undergone an unprecedented transformation and their cultural ethos has been reduced to the status of folklore.

In the sectarian structure the Sunni Muslims account for 25 per cent of the population, while Twelver Shia accounts for 50 per cent. Ismalia accounts 15 per cent and only 10 per cent remains the practising Nurbakshi Sufi order. The latter is clearly identifiable as a distinct religious sect or community, notwithstanding its closeness to Twelver Shi'ism. Within the above group ethnic, sub-sectarian and caste affinities exist. The major social divisions are along caste lines, i.e. Yashkun, Shin, Ronu, Kremin and Dom. Yashkuns form an

[8] "Northern Areas" to get Constitutional Power, *Dawn*, January 17, 2007.

overwhelming majority of people who follow either Molai or Shia sects, and only a few follow Sunni Islam.

Ismaili Tradition

The propagation of Islam in the region was started in the 12th century. The early Sunni tradition was introduced through the spiritual centre in Central Asia. Sometime in the 13th century, the ruler of Badakhshan region, an Iranian origin, invaded Gilgit and established the Trakhan dynasty. The ruler converted the people into Ismailia faith. The believers of this sect were called Mughli or Maulai. Today, the entire population of Chitral, Gilgit, Kuh, Ghizar, Yasin, Punial and even Hunza are Ismailia. They pay special attention to the Shia doctrine of *Taqqiah* or concealment in the time of danger. The propagation of the Ismailia faith continued throughout medieval and modern times. Today the head of this sect is Agha Khan, the leader of the Khoja community in Mumbai.

Nur-Bakshia Heritage

The Nur-Bakhshia is a branch of the Kubrawiya Sufi order that emerged in Iran in the 15th century. This Sufi order had a large content of Shia doctrine as evident from its special veneration for Ali in Abi Talib. This sect is associated with the famous Persian sage Amir Kabir Syed Ali Hamdani. He was a great missionary saint who was believed to have visited Kashmir in 1374 to propagate Islam in Hindustan (Indian subcontinent). However, the actual founder of the Nur-Baskshia was Syed Muhammad Nur-Baksh (1393-1465), who was a disciple of Hamdani's principal successor Khwaja Ishaq Khuttalani. Syed Mohammad Nur-Baksh evolved a unique Shia-Sufi synthesis, which closely resembled the syncretic versions of Hinduism and Buddhism. Syed Nur-Baksh was purged several times and exiled from Persia for popularising his Sufi order.[9]

The Muslim historiographers doubt whether Hamdani or Nur-Baksh themselves ever visited the western Himalayan region. However, it was clear that a disciple of Syed Mohammad Nur-Baksh, Mir Shamsuddin-Iraqi, who died in 1627 and was possibly the first to have successfully propagated the Nur-Bakshia order in Baltistan. It is believed that in Iran, the country of its origin, Nur-Bakshia got completely merged with the Shias some decades after the Safavid dynasty made Twelver Shi'ism the state religion. Similarly, in the Valley of Kashmir too the Nur-Bakhsia Sufi order disappeared during the reign of the Chak dynasty. It is believed that the Sunni invader of Kashmir, Mirza Haidar Dughlat (who was a Kazakh) severely persecuted the Nur-Baksh order in Kashmir in the mid-16th century. Nevertheless, in Baltistan the Nur-Bakshia has survived till this day as a sect with doctrines of its own.

The Nur-Bakshia as a unique brand of Islamic culture is deeply rooted in the contemporary history of Baltistan. Some of the important *Khanqahs,* or retreat centres are well preserved in places like Shigar, Kiris and Khaplu. It is believed that the sect survived from the onslaught of other proselytes of Shias and Sunnis owing to Baltistan's geographical remoteness much like Buddhism survived in Ladakh from the Hindu revivalism that reached up to Kashmir in the 7th century.

---

9 For more details see Adreas Rick, "Noornbakshis of Baltistan; Revival of the Oldest Muslim Community in the "Northern Areas". Also see the biography of Hazrat Shah Syed Mohammad Noorbaksh. Baltistan, *Jeeva net.*

One of the most important sources of Nur-Baksh doctrines is the book *Al-Fiqh Al-Ahwat*, which means the all-encompassing Fiqh, which strives to unify all Muslim sects. They possess an elaborate corpus of rules for worship and daily life reflecting Sufi heritage with elements of both Sunni and Shia law. Nur-Bakshia's emphasis on love, tolerance, divine love and meditation augured well with the Baltis' Buddhist background. In fact, the Sufis built the *chaqchan* or shrines on the Buddhist *stupas* and monuments, which can be seen in Khaplu and other areas in Baltistan. In fact, many Nur-Bakshis both in the Baltistan and Kargil area continue to keep the old Buddhist Tantric figures and images in the fear that they may harm the people in case of any disrespect of their past belief. Even till date the villagers of Chiktan and Shakar in Kargil share a mixed religion of both Buddhism and Shia Islam. Often both communities worship a common *Lha* (Protector God) and consult each other's priests in difficult times.

Shi'ism and Baltis

However, this is not to suggest that efforts have not been made to undermine the practice of Nur-Bakshia Sufi tradition. Historical evidences suggest that it was during the Mughal period in the 17th century, Persian Shia clerics made inroads into Baltistan and discouraged Sufi meditation, song and dance practised by the Baltis. Some even suggest that in the 16th century, Skardu rulers Ghazi Mir and Ali Sher Khan Anchan were already Twelver Shias. On the other hand, contemporary scholars claim that the entire Baltistan had remained Nur-Baksh until the last decades of the 19th century, when an energetic Shia cleric, Sayyid Abbas Al-Musawi from Gol, who settled in the village of Chutron in Shigar valley after 1900, converted thousands of Baltis to Shi'ism. Subsequently, more and more

Baltis came under the influence of Shi'ism primarily due to increased opportunity among the Baltis to have received higher religious education in Iraq, Iran and in Northern India.

The educated Baltis were zealous enough to adopt the practice of seeking guidance from living religious authorities, the Mujtahids, relating to daily lives, while denouncing the Nur-Bakshia practice of consulting a "dead Mujtahid". Similarly, the practice of ceremonies during the month of Muharram commemorating the sacrifice of Imam Husain became more elaborate because of their increasing contacts with the Shias. Since the late 19th century proselytisation of Sunni tenets among the Shias also increased following the arrival of "Mullah Peshawar" in Baltistan around 1875. He encouraged Baltis to opt for higher education in the Sunni schools in Northern India. As a result, dozens of such Nur-Baksh students returned as converts to Sunni Islam. Several families in Kiris and other areas got converted to the Ahl-i Hadith sect of Sunni Islam. It is said that many Balti leaders deliberately concealed their conversion to Shi'ism or Sunni faith in the fear of losing respect among their Nur-Baksh fellow villagers.

Two main factors contribute to the easy conversion of the Nur-Bakshia into either Sunni or Shia. First is their liberal attitude towards both Shia and Sunni sects. Second is their relative economic backwardness, which prompt them to change their old tradition in favour of new proselytising Muslim sects including their refuge into Wahabism. The 1911 census of India report indicated complete absorption of Balti Nur-Bakshis into other sects. This has even happened in remote villages in Shigar and Kharmang valleys. The modern Shia literature and printed books also claimed the Nur-Bakshi as part of Shi'ism, contending that Sufi orders are not sects but rather contemplative practice lineage that exists within both the Sunni and Shia sects. Both Sunni and Shia authors also portray Syed Muhammad Nur-Baksh as a follower of their own persuasion respectively. Moreover, since Baltistan came under Pakistani occupation in 1948, the proselytisation by Sunnis and Shias among the indigenous Balti Nur-Bakshias has become more pronounced.

Nur-Bakshia Reassertion

Ironically, perhaps owing to fast occurring in Baltistan and its exposure to the world outside, attempts are being made by the people to resist their forceful conversion into other sects and instead striving to revive their traditional Nur-Bakshia tradition. Some pioneering work to revive and modernise the Nur-Baksh has been done by Maulwi Hamza Ali from Khaplu who in his several writings refuted the attempts by Shias and Sunnis to absorb the Nur-Baksh teachings. Since the 1970s, an organisation called Nadwat-I Islamiya Nur-Bakshia, has been actively promoting the publication of Nur-Bakshia literature. A journal called *Nawa-I-Sufiya*, tries to create awareness among modern Baltis about their own past Sufi Nur-Baksh heritage. Similarly, a Nur-Bakshi *Dar Ul-'Ulum* has been established in Karachi in 1990, which intends to prevent Baltis converting to other sects. Incidentally, other non-Nur-Bakshia religious schools have also become reluctant to accept Nur-Bakshia students. The modern educated Baltis reject the assertion that the Nur-Bakshi is part of other sects. Instead, the mushrooming of new organisations tries to compete with Shia and Sunnis in establishing religious schools, besides reviving and renovating the historic *Khanqahs*. Attempts are also being made to strengthen Sufi traditions such as *etikass* or meditation retreats and *mehfils* or song and poetry recitals. It is reported that over 1000 Balti youth undergo intensive *etikaaf* retreats every year. Although the rate of Balti conversion into other sects has slowed down since the 1980s, they are still under constant strain and pressure from stronger groups. The huge modern-style mosques and *Imambargahs* construction in Skardu and other places outshine the old *Khanqahs*. Until recently sectarianism was non-existent among the hitherto peaceful Balti population. Such an attitude is fast creeping into them as the awareness among the Baltis grow for protecting their cultural and political identity. In 1986, sectarian violence erupted over the issue of control of the Khaplu *chaqchan*.

III

Baltistan in Perspective

It needs to be emphasised that Baltistan's history is one of the oldest once. The region is identified by some with the Aparytae of Herodotus. Its reference is found in the ancient Inner Asian Epic of King Kesar and in Ptolemy's Byaltae. If the Chinese called the region Palolo, the Dards called it Balor. For the Arabs, it was Baloristan and for the Tibetans, it was *Nang-kod*. Mughal historians called it *Tibet-i-Khurd* or "Little Tibet." The Mons (Indo-Aryan group) made Baltistan a hub of Buddhism – evolving a triangular relationship among Kashmiri, Gandhara and Turfan Schools.

The Tibetans ruled over Baltistan in the 9th-10th centuries when a local Skardu chieftain took over.[10] Historians believe that a young Egyptian adventurer, Ibrahim Shah reached Baltistan in the 13th century and married the last princess of Skardu. Ibrahim Shah later founded the Makpon dynasty. It was during Makpon Bokha's reign (15th century) that a Sufi saint, Mir Shamsuddin-Iraqi introduced Nur-Bakshia of Kubrawiya Sufi order in Baltistan.[11] Mughal rulers, Mirza Haider Dughlat (1532) and Sultan Syed Khan Kashgari (1531) invaded Baltistan and Ladakh around this period. Historians say that Persian Twelver Shia clerics made inroads into Baltistan in the 16th-17th century; others believe that Baltis practised Nur-Baksh

[10] Richard M. Emerson, "Charismatic Kingship: A Study of the State Formation and Authority in Baltistan", *JCA.*, Vol.VII, No.2, December 1984, pp. 95-134. G.T. Vigne, "Travels in Kashmir, Ladakh, Iskardo", London, 1842, Vol. II, p.251. Also see Alexander Cunningham, *Ladak*, New Delhi, Reprint, 1977, p.35.

[11] Hashmatullah Khan, *Tarikh-i-Jammu*, p. 449.

until the 19th century, when Sayyid Abbas Al-Musawi (1900) converted them to Shi'ism.

Baltistan's most powerful Makpon, Ali Sher Khan Anchan (1590-1625) conquered Ladakh and took Gyalpo Jamyang Namgyal to Skardu under captivity. Anchan later gave his daughter, Gyal Khatoon in marriage to Namgyal. Anchan's descendants ruled the Balti kingdom and maintained close political and cultural ties with Ladakh. He also conquered areas up to Chitral and brought many Shinas/Dards to serve him. In 1779, the Afghans also invaded Skardu but could not last long. In 1840, Baltistan along with Ladakh finally fell under Zorawar Singh and became a part of Jammu and Kashmir. Baltistan, Ladakh and Gilgit were one "frontier district" to be separated in 1901 into a separate Ladakh Wazarat. Skardu became the winter capital of Ladakh Wazarat. In 1947, Pakistan under "Operation Sledge", headed by Lt. Col Ehsan Ali, annexed Baltistan with force. Paksitan conferred Ehsan Ali with *Sitara-i-Jurrat* for conquering Baltistan.[12]

The Baltis are of Tibetan origin, akin to the Ladakhis and Purig-pas of Kargil. The Baltis, even today, speak the most archaic form of Tibetan. Their music, dress, food, folklore, epics, etc. are the same as those of Ladakh. In fact, the radio programmes of Leh and Kargil find a bigger audience across the border. This ancient land, however, remained a cul-de-sac for quite a long time ever since the intertwining relationship between two "Little Tibets" came to an abrupt end in 1948. The cease-fire line divided a thriving Himalayan nation that survived for centuries.

---

[12] A.N. Dani, "History of "Northern Areas" of Pakistan", National Institute of Historical and Cultural Research, Islamabad, 1989, p. 376.

Baltistan particularly suffered ruthless cultural and political purges under Pakistan. It's tagging with Gilgit distorted the culture. The Karakoram Highway brought forays of Punjabis and Wahabi zealots. Baltis' demand for 'self-rule' or 'civil rights' is also as old as the independence of Pakistan. But since the 1990s, demand for complete independence has become more vocal. Nawaz Khan Naji's founded Balwaristan National Front (BNF) has a flag depicting icy mountain peaks with an Ibex as the national symbol of people from Chitral to Ladakh. *Inter alia*, the Karakoram National Movement (KNM), Boloristan Democratic Front (BDF), Gilgit-Baltistan National Conference (GBNC) and "Northern Areas" United Front (NAUF) endure anti-Pakistan rhetoric; even seek return of territory from China. The struggle has become more intense since the High Court landmark judgement that ""Northern Areas"" belonged to Jammu & Kashmir State. The Baltistanese amply blamed India for not realising its claim over the area with action.

Balti National Reassertion

Historically and culturally Baltistan had an intertwining relationship with Ladakh. Both belonged to one cultural and ethnic complex. Notwithstanding the Islamisation, Baltistan and Ladakh had a cordial and harmonious relationship and protected their mutual security interests until Pakistan annexed the former in 1948. In the past, intermarriages between the two communities including between the royal families were common. Many of the traditions and customs and day-to-day social conducts were flexible. The valleys of Baltistan produced high quality apricots that had high value in the bazaars of Kargil and Leh. The cease-fire line brought the relationship to a complete standstill. The partition of India and Pakistan not only divided one nation but also a civilisation that thrived in complete protection in the high Himalayan region.

Essentially, the Baltis are ethnically and linguistically of Tibetan origin, akin to the Ladakhis and Purigs. The Baltis even today speak the most archaic forms of Tibetan. Balti had no script of its own. However, in the 8th century they adopted the Tibetan script and continued to use it till they came under the influence of Islam in the 14th-15th centuries. Over 65 per cent of Baltistan's population is Balti – the native of *Balti-Yul* or Balti as described by Ladakhis. Over the years, the Kashmiri influence led the Persianised to call it Baltistan. The present-day Balti language is heavily influenced by Persian, Urdu, Turkish and Burushaski literatures. However, the Balti dialect is still spoken by people inhabiting the six major valleys in Baltistan like Skardu, Rongdu, Shigar, Khapulu, Kharmang and Gultari. In India, people in Turtuk and some pockets in Kargil speak Balti dialect. The Baltis constitute about 3.2 per cent of the Leh population. A small community of Balti also lives in the neighbouring villages of Chuchot and Thikse in Leh. During the 1971 Indo-Pakistan war the soldiers of Ladakh Scouts liberated five Balti villages of Turtuk, Tyakshi, Chalungkha, Thang and Pharol from Pakistani control to integrate with Ladakh.

Baltistan remained cut off from the world outside. Over the last 50 years, both the physical and political isolation ensured Baltistan's complete absorption into Pakistan without the world knowing about the cultural and political purges ruthlessly brought about there by Pakistani authorities. Baltistan suffered not only due to the cessation of cultural ties with their diaspora in Ladakh but also because Pakistan forcefully tagged it with Gilgit to form what is today known as the "Northern Areas" of Pakistan. The completion of the Karakoram Highway linking Pakistan with China in 1978 had led to forays of Punjabis and other Pakistanis into Baltistan. Consequently, a large number of Sunni and Wahabi missionaries intruded into the area for religious conversion. On the other hand, the success of the Iranian Revolution bolstered the activities of the Shia faith, leading to the formation of the Tehrik-I-Jaffaria Pakistan (TJP), which is the most popular political body today in Baltistan.

Things are fast changing though amidst Balti reaction to the growing domination and assertion by *imamas* to erase Baltistan's pre-Islamic national identity. There is silent but fast growing yearning among the Tibetan origin Baltis to revive their old cultural roots. These include their attempts to revive the traditional rituals like *Me-phang*, fire ritual, a move to preserve and protect Skardu's ancient Buddhist monuments, rock carvings and other related heritage. A growing section of modern Balti scholars are trying to protect their Tibetan language from the growing linguistic influence of Urdu and Punjabi. In sharp contrast to their brethren in Ladakh and Kargil, the Baltis realise that their identity is fast eroding and their dress, customs and even wedding ceremonies have become Punjabised. Many Balti scholars complain that "Arabic is quite inadequate to bring out the richness of the Balti language" and assert that if their unique and rich history and culture is to be preserved, they will have to revive the Tibetan script again.[13]

Ali Sher Khan Anchan is already being resurrected as the legendary hero and a symbol of modern day Balti identity. A famous Balti intellectual, Mohammad Hasnain, professionally

---

[13] T.A. Khan, "Little Tibetan: Renaissance and Resistance in Baltistan", *Himal* May 11, 1998.

a textile engineer, now settled in Lahore, has already changed his name in Tibetan. He is now called Senge Tsering and has taken to the task of popularising the Balti language and literature. Another person is Syed Abbas Kazmi, who is working for the restoration of ancient Balti monuments. The Baltis Students Federation (BSF) uses the *yung-drung* (swastika), an ancient Bon symbol as the party's logo.[14] Several writings about Baltistan refer to the growing cultural renaissance of the people in the region and their efforts to re-establish their links with the Tibetan world, especially with the Ladakhis. Owing to the political barrier, these enthusiastic Baltis are making contacts through international organisations, which are engaged in the promotion of Ladakhi and Tibetan language and history. It is believed that these scholars find it easier to be in touch with Tibetans through Kathmandu.

There is also a growing interest among the Ladakhis and Purig-pas (Kargilis) for resuming old contacts with their kin across the border. Ladakhis too realise that their own identity is linked more with Baltistan than with proper Tibet. Even today, Baltis and Ladakhis share several non-religious affinities such as language, music, dress, food, folktales like the *Kesar* epic and other popular pre-Buddhistic Bon customs. The All India Radio programmes broadcast from Leh and Kargil are extremely popular among the Baltis in Baltistan. Though there have been no significant contacts between the two communities so far, scholars and intellectuals from both sides do meet and share each other's perceptions, whenever they get a chance to meet at international conferences. (Two Ladakhi scholars were invited to participate in a conference in Islamabad in 1993, but Pakistani authorities barred them from visiting Skardu.

---

[14] Ibid.

Since the mid-1980s, there also exists an International Association for Ladakh Studies (IALS).[15] There is tremendous scope for the scholars, social scientists, politicians, and policy makers to work in the direction of resuming the contacts between the divided ethnic groups. If any proactive policy is to be followed with respect to Pakistan, it should be in the field of language, ethnicity and language. When we are engaged in a conflict with Pakistan, especially along the ethnic frontiers, it would be useful to be armed with the knowledge of the forces at work.

Linguistic Pattern

Two broad families of languages are being spoken in different dialects by the people of NA. There have been, however, a high degree of transformations in the language structure as well as in the use of vernaculars. Under the Pakistani rule the use of Urdu, Punjabi and Pushto have become *lingua franca*, threatening the very survival of some of the most ancient and archaic dialects belonging to the Indo-Aryan, Dardic and Tibetan family of languages. For example, in Gilgit, the *lingua franca* is Shina and Burushaski. In Chitral the mother tongue is Khowar, a branch of Shina. In Yasin, people speak different dialects like Ishkoman, Shina, Khowar, and Burushaski. Shina is also the main dialect in Chilas and other areas of Indus Valley. A significant number of populations in Chilas and adjoining areas speak Kohistani, again a branch of the Dardic family mainly spoken in Kohistan. But in Hunza the main language is Burushaski and Domaaki, which are supposed to be of Indo-Aryan origin. However, in the upper

15 Several IALS Congresses were already held in various European and American cities. The IALS try to differentiate between Ladakh studies and Tibetan studies. The concept of Ladakh studies includes the area studies of Western Himalayas including Baltistan but not Gilgit.

part of Hunza Valley, an Iranian dialect Waki is commonly spoken. In Baltistan the *lingua franca* is Balti, which is an archaic form of Tibetan akin to Ladakhi and Purig. There are also nomadic people like Gujar (herdsmen) who speak Gujari language. Gujar, Khirghiz, Kashmiri and some others are foreign languages, which have entered later. However, in the urban areas, even the local people have adapted to the use of Urdu, Punjabi and Pushto languages. The spatial distribution of languages in the Pakistani held Jammu & Kashmir is very fascinating and intricate. Some of these native languages belong to the most archaic Indo-Aryan and Dardic family of languages and are closely associated with the rich history of the Gandhara civilisation. However, these indigenous languages have been facing constant pressure from exogenous forces. The imposition of Urdu has become more intrinsic because of commercial purposes following the construction of the Karakoram Highway linking Pakistan with China through the PoK.

ARYAN (DARDS)

The Dards belong to the Aryan race, but are quite different and distinguishable from the people of other Indo-Aryan origins such as Kashmiris, Dogris, Paharis and Chibhalis. The original home of Dards was said to be the Hindu Kush Mountains, but today Dardic-speaking people are found in Chitral, Swat, Gilgit, Hunza, and other areas of PoK. Many scholars also tend to call the area Dardistan. The Dardic-speaking region is also being described as Kafiristan, the land of infidels, describing the practice by the people of the region of pre-Islamic beliefs such as Buddhism and Bon religion. There are several sub-divisions of Dards depending on the areas they inhabit and the dialect they speak. They are:

Shin	Shina is predominantly spoken in Gilgit region. It is also spoken in the Ishkoman valley and in Hunza. The Shina-speaking elements are also found in Baltistan and some villages along the Indus valley in Ladakh. They are locally known by Ladakhis as Brokpas. Some of the popularly known Shina dialects are Phalura, Savi, Tangir and Palas, spoken in Chitral, Kunar Valley in Afghanistan, Tangir and Palas respectively.
Khowar	Khowar is one of the prominent dialects of the Dardic family of languages and is spoken by people in Chitral. However, several communities in Gilgit and Yasin also speak Khowar.
Astori	The dialect of Shin spoken in Rondu and Skardu is called Astori.
Chilas-Darel	The dialect is spoken in the Khurmang area of PoK.
Yashkin	Yashkin tribes inhabiting the Haramosh area speak a branch of Shin or Gilgiti dialect. Yashkins are also known as Brusha in Khurmang, Nagar and Hunza.
Maiyan	A Dardic dialect spoken in the Indus-Kohistan area. It is also known as Kohistani, mostly spoken by Shinas settled in the Valleys of Duber and Kandia on the right bank of the river Indus.

Rom	The Dards settled in Baltistan region are known as Rom. They trace their origin to Shins of Gilgit and Astor. The Rom is divided into four sub-castes: Sharshing - Gabur - Doro - Yudai. The Roms do not intermarry with Yashkins.
Ronu	Rono is the most honoured caste among the Dards. They are next to the ruling family and often the Wazirs are chosen from the Rono families. They give their daughters in marriage to the ruling families. In small numbers they exist in all parts of present-day "Northern Areas", such as Gilgit, Hunza, Nagar, Punial and Yasin. They are also found in small numbers in Chitral, where they are known as Zandre. In Nagar and Yasin they are called Hara.
Yashkun	It is the most predominant caste among the Dards. The entire population of Hunza, Nagar, Punial and Yasin belong to this caste. Besides, they form a significant part of Gilgit, Darel and Astor population. The Yashkuns are agriculturists. A caste difference exists between Yashkuns and Shins. A Shin may marry a Yashkun woman, but no Yashkun can marry a Shin woman.

Brokpa	The Dards or Shins in Ladakh region are called Brokpa – a Tibetan word meaning Highlanders or synonymous with herdsmen or shepherds. It is the name given by Baltis to the Dards. The Baltis are of Tibetan origin and consider themselves as superior to the Brokpas and generally intermarriages between the Brokpas and Baltis are avoided. For centuries, Brokpas and Dards have been living in harmony. In fact, before the Tibetan invasion the Dardic-speaking people, whom the Tibeto-speaking population later subjugated, inhabited the entire region of Ladakh.
Buddhist Brokpa	Although the Dards in Ladakh continue to practise their customs and ancient rituals, they have come under the influence of other religions such as Tibetan Buddhism, Shiasim and Sunni Wahabism. The Brokpas settled along the Indus river are lately converted to Buddhism. However, socially they do not interact with either neighbouring Ladakhis, Buddhists or Shia Baltis. The Buddhist Brokpas mainly live in Dha, Hanu, and Bema villages along the Indus river. The Buddhist Brokpas continue to practise their pre-Buddhistic beliefs, rituals and customs.
Shia Brokpa	The Brokpas who have come into close contact with Baltis in Kargil and also in Baltistan region have been converted to Shia Muslims over the years. In Ladakh, the places near Kargil such as Batalik, Silmo, Lalung, Chulichen, Dartsik and Darkon are Shia Brokpas. Similarly, Shia Brokpas are also found across the border in Baltistan. However, the Brokpas who have embraced Islam lost their original culture identity.

Sunni Shin	The Shins or Shinas who inhabit the Dras area of Kargil have been practising the Sunni faith. Unlike the Buddhist Shinas, those in Dras have lost their tribal customs and rituals. They have been under the influence of Kashmiris and Baltis in the recent past and therefore speak Urdu or Kashmiri dialect.
Mon	The Mons belonged to the most ancient Indo-Aryan race. They were the original inhabitants of the ancient kingdom of Zen Zan, which included the vast area of Lahul-Spiti, Ladakh, Zanskar, Baltistan, Swat-Gilgit region. The Mons perhaps practised Kashmiri type Buddhism as evident from their use of inscriptions in Brahmni character. The Mons called the Kashmiris Kyirs, Tibetans as Zun-Zan, Baltis as Tu-ruk. They called themselves Manus or Desi-si-manus, or the inhabitants of the land of aboriginals. Though they look quite similar in appearance to Kashmiris, but they were not of Kashmiri descent. Presently, there are only a few hundred Mons surviving in the Central part of Ladakh in the whole area. Ever since the Dards and Tibetans had subjugated the Mons, they have been reduced to a minority race and treated with scant respect by both Ladakhis and Baltis. In Ladakh, their profession is confined to the role of musicians and carpenters. No intermarriages take place between the Mons and Ladakhis.

NON-DARDIC (Indo-Aryan)

Domaaki	Domaaki is the language of the Domas, who are considered a lower caste by the Dards and are usually blacksmiths, musicians, etc. They belong to Burushaski and Shina-speaking communities. They are like European gypsies found throughout the Dard countries, particularly in Gilgit, Yasin, Chilas and Nagar areas. It is non-Dardic but an Indo-Aryan language. Domas are bilingual and speak other languages like Urdu, Shina and Burushaski. Domaaki is a dying language.
Burusha-ski	Another non-Dardic language spoken in the Hunza Valley as well as in parts of Nagar. It is an archaic dialect. Burushaski is not a written language but it has a lot of folk literature.
Wakhi	The Wakhi belongs to the Pamirian branch of the Iranian language. It is mostly spoken in the Upper Valley of Ishkoman, Upper Hunza Valley and Upper Yarkun Valley, who have an affinity with people living in the Wakhan Corridor of Afghanistan.

TIBETANS

Baltis	Over 65 per cent of Baltistan's population is Balti – the native of Balti–Yul or Balti as described by Ladakhis. Over the years the Kashmiri influence led to Persianise the Balti to call it Baltistan. The early reference to Balti is found in Ptolemy's Byaltae dating back to the second century BC. The Chinese literature described the whole region of present-day Gilgit and Baltistan as Palolo, with distinction made of little or big Palolo, perhaps referring to Baltistan and Ladakh. The Dards called the Balti area Balor and the Arabs rendered it Baloristan. While the Tibetans called it Nang-kod. Essentially Baltis are ethnically and linguistically of Tibetan origin, akin to the Ladakhis and Purigs. The Baltis even today speak the most archaic forms of Tibetan. Balti had no script of its own. However, in the 8th century they adopted the Tibetan script and continued to use it until they came under the influence of Islam in the 14th-15th centuries. The present Balti has been heavily influenced by Persian Urdu, Turkish and Burushaski literatures. However, the Balti dialect is still spoken by people inhabiting the six major valleys in Baltistan like Skardu, Rongdu, Shigar, Khapulu, Kharmang and Gultari. In India, people in Turtuk and some pockets in Kargil speak the Balti dialect. Balti constitute about 3.2 per cent of the Kargil population. A small community of Balti also live in the nearby villages of Chuchot and Thikse in Leh.

Purig	In Tibetan Pu-rig means Tibetan-race. Purig is a sister ethnic group of Balti and Ladakhi. The Purig-pas are the inhabitants of Suru, Dras, Wakha and Shakar-Chiktan valleys in Kargil district. The Purig speak the same archaic forms of Tibetan dialect like the Baltis in Baltistan and Ladakhis in Ladakh with minor differentiation. Like the Baltis they were earlier Buddhists. Presently they practise the Nurbakshia sect of Shiasm. However, some have directly come under the influence of Shiasm in the recent past, which threaten the existence of their original Sufi Nurbakshia faith. The majority population of Kargil, some 60,000 people is Prig-pas, which accounts for 70 per cent of the district's population.
Chang-pas	Chang-pa means easterner and is basically Ladakhi. The Chang-pas are inhabitants of the eastern flank of Ladakh. The Chang-pas speak the same Tibetan dialect as Ladakhi with little variation. The Chang-pas are mostly nomads and live in tents in the eastern plateau areas of Ladakh. They are closer to Tibetans in Tibet than the Ladakhis.
Argon	The Argons are hybrids between the Kashmiris and the surrounding native races. There are Argons between Kashmiris and Baltis in Kargil. Similarly, Argons in Leh are between Kashmiris and Ladakhis or between Ladakhis and Yarkandis or Kashgaris.

CHAPTER 2

JIHADI GROUPS IN POK: POST-EARTHQUAKE DYNAMICS

Kanchan Lakshman[1]

The earthquake of October 8, 2005, brought Pakistan-occupied Kashmir (PoK), which is also referred to as 'Azad Jammu and Kashmir (AJK)' by Islamabad, to the centre-stage with focused global attention.

The region, a hotbed of Islamist militancy, continues to simmer. More importantly, events and developments in PoK have a direct impact on the ground situation in Jammu and Kashmir and to the India-Pakistan 'peace process.'

Many in South Asia had hoped that the earthquake, which killed tens of thousands of people and affected millions on both sides of the Line of Control (LoC) would put a halt, at least momentarily, to the *Jihadi* campaign in Jammu and Kashmir (J&K) and allow for unhindered relief and rehabilitation operations. Some fantasists went so far as to see in this natural disaster a 'window of opportunity' for dramatic cooperation and an improvement of relations between India and Pakistan.

---

[1] Kanchan Lakshman is a Research Fellow, Institute for Conflict Management, New Delhi and Assistant Editor, *Faultlines: Writings on Conflict and Resolution*. Opinions expressed in this essay are solely of the author.

However, the terrorist crusade, evidently, recognises no bounds and is not constrained by the humanitarian crisis in the wake of natural disasters. The continuing terrorist violence in Jammu and Kashmir since the quake is an indication that the *Jihad* will not be slowed down even by natural calamities. That terrorist groups would continue to maintain the now consistent and calibrated levels of violence is evident from the fact that 1315 people, including 411 civilians and 199 security force (SF) personnel have died in J&K since October 2005 (data till December 31, 2006).[2]

In the immediate aftermath of the earthquake, on the ground in J&K, the terrorists also took advantage of the earthquake relief operations along the LoC. This was primarily intended to disrupt relief and rescue operations in the quake-hit Valley. It was also an attempt to bolster the ranks of the *Jihadis* and mark their presence, especially after a significant loss of men and material in Pakistan and PoK. The challenge for the security establishment in J&K was consequently two-fold: maintaining their guard even as they struggled to complete relief and rehabilitation work before the onset of winter. And the terrorists' strategy was directed towards attempting to take advantage of this and negate the balance that the security forces were maintaining. To that end, there were some high-profile incidents of terrorist violence in the immediate aftermath, although the overall level of violence did not see any drastic increase, primarily due to snow in the higher reaches and because of the cumulative impact of the earthquake. Some of the major incidents[3] in the immediate aftermath and during the year 2006 are as follows:

---

[2] Source: Institute for Conflict Management database. See South Asia Terrorism Portal, www.satp.org.

[3] Timeline 2005-2006 of Jammu and Kashmir, South Asia Terrorism Portal, www.satp.org.

October 18, 2005: Terrorists assassinate the Jammu and Kashmir Minister of State for Education, Dr. Ghulam Nabi Lone, while CPI-M legislator, Mohammed Yousuf Tarigami, escaped unhurt in a similar attempt in the high-security Tulsibagh area of capital Srinagar. Two SF personnel and a civilian are also killed in the incidents, for which the Islamic Front and Al-Mansooran have claimed responsibility.

November 2, 2005: A few hours before the swearing in of Ghulam Nabi Azad as the tenth Chief Minister (CM) of J&K, a *Fidayeen* (suicide squad) terrorist detonated a powerful car bomb in the Nowgam area of capital Srinagar near the old residence of outgoing CM, Mufti Mohammad Sayeed, killing at least 10 people and injuring 18 others.

November 15, 2005: Six persons are killed and 90 others sustain injuries when terrorists targeted the former Minister and PDP leader Ghulam Hassan Mir's public meeting with a grenade explosion at Tangmarg in the Baramulla district.

May 1, 2006: Suspected Lashkar-e-Toiba terrorists kill 22 Hindus in the mountain hamlets of Kulhand and Tharva in Doda district and 13 at Lalon Galla, a high-altitude meadow above the town of Basantgarh in the Udhampur district.

July 8, 2006: Five persons are killed and 42 others are injured in a terrorist attack outside a shrine at Kulgam. Senior National Conference leader and former legislator Ghulam Nabi Dar is among the dead, while former Minister Sakeena Itoo suffered minor splinter injuries in the attack.

October 5, 2006: With 10 fatalities – seven SF personnel, two terrorists and one civilian – the overnight gun-battle between the holed terrorists and troops in the business hub of

Budshah Chowk in capital Srinagar ended in the afternoon. Approximately 30 people sustained injuries in the suicide attack.

Major General M. S. Balhara, General Officer Commanding Kilo Force in J&K, stated on October 16, 2005: "We have intercepted many messages of militants in North Kashmir and they all indicate that around 600-700 militants were killed in the quake. The control stations of Lashkar-e-Toiba and Hizb-ul-Mujahideen have been destroyed, too, across the Line of Control opposite Kupwara sector. The launching pads of militants have also been smashed by the quake."[4]

While authoritative assessments are unavailable, a fair amount of damage is reported to have occurred to some terrorist training camps in Pakistan and PoK.[5] According to sources, camps of groups such as the Jaish-e-Mohammed (JeM), LeT, Tehreek-ul-Mujahideen (TuM), HM and Al-Badr, which were located within a radius of 10 kilometres from the epicentre of the quake in Muzaffarabad, were damaged.[6] A wireless intercept of the TuM indicated that one of the outfit's buildings near Muzaffarabad, the capital of PoK, had been destroyed and some cadres were buried under it. The Harkat-ul-Mujahideen (HuM) training centres at Balakot and Batrasi (North West Frontier Province [NWFP]), the JeM camp at Attock (Punjab province), Al-Badr's at Oghi (NWFP), an LeT camp at Mansehra (NWFP) and an HM recruitment camp at Jungle-Mangal (PoK) were also damaged.[7] While the exact number of destroyed camps is yet to be ascertained, it is safe to assume that significant destruction would have occurred to

[4] "About 700 militants dead: Army," *Indian Express*, Delhi, October 17, 2005.

[5] Kanchan Lakshman, "Jihad after the Quake," *South Asia Intelligence Review*, Volume 4, No. 15, October 24, 2005, South Asia Terrorism Portal, www.satp.org.

[6] Ibid.

[7] Ibid.

the *Jihadi* infrastructure since the whole city of Muzaffarabad, capital of PoK, was flattened. Sources said that communication centres of the HM (near Muzaffarabad) and TuM were among those that suffered severe damage. However, the destroyed camps and *Jihadi* infrastructure have been reconstructed gradually and the levels of such an infrastructure have now been restored to the pre-quake period.[8]

The state's acts of commission and omission in the post-earthquake period sparked off enormous hostility against the Pakistan Army and the regime of President Pervez Musharraf. Indeed, it is this animosity that conferred legitimacy on the *Jihadi* presence in the day-to-day chores of rescue and relief. Jama'at-ud-Da'awa (JD), the parent organisation of the LeT, is reported to have diverted a considerable part of its network towards relief efforts. Among the other Islamist groups that have contributed to quake relief are the Karachi-based Al-Rashid Trust (ART), one of the 27 groups and organisations listed by the US State Department on September 22, 2001, for their involvement in financing and supporting a network of international Islamist terrorist groups; and the charity wing of the Jamaat-e-Islami.[9]

For the Jihadi organisations the earthquake was a godsend and those that were formally banned by the Pakistan government were fully operative and highly visible in all earthquake zones, both in PoK and NWFP.[10] "In open bazars and town centres one sees the Lashkar-e-Tayyaba (aka Jamat-ud-Dawa), Jamat-e-Islami, Jaish-e-Mohammed, Sipah-e-

---

8 Interview with senior police official in New Delhi, December 14, 2006.

9 Kanchan Lakshman, "Jihad after the Quake," *South Asia Intelligence Review*, Volume 4, No. 15, October 24, 2005, South Asia Terrorism Portal, www.satp.org.

10 Pakistan Earthquake Relief Effort, http://www.pugwash.org/reports/ees/earthquake2005/dec8update.htm

Sahaba, Al Rasheed Trust, and others. They flaunt their flags and weapons, and drive in SUVs and vehicles, presumably given to them by the Pakistan army and intelligence agencies."[11]

The growing power of *Jihadi* groups was particularly evident in the aftermath of the earthquake in PoK, when the LeT, in its new garb as the Jamaat-ud-Dawa, emerged as the most prominent organisation in relief operations. Reports indicate that General Musharraf had, in fact, called up LeT chief, Hafiz Mohammad Saeed immediately after the quake, and emphasised Islamabad's reliance on the *jihadis*, both for relief operations and temporarily for 'defence' along the LoC, in view of the massive damage the Pakistani Army infrastructure had suffered.

The Musharraf regime's vacillating and deficient response led people to seek assistance from the *Jihadis*. The JD, according to credible Pakistani reportage, emerged as the most "effective relief agency that has built up an excellent rapport with the victims." In Muzaffarabad, JD activists, numbering around 350 and connected through wireless telephony, managed 16 ambulances, motorboats, mobile X-ray machines/operation theatres, were feeding approximately 3,000 people daily, according to the Pakistan Media Monitor.

While relief efforts by groups such as the JD provided much-needed succour, the inevitable gratitude of grief-stricken families has come in handy for the larger goals of the *Jihadis*. According to a senior police official in J&K, Islamist extremists, during 2006, did resort to considerable recruiting for the *jihad* from amongst the quake-affected populace.[12]

---

[11] Ibid.

[12] Interview with senior police official in New Delhi, December 14, 2006.

More insidious is the hidden and potentially long-term impact of the natural disaster on the socio-political landscape of the region, which has for long been the epicentre of the Kashmir *Jihad.* For instance, the quake destroyed almost all the schools in PoK. District Bagh (100 kms from Muzaffarabad) had 341 schools for a population of 500,000, while Muzaffarabad had 1,512 schools for a population of 900,000 people. Virtually all school buildings in these areas were flattened out, and thousands of students face an uncertain future, especially with the Pakistan Prime Minister Shaukat Aziz himself indicating that reconstruction and rehabilitation 'would take decades'. The *Jihadi* groups, within such a milieu, find it far easier to bolster their ranks. According to Mohammad Amir Rana, there are more than 1,200 *madrassas* (seminaries) in PoK being run by groups like the LeT, JeM, HM, Al-Badr, Jamiat-ul-Mujahideen, Al-Barq, Harkat-ul-Mujahideen and Jamaat-e-Islami (some of these, would, no doubt, also have been damaged or destroyed by the earthquake). Further, the extremists also propagated the view that the quake was the 'punishment of God' (Azab-e-Elahi) for abandoning the *Jihad.*

And while the government banned adoption of quake-hit children, groups like the Muttahida Majlis-e-Amal and JD announced, through mosque loudspeakers, banners and pamphlets, that they would adopt children orphaned by the earthquake. "The Jamatud Dawa has a huge complex at Misrial Road in Rawalpindi, by the name of Maaz bin Jabal. We will set up colonies in the complex where these children would be put up according to their age. Various *ayahs* (nursemaids) will raise them, ensuring motherly love," said Zafar Iqbal, head of the JD's 'education wing'.

With the state's writ undermined by its ineffective responses to the earthquake, and with popular frustration and anger against the regime growing, the terrorist groups easily occupied the space created by the humanitarian crisis, and also became more brazen about their activities. More significant, however, was Islamabad's continuing ambivalence towards the *Jihadis*. While President Musharraf told CNN on October 20, 2005, that banned religious groups would not be allowed to conduct relief efforts in the quake-stricken areas, the Interior Minister Aftab Khan Sherpao, while acknowledging the role of Islamist groups, declared, they are "the lifeline of our rescue and relief work."

While the quake undoubtedly inflicted some damage on the *Jihadi* infrastructure in Pakistan, the setback was momentary, and was more than compensated by the emerging circumstances and by the accelerated replenishment rate of cadres. There was also the renewal of state support after a modicum of stability was achieved on the relief and reconstruction front. The Union Minister of State for External Affairs, E. Ahamed, informed the Lok Sabha on August 2, 2006, that at least 52 terrorist training camps were operating in Pakistan and PoK.[13]

There was more evidence in 2006 that the 'footprint' of every major act of international Islamist terrorism invariably passes through Pakistan.[14] For instance, a UK-based Islamic charity organisation remitted a huge amount of money to three individuals in three different bank accounts at Mirpur in Azad Kashmir, in December 2005 with the sole purpose of helping its recipients and their organisations carry out the aircraft bombing plan in the UK, sources told *Daily Times* on August

[13] "52 terrorist camps in Pakistan & PoK," *The Hindu*, Chennai, August 3, 2006.

[14] K.P.S. Gill, *Islamist Extremism and Terrorism in South Asia*, New Delhi: Institute for Conflict Management, p. 1.

11, 2006.[15] An investigation carried out by *Daily Times*[16] showed that Muslim Charity of UK remitted not so long ago a huge amount of money under the head of "earthquake relief" to the accounts of three individuals in three different banks – Saudi Pak Bank, Standard Chartered and Habib Bank Ltd. One of these banks is UK-based and has its presence in PoK because of a huge number of British citizens of Kashmir origin in UK. The money was transferred from UK to banks in PoK reportedly through Barclays Plc.

There has been some churning as far as the socio-political milieu is concerned in PoK. Islamist clerics reportedly told aid agencies to dismiss all local women employees or face violent protests. According to *Daily Times*, the threat was given to district officials and non-governmental organisations in Bagh on August 22, 2006. "We have told the administration that we will not allow NGOs to exploit our women and asked them to give a date suitable to them for removal of all female workers," Syed Atta Ullah Shah, prayer leader of the Bagh central mosque, told AFP. "They hire beautiful girls and take them to Islamabad for enjoyment. They keep women in offices as decoration pieces because we know that women have no work and there is no such work that men cannot do," Shah said.

According to the Union Home Ministry's "Status Paper on Internal Security Situation" (presented in Parliament on November 30, 2006), the terrorist infrastructure in Pakistan and Pakistan-occupied Kashmir is yet to be dismantled and is being "used by Pak-based and Pak ISI-sponsored outfits like JeM [Jaish-e-Mohammed], LeT [Lashkar-e-Toiba], Al-Badr, HM

---

15 "'Quake money' used to finance UK plane bombing plot," *Daily Times*, Lahore, August 12, 2006.

16 Ibid.

[Hizb-ul-Mujahideen], etc."[17] The *modus operandi* is recruitment of Indian youths by the LeT and Bangladesh-based Harkat-ul-Jihad-al-Islami (HUJI-BD) for training in Pakistan and PoK and then sending them back to India for sabotage and subversive activities.[18]

The militant infrastructure across the LoC in PoK is intact which was evident from the more recent infiltration attempts in the Uri sector of Baramulla district, the Army said on January 12, 2007, according to Press Trust of India.[19] "Despite confidence-building measures between India and Pakistan, militants continue to get support from the other side of the Line of Control. This has been proved by the recent infiltration bids in Uri," General Officer Commanding of the 15 Corps of the Army, Lt. Gen. A. S. Sekhon, told reporters at the Raising Day of the Corps in Srinagar.

The Army commander said as per intelligence reports, terrorist infrastructure like training camps, launching pads and communication hubs were intact across the LoC.

Fatalities of Terrorist Violence in J&K, 2007

	Civilian	Security Force Personnel	Terrorist	Total
January*	11	7	24	42

*Data till January 28, 2007

---

[17] Kanchan Lakshman, "India: Darkness and Light," *South Asia Intelligence Review*, Volume 5, No. 25, January 1, 2007, South Asia Terrorism Portal, www.satp.org.

[18] "LeT, JeM use Bangladesh, Nepal for anti-India activities," *Times of India*, New Delhi, December 3, 2006.

[19] "Militant infrastructure still intact in PoK: Army," *Daily Excelsior*, Srinagar, January 13, 2007.

Fatalities of Terrorist Violence in J&K, 2006

	Civilian	Security Force Personnel	Terrorist/ Militant	Total
January	11	9	49	69
February	11	7	43	61
March	14	13	43	70
April	37	16	38	91
May	75	13	52	140
June	49	11	54	114
July	36	10	63	109
August	23	24	59	106
September	28	22	61	111
October	21	23	64	108
November	24	17	43	84
December	20	3	30	53
Total	349	168	599	1116

Fatalities of Terrorist Violence in J&K, Post-Quake 2005

	Civilian	Security Force Personnel	Terrorist/ Militant	Total
November	42	16	43	101
December	20	15	63	98

Source for data: Institute for Conflict Management Database.

Despite the declines in indices of violence, J&K continues to suffer from high levels of violence and subversion. Pakistan's military regime, which was forced to scale down its proxy-war under intense international scrutiny, has nevertheless shown no indication of dismantling the vast infrastructure of terrorism on its soil. Amidst the hype on people-to-people contacts and confidence-building measures (CBMs), it is evident that the reduced levels of violence in J&K primarily reflect a tactical rather than strategic shift in the Pakistani calculus, as a two-pronged strategy of parallel talks and terrorism is pursued by the Musharraf regime to secure its ambitions against India.

Talks between India and Pakistan thus continue under the aegis of the Composite Dialogue, even as terrorism in J&K, and sporadically in other parts of India, persists. At the same time, Pakistan has been complaining bitterly about the slow pace of 'progress' towards the goals it seeks to secure on the negotiating table, having failed to achieve these through its vicious campaign of terrorism over 17 years. The peace process, consequently, remains, tactical rather than substantive, as the hiatus between the rival positions on Kashmir remains unbridgeable, and much of the 'progress' has been in peripheral areas, such as the restoration of communication links, people-to-people exchanges, Track Two diplomacy and a range of confidence-building measures. At the same time, the ground situation in J&K remains a cause for concern, as a stream of infiltrators continues to find its way into the terror-wracked State. While the various CBMs currently operational between the two countries may have strengthened processes of 'emotional enlistment', have failed to alter India's and Pakistan's stated positions on the Kashmir issue, or to change the fundamentals of the conflict in and over Kashmir. An end to the bloodshed in the State, consequently, seems as unlikely today as it was at any given point since the dramatic escalation of the militancy in 1989-90.

According to the *Human Rights Watch,* "The post-earthquake role of militant organisations underlines the continuity of the military-militant relationship in Azad Kashmir. Pakistan's two-track policy on the militant groups operating in Jammu and Kashmir State–assurances of roll-back for international consumption but only a scale-down and lower visibility in the theatre of operations–appears to be continuing. The Pakistani military apparently saw the earthquake as an opportunity to craft a new image for the militant groups rather than as an opportunity to disband them."[20]

---

20 ""With Friends Like These..."Human Rights Violations in Azad Kashmir," http://hrw.org/reports/2006/pakistan0906/3.htm.

CHAPTER 3

Sectarian Violence In The Northern Areas

D. Suba Chandran[1]

Recent years have witnessed a sudden spurt in the sectarian violence in the Northern Areas, especially in Gilgit region. While during the 1980s, there was only one major sectarian violent incident, since 2003, there have been a series of events. During 2004 and 2005 alone, more than 100 people were killed in the sectarian violence. What started with a controversy over the focus of curriculum in the schools in mid-2003, increased the sectarian fault line and snowballed into a serious conflict, pitching one group over the other. Unlike the 1988 incident, the recent violence does not seem to be a one-off event that will die soon. The violence seems to be spreading and has been witnessing killings and counter killings. Worse, the violence in the Northern Areas is also having its echoes elsewhere, for example, in Karachi.

Why are the Northern Areas facing sectarian violence today, when the different communities of Gilgit and Baltistan have lived in peace and remained united all these years?[2] What are the major sources and causes of sectarian tensions in the

---

1 Dr. D. Suba Chandran is Assistant Director at the Institute of Peace and Conflict Studies, New Delhi. Currently he is a Visiting Fellow at the Centre for Strategic and Regional Studies, University of Jammu

2 The only exception being the sectarian carnage that took place in 1988 in Gilgit. Except that incident, one could even conclude, that there was sectarian harmony until the 1990s in these regions. According to the ICG report, "prior to 1988,

Northern Areas? Are the fault lines inherent or being imposed? The first section of this essay, attempts to profile the major sectarian violent events in the Northern Areas. The second section makes an effort to map the various reasons and causes for this sectarian violence. The last section provides a set of conclusions and forecasts.

---

sectarian tensions were rare and did not result in armed conflict. Shias and Sunnis had coexisted peacefully. Intermarriages were frequent, and the resultant ties of kinship took precedence over sectarian differences. Historically, too, ethnic ties and tribal loyalties were more important than sectarian identities. After 1988, however, Gilgit gradually changed from a peaceful tourist destination into a battleground for Sunni and Shia militants." See International Crisis Group Report, *Discord in Pakistan's Northern Areas*, April 2007.

I

Sectarian Violence in the Northern Areas: A Profile

The first major sectarian rift in the Northern Areas took place in 1988, when a minor incident was purposefully allowed to boil over and exploited by external factors. But, it subsided and there was peace in the 1990s, however uneasy, it may have been. In this decade, since 2003, there have been a series of bloody sectarian events.

The 1988 Violence

The 1988 sectarian violence in the Northern Areas started with an issue that is generally associated even today with the sighting of the moon and observing the fast during Ramadan. There has always been a difference in opinion in terms of sighting the moon, which happens all over Pakistan. In 1998, amongst the Shia community, the scholars sighted the moon, hence broke the fasting, while the Sunnis were still observing it. This led to minor violence, but the issue was amicably settled and for four days, there was peace. What followed then, is best explained in the following words of the local media, quoted in *The Friday Times*:

> "Zia exploited a minor issue of moon-sighting and observance of Ramadan fasting and masterminded the murder of 700 innocent people that included women, elders and children…a huge lashkar [army] of 80,000 Sunni extremists was sent by Zia-ul-Haq's government to annihilate the Shias. Villages inhabited by the Shias

> – Jalalabad, Bonji, Darot, Jaglot, Pari, and Manawar were completely ruined. Even their animals [livestock] were slaughtered. The Laskhar had travelled a long distance from Mansehra to Gilgit and the government did not stop it. Instead, it put the blame on RAW and CIA."[3]

The ICG report, published recently, stated the following on this incident: "For three days, they (the Sunni militants) killed, looted and pillaged with impunity while the authorities sat back and watched. Although contingents of the paramilitary Frontier Constabulary (FC) were eventually sent in, they too looked the other way while Sunni attackers wreaked havoc. By the time army units were sent in to quell the violence, at least 150 people were killed, several hundred injured and property worth millions of rupees destroyed."[4]

Ironically, according to a report, it was General Musharraf, then a Brigadier with the SSG, was chosen by General Zia-ul-Haq in May 1998 to bring down the Shias; Musharraf, recruited several thousands of Sunni tribals from the Afghan borders, and let them loose against the Shias.[5] According to the same report, "the Balawaris also remember Musharraf as the man who played a key role in changing the demographic composition of the area. He brought large numbers of Sunni businessmen from Punjab and the NWFP and helped them to set up business in the Northern Areas."[6]

---

[3] Mohammad Shehzad, "Textbook controversy in Gilgit," *The Friday Times,* July 4-10, 2003, Vol. XV, No. 19.

[4] International Crisis Group Report, *Discord in Pakistan's Northern Areas*, April 2007.

[5] Sultan Shaheen, "Free Balawaristan movement gains momentum," http://www.jammu-kashmir.com/insights/insight20000206b.html.

[6] Sultan Shaheen, "Free Balawaristan movement gains momentum," http://www.jammu-kashmir.com/insights/insight20000206b.html.

Why did Zia want to use this minor issue to initiate a major sectarian conflict, for after this attack, the sectarian peace was shattered? Two factors could be attributed towards Zia's efforts to increase the sectarian fault lines in the Northern Areas. First, ever since the Northern Areas came under the control of Pakistan, Zia, for the first time, took effective steps to formally and officially integrate the region into Pakistan. Until then, the rulers of Pakistan put forward a bogus reason for not providing any constitutional or political status to the Northern Areas – that the region was a part of Jammu and Kashmir, which is disputed, hence no administrative change could be introduced. Zia, for the first time decided to change this bogus argument and formally annex the Northern Areas with Pakistan. In fact, he was the first military ruler to extend the martial rule to the Northern Areas in 1977. Zia also attempted to keep the Northern Areas away from the Kashmir dispute. According to a report published in Islamabad, Zia on May 9, 1982 told the correspondents in Quetta, "Kashmir has been a disputed issue, but so far as the Northern Areas are concerned, we do not accept them disputed."[7]

As a part of formally integrating the Northern Areas with Pakistan, Zia, for the first time nominated three members from the region as observers in the *Majlis-e-Shura*, and even made the following observation during his inaugural speech at the second session of the *Shura:* "I am not talking of Kashmir; I am talking about the Northern Areas, *which make a part of Pakistan.*"[8] (Emphasis added) Zia also had plans to give

[7] Quoted in the IPS Task Force Report, "Northern Areas of Pakistan: Facts, Problems and Recommendations," *Policy Perspectives,* April 2004, Vol.1, No.1, p.121

[8] GM Mir, "Future of Gilgit and Baltistan," *Daily Nawai Waqt,* October 19, 1982, quoted in the IPS Task Force Report, "Northern Areas of Pakistan: Facts, Problems and Recommendations," *Policy Perspectives,* April 2004, Vol.1, No.1, p.121.

representation to the Northern Areas in the National Assembly and the Justice Ministry was directed to remove all hurdles in providing this.[9]

Thus, it is clear, that Zia wanted to integrate the Northern Areas formally with Pakistan and make its people Pakistanis. The sectarian streak in Zia, perhaps could have guided him to make the Northern Areas not only a part of Pakistan, but also change the sectarian nature of this region. This could be one reason, for why Zia used a minor incident to blow over in the Northern Areas. Fortunately for the Northern Areas, his untimely death provided the space for uneasy peace for at least another decade.

The second reason, for the 1988 violence in the Northern Areas, perhaps could be the general sectarian upsurge in Pakistan.[10] This sectarian madness all over the country, perhaps also pulled the Northern Areas into it. Thanks to the *jihad* against the Soviet Union and the worsening of Pakistan-Iran relations in the 1980s, the sectarian peace all over Pakistan was completely shattered, with 1988 becoming a major benchmark year. There was sectarian violence all over Pakistan during this period, especially led by the Sunni fundamentalists in Shia-dominated regions including Karachi, parts of Punjab and NWFP and Khurram Valley in the Federally Administered Tribal Agencies (FATA) of Pakistan. The Shia groups responded to this, by forming their own radical organisations. Thus the Sipah-e-Sahaba (SSP) and Sipah-e-Muhammad

---

[9] See-IPS Task Force Report, "Northern Areas of Pakistan: Facts, Problems and Recommendations," *Policy Perspectives,* April 2004, Vol.1, No.1, p.121.

[10] For a brief analysis of sectarian violence in Pakistan, see Suba Chandran, "Sectarian Violence in Pakistan," IPCS Issue Brief 09, August 2003, http://www.ipcs.org/newIpcsPublications.jsp?status=publications&status1=issue&mod=d&check=13&try=true.

Pakistan (SMP) had their origins linked to this general sectarian upsurge of this period.[11]

Thus whatever happens in Pakistan in terms of sectarian violence, it reverberates in the Northern Areas. One could see this pattern being repeated in the recent years as well. In the recent period, Pakistan witnessed a sudden increase in sectarian killings; more than 200 people were killed in 2004 alone.[12] In 2005, there was the maximum number of killings in the Northern Areas, starting from the killing of Agha Ziauddin Rizvi in January. One could easily establish a correlation between the sectarian violence in the Northern Areas and elsewhere in Pakistan in the recent years, especially since 2003.

2003-05: Violence Over the Curriculum Controversy

The sectarian tensions started during mid-2003, when the government decided to introduce the new curriculum. Though this issue was boiling slowly for at least three years before 2003, real seeds of violence were thrown during this year. In June 2003, Agha Ziauddin Rizvi, Khateeb of the Imamia Mosque, made a serious note on the new syllabus; he was reported to have said that the syllabus would affect over 75 per cent of the population in the Northern Areas and the issue was not only confined to Islamiat textbooks, but also include

---

[11] The SSP was founded in 1985 by Maulana Haq Nawaz Jhangvi, Maulana Zia-ur-Rehman Farooqi, Maulana Eesar-ul-Haq Qasmi, and Maulana Azam Tariq. See "In the Spotlight: Sipah-I-Sahaba Pakistan (SSP),"

http://www.cdi.org/program/document.cfm?documentid=2308&programID=39&from_page=../friendlyversion/printversion.cfm; and "Sipah-e-Sahaba,"

http://www.satp.org/satporgtp/countries/pakistan/terroristoutfits/ssp.htm; The SMP is believed to be founded in early 1990s. See "Sipah-e-Mohammed Pakistan,"

http://www.satp.org/satporgtp/countries/pakistan/terroristoutfits/SMP.htm

[12] See Samina Ahmed, "The Sectarian Challenge," *Newsline,* April 2005, p.35.

other textbooks of Urdu, History, English and even the drawing books.[13] According to him, this new syllabus was designed to promote and preach the thoughts of a particular sect.[14] According to the Curriculum Reform Committee of the Northern Areas, Gilgit the following are the major points of controversy relating to the textbooks:

- *"The incident of wahee (revelation) has been described in a ridiculous manner that shows the Prophet himself was not sure about his prophethood. Islamiat, 4th grade, 22; Social Studies, 4th grade, 115; Urdu, 8th grade, 14.*
- *Abraham's father Azar has been described as worshipper of idols. Islamiat, 6th grade, 62.*
- *The Prophet was said to have missed his prayer during the battle Khandaq. Islamiat, 5th grade, 43.*
- *The Prophet's wife Ayesha has been projected as superior to all other women of the Prophet's family through fake ahadiz (sayings of the Prophet). Urdu, 7th, 9-10.*
- *The Sunni caliphs have been presented as Khulfa-e-Rashideen unopposed by Shias. [The Shias do not recognise the first three caliphs as Khulfa-e-Rashideen.] Urdu, 3th grade, 89; Arabic, 7th grade, 46; Social Studies, 7th grade, 12-14.*
- *The Caliphs [that are not recognised by Shias] have been eulogised through titles such as Siddique-wa-Amirul Momineen [the First Caliph Hazrat Abu Bakar Siddique] and Farooq-wa-Amirul Momineed [the Second Caliph Hazrat Umar Farooq]. Shia claim such titles are only for Hazrat Ali [the Fourth Caliph]. Urdu, 4th grade, 77; Islamiat, 4th grad, 25; Arabic, 8th grade, 27.*

---

[13] "Week's deadline for recasting syllabus," *Dawn*, June 4, 2003.

[14] "Week's deadline for recasting syllabus," *Dawn*, June 4, 2003.

- *The Sunni Caliphs have been glorified through special chapters that pay them a rich tribute. No such tribute has been paid to the Shia Caliphs.*
- *It is a fabricated statement that the Prophet asked the First Caliph to lead the prayer when he [the Prophet] was ill. Islamiat, 5th grade, 59-60. Islamiat, BA, 294.*
- *The contribution and sacrifices of Hazrat Ali have been faded out deliberately.*
- *Yazid has been totally exonerated from Karbala and the entire blame has been shifted to Ibn-e-Ziyad. Urdu, 8th grade, 105.*
- *Khalid bin Walid has been praised more compared to Hazrat Ali. It is untrue that the Prophet had bestowed him [Walid] the title of Saif Ullah. Urdu, 7th grade, 30-33.*
- *Sunni procedure of ablution has been featured in Islamiat, Urdu, 9-10th grade, 157.*
- *The addition of prayer is better than sleep. Islamiat, grade 8th, 8.*
- *Sunni procedure of prayer is features. Islamiat, 2nd grade, 15; Urdu, 3rd grade, 57.*
- *A picture that depicts the Sunni style of saying prayer. Urdu, 2nd grade, 18.*
- *Such sayings of the Prophet have been quoted that have been recorded by the Sunni historians.*
- *The Islamiat of 12th grade promotes the Sunni school of thought.*
- *The Prophet's uncle Hazrat Abu Talib has been described as non-Muslim. Islamiat, BA, 231."*[15]

---

[15] Quoted in Mohammad Shehzad, "Textbook controversy in Gilgit," *The Friday Times*, July 4-10, 2003, Vol. XV, No. 19.

The main demand of the Shia community, as detailed elsewhere was the following: "The long-lasting peace in this mountainous region cannot be guaranteed unless and until necessary changes as proposed by the Shia community are brought about and made part of the Islamiat syllabus...We are not against the existing Islamiat and other syllabi but Shia students should not be forced to study the present syllabus as we deem this to be controversial and a cause of sectarian rift. We want a syllabus reflecting our beliefs."[16]

In July 2003, in Skardu, locals, including hundreds of school students from the Shia community organised a rally to protest against the committee to review the Islamiat curriculum; the committee was constituted by the Northern Areas administration.[17] Their demand was to include a Shia leader in the committee, so that the news syllabus in the textbooks in the Northern Areas is acceptable to the Shia community.

During mid-2004, there were clear signs of the forthcoming violence. In June 2004, after failing to reach an understanding with the government, the Shia community led by Aga Ziauddin Rizvi and Didar Ali, then a member of the Northern Areas Legislative Council, decided to stage a rally. The government immediately imposed an indefinite curfew and deployed the Army, which was breached. This event witnessed by the local people damaged the offices of the Police Recruits Training Centre, and Radio Pakistan; in the following shootout, one person was killed and six others injured.[18] The stalemate

---

[16] "Shia leader demands separate syllabus," *Dawn,* May 14, 2004.

[17] "Representation on curriculum body sought," *Dawn,* July 1, 2003.

[18] See "Curfew imposed in Gilgit; one killed," *The News,* June 4, 2004; "Curfew in Gilgit; protester killed," *Dawn,* June 4, 2004.

continued, with no understanding being reached between the government and the Shia community. In December 2004, a meeting was held, in which reopening of the schools, which were closed in June was discussed. The heads of institutions could not give an assurance, that their students would not engage in violence or protests once the schools were reopened.[19]

However, the killing of Aga Ziauddin Rizvi, who was spearheading the curriculum issue, in January 2005, sparked a new round of violence during that entire year. In March 2005, Sakhiullah Tareen, who was just removed from power as the IG police of the Northern Areas was killed. Tareen was considered "to be imbued with extreme Sunni views and was inspired by the Taliban's sectarian politics from his days as a Pakistani diplomat in Afghanistan" and killing was seen "certainly as an act of revenge for the killing of Rizvi in Gilgit by Sunni fanatics."[20]

Finally the curriculum issue was resolved in April 2005. The Northern Area Syllabus Issue Committee agreed to withdraw the textbooks of Islamiyat and Urdu of the Punjab Textbook Board and approved the books of NWFP Textbook Board and the National Book Foundation, as the latter were acceptable to the sects.[21] The schools were reopened in April 2005, but unfortunately the damage had already been done, as the sectarian violence continued throughout the year.

In July 2005, near Chilas, a NATCO bus travelling from Gilgit to Rwalapindi was attacked and four passengers were

---

[19] "Reopening of Schools delayed," *Dawn,* December 24, 2004.

[20] Khaled Ahmed, "The trouble in Gilgit," *The Friday Times,* July 8-14, 2005, Vol. XVII, No. 20

[21] "Gilgit schools reopen today after one-year," *The News,* April 19, 2005.

killed.[22] Between January and July 2005, according to a news report, there were at least a dozen of such attacks along the KKH, killing more than 15 people.[23] In most cases, such attacks along the Karakoram Highway, especially in the lower part around Astore and Chilas are blamed on robbery and bandits. However, most of the attacks were carried out by the Sunni fundamentalists who are in a majority in these regions. Astore today has almost 100 per cent Sunni population, whereas Chilas has 90 per cent. This region has become a hub of Sunni fundamentalists and radicals over the years, and ever since 9/11 one could see a pattern in their increased activities along the KKH. Perhaps they understood the economic and strategic significance of the KKH ever since they blocked the highway and occupied the Chilas airstrip protesting against the US-led coalition forces' air strikes in Afghanistan in 2001 after 9/11.[24] People who suffered the most out of this blockade were those living beyond Astore, as essential commodities including wheat flour, fuel and related items suddenly became unavailable, not even giving time for the locals to stock them.

Even the devastating earthquake in October 2005, which affected the "AJK" and parts of NWFP and Northern Areas and the emotional outpour towards it, did not affect this region, as it was embroiled in its own sectarian violence. In fact, there was a fresh round of sectarian violence during October 2005. An analysis of this round of violence will prove the State's lethargy or highhandedness if not complicity in sectarian violence in Gilgit. On October 11, 2005, when the rest of Pakistan and PoK were counting the dead bodies of the

---

[22] "Four killed as bus ambushed on KKH," *The News,* July 19, 2005.

[23] "Bus ambushed on KKH; four killed," *Dawn,* July 19, 2005

[24] See "Blockade of Chilas airstrip, KKH continues," *Dawn,* October 31, 2001; "Blockade of KKH enters second week," *Dawn,* November 2, 2001.

earthquake, armed militants in the outskirts of Gilgit opened fire on a bus, killing one passenger and injuring seven others.[25] The police apprehended one of the attackers. However, the trouble broke out, when the attacker was taken away from the local police by the military.[26] A group of Shia students, suspecting that the government was protecting the attackers or their identity, attempted to prevent the rangers from shifting the militant from Gilgit's District Headquarters Hospital to the Combined Military Hospital. A Shia student in the ninth class was detained and tortured by the Rangers; on 13th October; students held a demonstration demanding the release of the student who was detained. In the process there was a firing and a cross firing from both sides leading to twelve deaths, including two Rangers.[27] The Human Rights Commission of Pakistan's (HRCP) Secretary General Iqbal Haider later announced at a press conference in Islamabad that the Rangers had "unleashed terror" on Gilgit's population.[28] Following this event, there were demonstrations and protests by the Shia community all over Gilgit.

This round of violence however did not spiral further, thanks to the efforts made by a local *jirga*, which included members from the civil society and representatives of the local administration who also attended the meeting. A section inside this *jirga* demanded withdrawal of paramilitary forces from Gilgit and according to a news report, "called for their replacement by a 'neutral and impartial force.'"[29] Such an

---

[25] "Two killed, 10 injured in Gilgit ambush," *Dawn,* October 12, 2005.

[26] Sarmad Abbas, "Unending War," *The Herald,* November 2005, p.32.

[27] See "Six die in Gilgit violence," *Dawn,* October 14, 2005; "Death toll in Gilgit violence soars to 12," *Dawn,* October 15, 2005.

[28] "HRCP demands Rangers in Gilgit cease fire," *Dawn,* November 3, 2005.

[29] "Peace efforts resumed in Gilgit, *jirga* reactivated," *Dawn,* October 25, 2005.

attempt was tried even before the violence broke out, led by Malik Mohammad Miskeen, the Northern Areas Legislative Council Speaker. The grand *jirga* reached an understanding on promoting peace and had even drafted an agreement which was to be signed by leaders and clerics belonging to both the Shia and Unni communities. This draft, was apparently approved by Agha Rahat Al-Hussaini, a Shia cleric, whereas Maulana Qazi Nisar Ahmed, the Sunni cleric and Amir of Tanzeem Ahle Sunnah wal Jama'at, Northern Areas and Kohistan, was yet to formally sign as he was away in Rawalpindi.[30] According to a *Herald* report, "the local administration itself did not allow Qazi Nisar to sign the agreement and knowingly kept him away in Rawalpindi until the violence broke out."[31] The State's complicity in sectarian violence is an important issue, which is subsequently discussed in the next section.

30 "Peace efforts resumed in Gilgit, *jirga* reactivated," *Dawn,* October 25, 2005.

31 Sarmad Abbas, "Unending War," *The Herald,* November 2005, p.33.

II

Understanding the Causes of Sectarian Fault Lines

What are the major causes of sectarian violence in the Northern Areas? Why would the sectarian violence suddenly flare up in the recent years, after being under the carpet, especially since the 1998 incident? The reasons are general, historical, strategic and specific, which are discussed below.

A. Absence of Governance

Absence of governance and lack of democratic institutions could be identified as a major reason for the sectarian violence in the Northern Areas. Numerous articles published in the Pakistani media in recent years have highlighted the fact that with no democratic and secular means to reach out to the government, the local youths are venting their anger through sectarian expressions. In a landmark decision on May 28, 1999, the Supreme Court of Pakistan ruled that "it was not understandable on what basis the people of the Northern Areas can be denied the fundamental rights guaranteed under the Constitution. We are of the view that the people of the Northern Areas are citizens of Pakistan for all intents and purposes. They have the rights to invoke any fundamental rights..."[32]

Despite these rulings, subsequent governments–democratic and political have not taken adequate measures to

[32] The Supreme Court verdict is discussed elsewhere in this book. See the chapter on the critique of the ICG report.

address the issue. Lack of proper constitutional and legal status to the region, thus is a major reason for the sectarian violence in the Northern Areas. Besides, whatever institutions are available, such as the Northern Areas Legislative Council (NALC), they do not wield any powers in reality and are toothless. Both these issues have affected the social and economic development of this region. These three issues are worth discussing in detail here.

Lack of Constitutional Status

The people of the Northern Areas have neither any constitutional rights nor any basic fundamental rights. They are neither the citizens of Pakistan nor of the "AJK". Neither the constitutional provisions of Pakistan nor that of the "AJK" is extended to the people of the Northern Areas. Subsequent reforms since the 1970s have proved both insufficient and inefficient.

As mentioned elsewhere in this book, four major efforts have been taken on reforming the administrative structure of the Northern Areas.[33] In the 1970s, Zulfikar Ali Bhutto introduced the first set of reforms; in 1974, he abolished both the Agency system existing then and the Frontier Crimes Regulation (FCR) which were the guiding rules. Instead he created a Northern Areas Council (NAC), whose members were directly elected. Gilgit and Baltistan became two districts. As mentioned above, Zia attempted to make the Northern Areas a part of Pakistan; had he not met with that fatal accident, perhaps, he would have accomplished the task. In 1994, almost two decades after the first set of reforms, the second set was introduced, during Benazir Bhutto's period. The NAC became

[33] The chapter on the critique of the ICG report deals with these issues as well.

the Northern Areas Legislative Council (NALC). Though the post-1994 reforms period witnessed the mobilisation of the Shia community under the Tehreek-e-Nafaz-e-Fiqah-e-Jafria (TNFJ), it did not lead to any major sectarian upheaval. Perhaps, the political representation of the TNFJ in the NALC (it won ten out of the 24 seats) addressed, at least initially some concerns of the community. However, the failure of Islamabad to transfer any real administrative and executive powers to the NALC made this exercise irrelevant.

In 2004, exactly after a decade, General Musharraf introduced the set of reforms in 2004, just before the election to the NALC. One is not sure, whether the package was to address the election concerns, so that the pro-military PML-Q could garner more seats. Whatever may be the real reasons, according to the 2004 package, the NALC's strength was increased, with three additional members to be elected by the originally elected 24 council members; increased seats for women by 33 per cent in districts and union councils by 33 per cent; an appellate court for Northern Areas established; the administrative powers of the Ministry of Kashmir Affairs and Northern Affairs transferred to the NA administration; and a new district Astore created.[34] Afzal Shigri, commenting on this reforms package wrote: "The package fell far short of the expectations of the people as the least that they wanted was the implementation of the judgement of the Supreme Court of Pakistan that had clearly directed that the people of the area must be given self-rule through its representatives and an independent judiciary to protect the fundamental rights of the people."[35]

---

[34] See "Musharraf announces uplift package for Northern Areas," *The News,* October 12, 2004; "NALC expanded, new district created," *Dawn,* October 12, 2004.

[35] Afzal Shigri, "Reforms Package for NA," *The News,* November 12, 2004.

Toothless NALC

The Northern Areas Legislative Council (NALC) is the highest decision-making body in the Northern Areas, but with no effective power. The power to make all decisions important or otherwise, rest with the Kashmir and Northern Areas Affairs (KANA), which is headed by a federal minister in Islamabad. The following, though mentioned in a later chapter in this work, is worth repeating here as well, for it will prove how powerless the NALC is. In 2003, *Dawn,* reporting the proceedings of the NALC highlighted the discussion. The first one was a demand from one of the NALC members, that the Speaker, Deputy Chief Executives and the Advisers should resign from the NALC, as they have failed to get the medical superintendent of DHQ Hospital in Gilgit to comply with an order of the NALC health adviser regarding the transfer of a doctor.[36] The second case, which was reported at the same meeting, was on similar lines. The food department officials refused to allow the NALC Adviser of the department from visiting and inquiring into the affairs of the department.[37]

Following the introduction reforms package in late 2004, a leading commentator on the Northern Areas writes what was expected the least from Islamabad: "The least that the government should do is to appoint the leader of the house as the Chief Executive of the NA with the powers of a Chief Minister of a province so that the governance of the region could be entrusted to the elected representatives of the people instead of an unaccountable bureaucracy."[38]

36 "NALC members ask cabinet to quit," *Dawn,* July 3, 2003.

37 "NALC members ask cabinet to quit," *Dawn,* July 3, 2003.

38 Afzal Shigri, "Reforms Package for NA," *The News,* November 12, 2004.

Social and Economic Underdevelopment

The above two issues have ultimately resulted in the social and economic underdevelopment of the region. According to an analyst with the Institute of Policy Studies, who has been engaged in publishing a report on the Northern Areas:

> "That the entire region of NAs does not have any kind of industry is an inescapable fact and there is no doubt that 85 per cent of the people live below the poverty line here. Local people are extremely poor, living in some of the harshest environmental conditions of weather and terrain. Often, summer temperatures exceed 40°C; whereas in the winter, the mercury may drop below 25°C. People mostly depend on government-offered jobs and join defence-related institutions to earn their livelihood. Before the nuclear explosions of 1998, tourism was the economic lifeline but the explosions mixed with the subsequent events of the 9/11 almost dried up the avenue. Resultantly, the unemployment and lack of equal opportunities have today created an explosive situation; there is widespread unrest and frustration amongst the masses."[39]

The balance sheet of the above failures is obvious. To quote Ershad Mahmud again:

> "The non-local chief secretaries had since long been the sole authority to run the areas on behalf of the federal minister while unchecked deputy commissioners

---

[39] Ershad Mahmud, "Challenges before the new government in NAs," *The News,* December 11, 2004. Ershad was a part of the IPS Task Force that prepared an in-depth report titled, "Northern Areas of Pakistan: Facts, Problems and Recommendations." See IPS Task Force Report, "Northern Areas of Pakistan: Facts, Problems and Recommendations," *Policy Perspectives,* April 2004, Vol.1, No.1. pp. 121-141.

> run district management answerable to the chief secretary instead of the deputy chief executive. It is widely believed that the NALC – the powerless legislative body – has been a bitter experience for the people of Gilgit and Baltistan. *The bureaucratic rule– mainly from the NWFP and the Punjab – has heightened the sense of alienation and completely eroded the notion of self-rule from amongst the people's minds.*"[40] (Emphasis added)

Clearly, there is alienation in the Northern Areas, due to the failure of governance, which gets reflected in sectarian terms, as other democratic forms of expressions have not yielded results. For example, the mainstream political parties of Pakistan do have a presence in the Northern Areas. The PPP is considered to have better influence amongst the locals, but the military regime's efforts to keep the party away played an important role in undermining the political process, thereby creating a vacuum and letting the sectarian organisations take over. Both in the 1980s and early years of this decade, Zia then and Musharraf now for various political reasons at the national level, did not allow the political parties in general, and PPP in particular, to effectively play a role on the election held to the NALC. As a result, the effectiveness of political parties as being the vehicle of domestic expressions got seriously curtailed. Even when there was a democratic dispensation at the national level, party/dispensation ruling in Islamabad always wanted to have its say in the Northern Areas. The 2004 election for the NALC reflects this reality at the ground level; the PML-Q acquired a majority in the NALC, after many of the independent members were either forced or lured to join the party. It is no coincidence that the sectarian

[40] Ershad Mahmud, "Challenges before the new government in NAs," *The News*, December 11, 2004.

violence in the Northern Areas got a fillip after the 2004 election to the NALC. There were sectarian rumblings before the 2004 election, but the way in which loyalties were purchased after it, perhaps made the NALC an ineffective institution of any democratic expression. Some of the independents, who won the election on anti-State sentiments, suddenly became staunch supporters of the regime.

Precisely for the failure of political parties, the sectarian groups are able to wield better influence over them, mainly due to the mosques and *madrassas* factor. With the mainstream education in the doldrums, as has been the case with Pakistan, there is an increased emphasis on the *madrassa* education, ultimately resulting in sectarian teachings and providing a fertile ground for the subsequent sectarian violence in the Northern Areas.

B. Sectarian Nature of Demography

The demographic nature of any region plays a vital role in maintaining peace or inducing violence. In the Northern Areas as well, the demographic profile of the region plays an important role. According to the April 2007 International Crisis Group Report on the Northern Areas, the region has a population of around 1.5 million; of this, approximately, 39 per cent is Shia, 27 per cent Sunni, 18 per cent Ismaili and 16 per cent Nurbakhshi.[41] Since there is no official break up of the sectarian break up of the districts, this research will rely upon two sources, quoted by Khaled Ahmed, a noted analyst in Pakistan and the International Crisis Group Report. Khaled Ahmed, quoting a book written by F.M. Khan titled the *History of Gilgit, Baltistan and Chitral: A Short History of Two Millennia*

[41] See ICG Report, Discord in Pakistan's Northern Areas, April 2007.

(2004), gives a district and region-wise breakdown of the Shia-Sunni composition in the Northern Areas; according to this, the sectarian population in Gilgit is 60 per cent Shia and 40 per cent Sunni; in Hunza 100 per cent Ismaili; in Nagar 100 per cent Shia; in Punial 100 per cent Ismaili; in Yasin 100 per cent Ismaili; in Ishkoman 100 per cent Ismaili; in Gupis 100 per cent Ismaili; in Chilas 100 per cent Sunni; in Darel/Tangir 100 per cent Sunni; in Astor 90 per cent Sunni and 10 per cent Shia; in Baltistan 96 per cent Shia, 2 per cent Nurbakhti and 2 per cent Sunni.[42]

The ICG report in a footnote, quotes Manzoom Ali's work titled *Atlas of the Northern Areas* (Gilgit, 2004), which according to the report is considered as the "the most accurate account of the Northern Areas' sectarian profile" by the local population. According to it, "Gilgit district is 54 per cent Shia, 27 per cent Ismaili and 19 per cent Sunni; Skardu district is 87 per cent Shia, 10 per cent Nurbakhshi and 3 per cent Sunni; Diamer district is 90 per cent Sunni and 10 per cent Shia; Ghizer district is 87 per cent Ismaili and 13 per cent Sunni; and Ghangche district is 87 per cent Nurbakhshi, 8 per cent Sunni and 5 per cent Shia. The district of Astore, carved out of Diamer district in 2005 and created after the publication of the Atlas, is believed to be 70 per cent Sunni and 30 per cent Shia."[43]

An analysis of sectarian attacks over the recent years will reveal, that most of the attacks are centred around two regions/districts – Gilgit, and Chilas and Astore. The reasons are not difficult to identify, why there is sectarian conflict in

[42] Khaled Ahmed, "The trouble in Gilgit," *The Friday Times,* July 8-14, 2005, Vol. XVII, No. 20.

[43] See the ICG Report, Discord in Pakistan's Northern Areas, April 2007.

these two areas, while the other regions are relatively peaceful. Those regions which have not witnessed the sectarian madness in the Northern Areas, including Hunza, Nagar, Punial, Yasin, Ishkoman, Gupis and to an extent even Baltistan, primarily or in most cases are homogeneous in terms of the sectarian composition. These areas are wholly dominated by the Shias or Ismailis, where there is no presence of the 'other'.

Whereas Gilgit, Chilas and Astore have become areas of sectarian violence for the following reasons. First, Gilgit is volatile, for the sectarian composition is not uniform; it has a 60 per cent Shia population and 40 per cent Sunni population. The sectarian fault line along with the State's support to one section (the Sunnis) has added the volatility of the situation. In case of Gilgit, as reported elsewhere in this essay, there are reasons to suspect that the State has joined hands with the Sunni fundamentalists. Second, the geo-strategic location of Gilgit, as explained subsequently is important for Islamabad.

Though the demographic distribution has been the same even before the 1980s, a crucial foreign policy decision of Pakistan in the 1980s and the 1990s, exploited this demographic profile, ultimately resulting in introducing sectarian violence in the Northern Areas. The use of *jihad* as an instrument vis-à-vis Afghanistan in the 1980s and vis-à-vis Kashmir in the 1990s, totally transformed this region, especially the Sunni–dominated Chilas and Astore in the Northern Areas. Not only were people from these regions recruited for the *jihad* in the 1980s and 1990s, but this period also witnessed a constant interaction between the local Sunni population and the sectarian and *jihadi* organisations including the SSP, Lashkar-e-Jhangvi, Lashkar-e-Toiba and the Jaish-e-Mohammad. All these organisations adhere to militant Sunni ideology, which consider not only the Shias, but even the Brelvi ideology as un-Islamic. Added to this interaction was the easy availability of small arms and light weapons in this region. These two factors, totally changed the Shia-Sunni interactions in the Northern Areas.

C. Geo-Strategic Importance of the Northern Areas

Is it possible, the absence of governance, lack of connectivity and assassination politics are a part of a larger plan to keep the Northern Areas under perpetual control? Is it possible, the sectarian violence is not a natural outcome or a collateral damage of the above, but deliberately orchestrated by Islamabad, so as to keep the Northern Areas divided on sectarian lines?

To answer the above questions, one should first look into the geo-strategic importance of the Northern Areas. This region is strategically important for Pakistan, for this is the only region, which has borders with Afghanistan (more importantly), China, PoK and India. None of the provinces in Pakistan have borders with all the three countries that matter to Pakistan – Afghanistan, China and India.

Pakistan's physical connectivity with its 'all weather ally' China – the mighty Karakoram Highway (KKH) runs through the Northern Areas. Gilgit, the administrative headquarters of the Northern Areas is a major staging point in the KKH. Pakistan since June 2006 has started a bus service between Gilgit and Kashhgar.[44] There are further plans to expand the economic cooperation between the two countries in this region. According to a report, China has promised to invest $350 enabling Pakistan to open its northern borders for trade with

[44] "Pakistan-China bus service inaugurated," *Dawn,* June 16, 2006.

China and Central Asian states.[45] The Sust dry port, a joint effort by Pakistan and China, built at the cost of $1.26 has been functional since 2005.[46] There are also grand plans to expand the KKH and have a railway and gas pipelines built along with it. General Musharraf has hinted in 2006 that building of such a connection would mark the ninth and tenth wonders.[47] If China and Pakistan could succeed building such a connection, undoubtedly it should be considered as the next world wonders.

The economic significance of the KKH is enormous, that if the road is closed even for a short period, the losses will be significant. For example, when this road was closed in 2003, because of the SARS threat in China, Pakistan and the Northern Areas had to bear the major brunt. According to a report, in one month "the traders in the Northern Areas suffered a loss of Rs.100m, the Northern Areas Transport Corporation (NATCO) lost Rs. 5 million, customs revenue collection fell by Rs. 49.18m, Rs. 800,000 was paid by the importers whose consignments were blocked and had to pay charges to truckers in China, and the hotels along the Karakoram Highway had lost around Rs1.8 million."[48]

Besides, the KKH is also significant for exploiting the tourist potential of this region. Though there are air services to Gilgit and Skardu from Pakistan, the bulk of the tourist movement takes place through the KKH. The fact that after 9/11 and the increasing sectarian violence in the region has

---

[45] Aoun Sahi, "Going the Karakoram way," *The News,*

[46] Sust is a town in the northern most part of the Northern Areas, 170 kms from Gilgit, in the Hunza region. See "Sust dry port starts functioning," *Dawn,* June 3, 2005.

[47] "Karakoram Highway's Gwadar link likely," *Dawn,* July 29, 2006.

[48] See "Border closure causes Rs156m loss," *Dawn,* June 7, 2003.

affected the tourist inflow, thereby forcing the Northern Areas Transport Corporation (NATCO) to reduce its fleet and workers will reflect the economic significance of the KKH. Before 9/11, the NATCO used to ply 12 services a week between Gilgit and Rawalpindi, which is reduced to only five now.[49] Today the KKH assume even more importance, for two other factors – the Chinese investments in the Northern Areas and also elsewhere, especially in Gwadar;[50] and the proposed rail line and gas pipeline.

The geo-strategic location of the Northern Areas is of paramount importance, from a military perspective, as was seen during the Kargil conflict in 1999. The Northern Areas is also strategically important for Pakistan's water security. Afzal Shigri, on both these issues, made the following important observations on why this region is important for Pakistan: "The FO's (Foreign Office) suicidal push to include this area in a future United States of Kashmir has serious repercussions for Pakistan. *The country's biggest reservoir and lifeline cannot be allowed to be situated in a weak and unstable political entity*. It is therefore vital that the constitutional status of this area is settled once and for all and this area is integrated in Pakistan with representation in the National Assembly and Senate and its own provincial set-up."[51] (Emphasis added) Elsewhere he also commented, "The NA comprise a very sensitive and important

---

49 Since 9/11, the tourist potential to the Northern Areas has reduced to ten per cent of the original inflow. This has resulted in NATCO terminating the services of 200 workers. One could also argue that this termination is due to poor administration of the NATCO; The NATCO fleet of buses include only 70 buses and 165 trucks, not all of them in plying conditions. See "'We should learn to respect tourists...'," *The News,*

50 The Chinese interests and investments are discussed separately in another chapter. See Jabin T. Jacob.

51 Afzal Shigri, "Bhasha Dam, the Northern Areas and Pakistan," *The News,* January 9, 2006.

region that opens up Pakistan to China and Central Asia."[52]

Now back to the question raised earlier in this section – is it possible that Islamabad is playing the sectarian card, so as to divide and rule the Northern Areas? Perhaps. It is possible, that Islamabad does not want such an important region to be under the total control of the local population, which has a Shia majority. The following analysis of Khaled Ahmed, one of the most noted critics in Pakistan is worth reading in detail on this issue. On the killing of Allama Rizvi, he wrote:

> "The story in Gilgit is that one injured attacker who was arrested by the authorities had revealed that the dead terrorist was Mukhtar Ahmad, the son of a pesh imam in Peshawar city, who had belonged to a banned religious *jihadi* organisation. On the day Allama Rizvi was murdered the authorities immediately cut off all telecommunication links of the Northern Areas with the rest of the country. The government also banned all air and road traffic into the region and stopped all journalists from reporting anything other than the official handouts. *This kind of quarantine simply encouraged the terrorists to widen their activity. Instead of siding with the people the government seemed to join the extreme elements of the sectarian divide against the common man.*"[53] (Emphasis Added)

Once again, the Northern Areas is the only region in entire Pakistan, where the Sunnis are in a minority. If this region is given a provincial status or an administrative set up like that of the "AJK", it is only natural, that the region will be ruled by

[52] Afzal Shigri, "Kashmir dispute and status of Northern Areas," *The News*, December 8, 2005.

[53] Khaled Ahmed, "The Sectarian State in Gilgit," *The Friday Times,* July 15-21, 2005, Vol. XVII, No. 21.

the Shias. A comparative analysis with what is happening today in the FATA will prove this point. It is argued elsewhere that it is in the interest of Pakistan that it allows Talibanisation of certain tribal agencies such as North and South Waziristan, so as to thwart any cross-border Pashtun nationalist feeling from emerging against Islamabad. Subsequently, it could also be argued that, it is in the interest of Pakistan that the Northern Areas are divided in terms of sectarian identities than a nationalist Balwaristan identity to emerge.

D. Missing Emotional and Physical Connectivity with Pakistan

Physical and emotional connectivity with the rest of Pakistan, or the lack of it, is yet another factor for the sectarian violence in the Northern Areas. In most cases, the rest of Pakistan is not aware of what is happening inside the Northern Areas. Islamabad plays a major role in keeping the major negative developments in the Northern Areas under strict media censor and also blacking out all forms of connectivity. The case of what happened after the killing of Allama Rizvi, as mentioned above, in terms of the government immediately disconnecting all telecommunication links of the Northern Areas with the rest of Pakistan will prove this point.

The region also suffers from physical connectivity with the rest of Pakistan in another sense. The Karakoram Highway that runs south from Gilgit has to pass through Sunni–dominated regions of Astore and Chilas, before reaching the major cities of Pakistan. With most of the people in the Northern Areas relying upon the roads, the safety and security of the passengers along with the drivers assume paramount importance.

According to Khaled Ahmed, "the Northern Areas Transport organisation runs buses between the Northern Areas and the NWFP. Most of its 72 Shia drivers have refused to get on the buses because they fear attacks on the way as the buses pass through Sunni-dominated areas like Kohistan and Diamir. One bus service was given personal guarantees by chief minister NWFP, but when its buses passed through Diamir on April 18, 2005, they were fired upon. One bus suffered when 16 passengers received bullet wounds and the Shia driver was killed. The NWFP government declared the incident a dacoity while it was clearly a case of sectarian violence."[54]

The media has also failed to adequately highlight what is happening inside the Northern Areas. To extensively quote Khaled Ahmed again, "the failure of Pakistani journalism to report and discuss sectarianism has much to do with the tragedy of Gilgit. The 'politics' of sectarianism is moulded by the 'policy' of both communities to blame the violence on the United States. The blame Ayatollah Sistani of Iraq put on the Americans for the 2004 ashura massacre (a simultaneous bombing in Karachi was also blamed by the Shia and Sunni communities on the US) was echoed with great admiration by a number of columnists in the Urdu press. This pall of self-deception and sheer mendacity has disabled the national press in examining in close detail the quarrel over the textbooks prescribed by the Musharraf government for the Northern Areas."[55]

---

54 Khaled Ahmed, "The Sectarian State in Gilgit," *The Friday Times,* July 15-21, 2005, Vol. XVII, No. 21.

55 Khaled Ahmed, "The trouble in Gilgit," *The Friday Times,* July 8-14, 2005, Vol. XVII, No. 20.

Because of the above factors, the rest of Pakistan is not aware of what is happening in the Northern Areas, or do not have sufficient time to turn their attention towards the same. Till today, there have been hardly any discussions inside the Parliament on the constitutional situation prevailing in the Northern Areas. The reforms package announced by General Musharaf was not the result of any major debate in the Parliament, but was one of his arbitrary decisions. Nor is the Parliament interested in discussing the pressing problems of the Northern Areas. When Gilgit was under the sectarian fire during 2004-06, there was hardly any discussion in the Parliament.

The other major issue facing the people of the Northern Areas – the water security, especially in terms of the Bhasha-Diamer dam, there is less sympathy for their position elsewhere in Pakistan. Ismail Khan, a noted columnist on this issue, commented: "The Northern Areas will foot the bill for all the social, economic and ecological costs of the Bhasha dam, while the NWFP will pocket the royalties. Very equitable." Nor was the construction of the Skardu dam, its economic, human and environmental impact on the people of the Nortehrn Areas was ever appreciated by the rest in Pakistan. It was even noted that the very people who oppose the construction of Kalabagh on the humanitarian issue, support the construction of the Skardu dam.

CONCLUSIONS

Will sectarian violence in the Northern Areas decline in the coming days? Unlikely, for the following reasons. First, as discussed earlier, Islamabad is unlikely to provide any useful reforms package that will satisfy the local population in the Northern Areas. Until the Kashmir dispute is resolved between India and Pakistan, the latter is also not likely to provide any constitutional status to the Northern Areas. Pakistan's rhetoric of the entire Kashmir a dispute region has created a minor quagmire for its direct administration of the Northern Areas as its fifth province. Alternatively, Pakistan is neither inclined to provide a "AJK" type status to the Northern Areas, for it will create a region with a Shia majority, having its own administration, where the Sunni Muslims are in a minority. These issues, as a result, the Northern areas will continue remain without any constitutional guarantee, whether under Islamabad or Muzafarabad, purely remaining a colony of Pakistan.

Second, the Northern Areas Legislative Council (NALC) will continue to remain a toothless body. The Chief Executive ruling over from Islamabad, KANA and the civilian bureaucracy will continue to be the main decision making, implementing and reviewing bodies. The NALC will continue to remain as an advisory body, though elected directly by the people. The local population, primarily Shia, having no proper avenues to express their feelings vis-à-vis the State, is likely to use the sectarian route.

Third, the strategic location of the Northern Areas, for military and economic reasons is crucial to Islamabad. As discussed above, the Karakoram Highway, its importance in linking Gwadar with China, the military importance of Baltistan and the forthcoming dams in Northern Areas – all are of vital importance to Islamabad. It is important from Pakistan's perspective, that there is no unanimous local voice against Islamabad and it is unlikely, that Pakistan will allow a region of this importance to be under the control of non-Sunni Muslims. As a result, the government is likely to use the much abused divide and rule strategy and support Sunni militant groups.

Fourth, there are no sings of Islamabad allowing an independent political process in terms of parties strengthening themselves at the grass roots level in the Northern Areas. The present political vacuum is likely to continue, with none of the mainstream parties including the PPP to strengthen themselves at the grassroots level and engage in serious politicking. In the absence of such democratic processes, the sectarian organizations are likely to fill the political vacuum, thereby becoming the primary vehicles of popular expressions.

Finally, Islamabad is also not willing to pursue tough measures vis-à-vis sectarian political at the national level. The sectarian groups and their parent or sister jihadi organizations along with scores of madrassas from where they find recruitment continue even today. There is a clear link between the sectarian groups at national level in Pakistan, with those in the Northern Areas. In fact every sectarian killing in Karachi always had an echo in the Northern Areas or vice versa.

For the above reasons, the sectarian violence in the Northern Areas are likely to continue. There may not be an organized formal conflict between the two communities, but the region will face a series of violent incidents, never letting the wounds of the previous attack to heal.

CHAPTER 4

DIAMER-BASHA AND MANGLA DAMS: THE EMERGING WATER CONFLICT IN POK

Seema Sridhar[1]

> *"Fierce competition for fresh water may well become a source of conflict and wars in the future."*[2]
>
> Kofi Annan

The adage of recent conception that future wars would be fought over the world's water resources seems to have taken ground, not only in states' strategic thinking but also in their patterns of development. Several reports in recent years have been identifying water as a potential source of conflict and have called for urgent mechanisms to ensure better mechanisms for management, and distribution of fresh water resources. For instance, the UN Global Security Report on "Water, Conflict, and Cooperation" by Alexander Carius, Geoffrey D. Dabelko, and Aaron T. Wolf mentions the scenarios where water has been and could be a potential source of conflict, as well as a source for cooperation, if concerted efforts are made towards this end.[3] Sandra Postel of the Global Water Policy Project, in her article "Dehydrating Conflict" in *Foreign Policy* (October

---

1 Seema Sridhar is a Research Scholar, School of International Studies, Jawaharlal Nehru University, New Delhi.

2 UN Secretary General Kofi Annan delivers World Water Day message, March 22, 2002.

3 Alexander Carius, Geoffrey D. Dabelko, and Aaron T. Wolf, "Water, Conflict, and Cooperation" UN Global Security Report, June 1999.

2001) emphasises the need for nations to take preemptive steps, rather than act in retrospect so as to steer clear of the impending crisis over water usage.[4] According to the United Nations World Water Development Report, there are 507 conflictive events over water and 37 among these involved violence, of which 21 consisted of military acts (18 between Israel and its neighbours). "Some of the most vociferous enemies around the world have negotiated water agreements or are in the process of doing so, concerning international rivers," says the report.[5] The Stockholm International Water Institute (SIWI) in its report, "Are Water Wars a Fantasy, or a Future Reality?" (August 29, 2005) warns that growing populations will fight over water resources to secure sufficient food production.[6]

The water wars prophecy is yet to be proven in South Asia, mega water projects have definitely led to agitations, protests and unrest due to their massive human cost and environmental impact. Jeffrey Sachs makes apparent the connection between drought caused by climate change in Darfur since the 1980s, abject poverty, and the current conflict in the region. Sachs argues that "crises that are fundamentally ecological in nature are managed by outdated strategies of war and diplomacy[7]. "Breaching Borders: The Role of Water in the Middle East

---

[4] Sandra Postel, "Dehydrating Conflict", *Foreign Policy*, October 2001.

[5] 'Water, a shared responsibility', The Second United Nations World Water Development Report, March 2006.

The triennial UN World Water Development Report is a joint undertaking of 24 UN agencies comprising UN-Water in partnership with governments and other stakeholders. The report was launched at the Fourth World Water Forum in Mexico City, Mexico.
See, http://www.unesco.org/water/wwap/wwdr2/index.shtml

[6] "Are Water Wars a Fantasy, or a Future Reality?", The Stockholm International Water Institute (SIWI), August 29, 2005.

[7] Jeffrey Sachs, "War Climates", *Opinion:Tom Paine*, October 23, 2006.
See, www.tompaine.com

Conflict" from the *Washington Report on Middle East Affairs*, argues that water constitutes the root of conflict in the Middle East. Going back to Israel's attempt to divert the Jordan River in 1953, the article claims Israel triggered conflicts with its neighbours to secure access to water supplies[8].

Developing countries are gearing up to harness as much water resources as possible; mega dam projects seem to be their response to the increasing demand for water. This has evoked widespread opposition from affected populations and has led to some of the most remarkable civil society movements in South Asia. The controversial Sardar Sarovar Project, part of the Narmada Valley Development Project led to one of the most extraordinary agitations in the form of the "Narmada Bachao Andolan" in India involving a large number of civil society groups, students, celebrities showing solidarity with the affected people.[9] In Nepal, after heated controversies the World Bank in 1995 famously withdrew from the controversial Arun III hydropower project.[10] The project was shelved thereafter. In Sri Lanka, the planned construction of the Upper Kotmale hydropower project – which is likely to destroy large areas of fertile land, displace hundreds of families and destroy pristine wetlands – has led to massive opposition

---

8 "Breaching Borders: The Role of Water in the Middle East Conflict", *Washington Report on Middle East Affairs*, September/October 2006.

9 Sardar Sarovar Project is a multipurpose Interstate Project of four States (Madhya Pradesh, Gujarat, Maharashtra and Rajasthan) funded by the World Bank. The Ministry of Environment & Forests, India accorded clearances to the project in 1987, after specifying certain conditions. It has caused widespread agitation owing to the large-scale displacement of local population and the failure of the government to fully rehabilitate the affectees.

10 Arun III, a 400-megawatt hydroelectric project on River Arun proposed in Nepal was shelved in 1995, after the World Bank Inspection Panel, constituted in 1994 to receive claims from citizens who believe they have been directly harmed by World Bank projects filed its report.

in Sri Lanka and abroad.[11] The Kaptai Dam in the Chittagong Hills in Bangladesh was inaugurated in 1962.[12] More than 50,000 acres of cultivable land and 18,000 houses were flooded to make room for its reservoir. No resettlement was provided for the 100,000 indigenous people from the Chakma and Hajong tribes who lost their lands and homes. Most of them migrated to India, in what they termed Bara Parang ("exodus" in the local Chakma language).

Water sharing has been an area of tension between countries. While India and Nepal have differences over the Mahakali River Treaty[13], and India and Bangladesh have contending interests over rivers Ganges and Brahmaputra.[14] As demands grow and supplies decline, conflicts over water are bound to take various hues ranging from opposition to large dams by indigenous populations, disputes over use of water resources between states for economic interest, to discords among regions within states threatening their political stability. Water issues between India and Pakistan have emerged

---

[11] The Upper Kotmale Hydropower project is a US $0.91 million project, initiated in the mid-1990s. It has been persistently opposed by environmentalists and the Ceylon Workers Congress (CWC), a powerful plantation union as it would uproot many people and affect other natural resources.
See, Feizal Samath, "Minimum support price", *Down to Earth*, August 15, 2005.

[12] The Kaptai Dam was built in 1964, in the Chittagong hill tracks, Rangamati, of the erstwhile East Pakistan, now Bangladesh. The dam displaced over 100,000 tribes– Hajongs and Chakmas, who were minority Buddhists.

[13] The Treaty on integrated Development of Mahakali River had been signed between the Government of India and Government of Nepal in February 1996, which came into force in June 1997 (Mahakali Treaty) . Pancheshwar Multipurpose Project on river Mahakali which is known as river Sarda in India is the centrepiece of the Mahakali Treaty. See, http://wrmin.nic.in/international/mkalitreaty.htm

[14] In December 1996, India and Bangladesh signed a 30-year India-Bangladesh Water Sharing Agreement. The treaty would determine the amount of water released by India to Bangladesh at the Farakka Barrage.

as one of the most contentious over the years, with both countries facing severe water and power scarcity in some of their regions. The Indus waters apportioned between India and Pakistan by the Indus Waters Treaty, 1960 have taken all the three above mentioned hues of conflict.[15] The situation of the Indus headwaters in the disputed region of Kashmir has intensified the complexity of the conflict associated with it. Water is also one of the most explosive issues within Pakistan amongst its provinces. It has spurred off conflict between the federal government and the provinces of NWFP, Sindh and Baluchistan and reinforced the anti-Punjab sentiment within all these provinces. Within Pakistan, the Kalabagh[16], Chashma Right Bank Canal Project[17], Skardu Dam[18], Akhori[19], Diamer-Basha and Mangla Dam Raising Projects are some of the most controversial mega water projects.

The Government of Pakistan's vision for large dams in Pakistan-occupied Kashmir (PoK) is of special significance as it entails sensitive bilateral concerns between India and Pakistan and it also determines the relationship between the people of PoK and Islamabad. This paper seeks to look into how the proposed increase in the height of the Mangla dam in

---

[15] Under the Indus Waters Treaty 1960, the flows of the three eastern rivers (Sutlej, Beas and Ravi) have been allocated to India, whereas, with minor exceptions, Pakistan is entitled to all the waters of the western rivers (Indus, Jhelum and Chenab).

[16] The US $6.1 billion Kalabagh Dam, with a live storage capacity of 6.1 MAF and an installed capacity of 24,000/36,000 MW, is proposed to be built on River Indus in Sindh, Pakistan.

[17] The Chashma Right Bank Canal Project is situated in Dera Ismail Khan District in NWFP at a cost of US $655 million.

[18] The Skardu Dam planned in the NA with a storage capacity of 35 MAF has been shelved temporarily owing to technical difficulties.

[19] The US $5 billion Akhori Dam Project in Punjab, with a live storage of 6.00 MAF and an installed capacity of 600 MW, is scheduled to begin in 2015.

that part of PoK designated as Azad Jammu and Kashmir (AJK) by Pakistan and construction of the Diamer-Basha dam, in the Northern Areas (NA) in PoK affect ties between PoK and Islamabad. How are inter-provincial relations in Pakistan influenced by these proposals? What are viable alternatives keeping in mind the sensitive political issues involved as well the real needs of a developing country reeling under water stress?

I

The Diamer-Basha Dam

The proposed Diamer-Basha project site is located about 314 kms upstream of Tarbela dam on the Indus River, 165 kms south of Gilgit in Chilas, in NA. Several political, strategic, economic and developmental considerations have exacerbated the complexities of the problem with Diamer-Basha. The people of the NA are against it as they feel that their interests and needs are being sidelined in this process, which has been elaborated upon later in the following sections of this paper.

The Diamer-Basha dam project is part of President Musharraf's Water Vision 2025, which foresees the construction of dams including Kala Bagh, Akhori, Munda, Gomal Zam and Kuram Tangi by 2015.[20] Pakistan's Water Vision is part of the World Water Vision of the World Water Council (WWC) or the Long Term Vision for Water, Life and the Environment in the 21st century. The World Water Vision is expected to subsume the Water Visions for countries and regions. In tandem with the development of the Water Visions, the Global Water Partnership (GWP)[21] has initiated the formulation of country and Regional Framework for Action

---

[20] The World Water Vision was presented by the World Commission on Water for the 21st century at the Second World Water Forum in March 2000 in The Hague, the Netherlands.
See, www.worldwatercouncil.org

[21] Global Water Partnership is a working partnership among all those involved in water management- government agencies, public and private institutions, multilateral development agencies and others. The GWP supports countries in sustainable management of their water resources.
See, www.gwpforum.org/

(FFA) which would constitute the building blocks for the formulation of Global FFA.[22] This would help in the achievement of the Water Visions in the year 2025.

The Diamer-Basha dam project is expected to augment water supply by creating significant storage capacity in the Indus valley between Rakhiot bridge[23] and Dasu-Sazin gorge in NA. It will have a mega reservoir to store 7.2 million acre feet (MAF) of water and would create an additional power generation capacity of 4,500 MW.[24] The ambitious project is strewn with technical difficulties and had been opted for, owing to the relentless opposition by its other provinces against the other mega dam projects proposed to be constructed in Pakistan. With a proposed height of 280 metres (990 feet above the river bed) and a reservoir area of 27,700 acres, it will be the highest roller-compacted concrete dam in the world, surpassing the highest dams in China, Japan and Colombia (425, 460 and 620 feet, respectively).

The Location Issue

The location of the dam, apart from involving technical difficulties calling for huge financial commitments, has also spurred off political controversy between India and Pakistan.

---

22 The Framework for Action for achieving the country's Vision of Water 2025, was prepared following an initial consultation at Islamabad on November 16, 1999 and a subsequent consultation at Lahore on January 13, 2000. These consultations were organised by the Pakistan Water Partnership (PWP) with the support of Global Water Partnership, after the PWP developed the Country's Vision for Water in the 21st century in June 1999.

23 The Rakhiot Peak is in the north face of the Nanga Parbat range in the Himalayas and is 7010 metres high.

24 Planning Commission, Government of Pakistan (September 2001), "Ten Year Perspective Development Plan 2001-11 and Three Year Development Programme 2001-04".

The location of the dam falls inside the disputed territory of Kashmir on the Pakistani side of the LoC. India has lodged its protests through diplomatic channels saying it would inundate large parts of land in Jammu and Kashmir which have been disregarded by Pakistan. India's position is that the proposed construction site of the Diamer-Basha project is in that part of the NA, which is part of the erstwhile Jammu and Kashmir state, hence an "integral part of India by virtue of its accession to it in 1947".[25] This objection is linked to the political resolution of the Kashmir issue and not related to the distribution of the Indus waters. It therefore falls outside the ambit of the IWT and Pakistan has rights of utilisation of the waters of the Indus River. India lodged its protests in March 2006, just before the scheduled foundation stone laying ceremony which eventually was postponed due to large-scale protests in the region. Eventually, the foundation stone laying ceremony was carried out in April 2006, for this mega project that was announced by President Musharraf in January 2006.[26]

The Basha dam owing to its geographical setting involves huge costs. The dam site is located on a pronounced bend of the Indus River, in a section with steep rock slopes.[27] It requires the laying of long distance transmission lines to connect the hydel power generated to the national grid and the transmission costs amount to 1 billion USD.[28] The project envisages

---

[25] E Ahamed, Minister of State in the MEA, "2910 Building of Diamer-Basha Dam By Pakistan", Rajya Sabha Q&As, Ministry of External Affairs, New Delhi, August 24, 2006. See, http://meaindia.nic.in/parliament/rs/2006/08/24rs10.htm

[26] Rana Qaisar, "Basha Dam will be built first: Musharraf", *Daily Times*, January 18, 2006

[27] Pakistan Water & Power Development Authority, "Annual Report 1999-2000", 2001.

[28] Ashfaq Mehmood, "Water Security", *Pakistan Development Forum*, May 11, 2006. http://www.pakistan.gov.pk/divisions/economicaffairs-division/media/S-6-ASHFAQ-Pre-3.ppt#

construction of a 9.26-metre wide and 247-metre long bridge at Thakot over River Indus on Karakorum Highway (KKH) as replacement of the existing one. The proposed bridge scope of work also includes approach roads of 717 metres in length. The construction of Thakot Bridge is a prerequisite for the construction of the Diamer Basha Dam as it would facilitate uninterrupted transportation of plant, equipment, machinery and materials for the construction of Diamer Basha Dam. It would also cater to the needs of the increased volume of normal traffic in future. The total cost of the widening of the KKH and construction of the Thakot bridge is estimated to be Rs 302.6 billion, including the costs of land acquisition and shifting of utilities which amount to Rs 30 billion.[29]

The project entails upgrading 323 kms of the Karakoram Highway and widening of 140 kms of the same.[30] As the existing structure was built in 1978, it needs renovation and some possible realignment in many sections. The National Highway Authority (NHA) would spend Rs. 9.52 billion for the relocation and upgradation of the Karakoram highway affected by the project of Diamer-Basha Dam.

Technical difficulties apart, the dam has come under strong opposition from the people of NA on several issues including royalty, displacement, compensation and resettlement, environmental hazards, loss of cultural and historical sites. These problems predominantly stem from a sense of political alienation wherein the NA do not have

---

29 Annexe 1, Government of Pakistan Planning & Development Division (Public Investment Authorisation Section) Report No. 23(1)PIA-I/PC/2006, Islamabad, the December 19, 2006.

30 "Nespak Profile: 1973-2003", website of National Engineering Services of Pakistan. See, http://www.nespak.com.pk/downloads/pdf/nespak_profile2003.pdf.

political representation in Pakistan and are not included in making decisions that affect them directly.

The Question of Royalty

Royalty is the most contentious of the issues around this mega project. It stems from the complex ethnic mosaic in Pakistan that gives way to politics of deprivation of one at the cost of the other. The storage structure of the dam, is to be situated in Chilas, in the NA; however, the hydro-electric power station is planned at Basha, in the NWFP. Initially, the project was named as Basha, but changed to the Diamer-Basha project in February 2006, Diamer being the location of the storage structure.[31] The NALC had been debating the issue for a considerable time and the issue was during their discussions regarding the legal status of the NA and constitutional rights of the people of the region. NALC members – Muzaffar Relay, Sultan Madad and Muhammad Iqbal – expressed their annoyance at the unanimous resolution passed by the legislative council regarding the construction of the proposed Basha Dam and renaming it as the Daimer Dam was ignored in total by the federal government.[32] The name Basha, people in NA believe, was chosen so that the entire benefit of royalty, ownership, employment and income of the project is enjoyed by NWFP. It was orchestrated to deny recognition to the region of Gilgit where the structure was to be constructed, submerging villages and displacing its people.[33] Based on the claim that the location of the hydroelectric station was in the province, which would be generating revenue,

[31] "Musharraf to lay foundation for controversial Basha Dam", *Times of India*, March 15, 2006.

[32] Ibrahim Shahid, "NALC resumes Basha Dam Debate", *Daily Times*, January 30, 2006.

[33] "Basha, Why not Diamar Dam?", http://www.balawaristan.net/damCond.html.

NWFP had been claiming royalty.[34] According to Article 161(2) of the Constitution of Pakistan,

> "The net profits earned by the Federal Government, or any undertaking established or administered by the Federal Government from the bulk generation of power at a hydro-electric station shall be paid to the Province in which the hydro-electric station is situated."[35]

Thus royalty accrues to the province where the power station is located and mention has not been made of the storage structure of the reservoir. It may also be noted that Article 161(2) refers to "Net Profit" and not royalties. This is a fundamental difference, as royalty is payment made for the exploitation of a resource and is payable whether or not any profits are made. By contrast, it may be the case that the rate determined by the Certificate of Capital Importation (CCI) is so low that there are no Net Profits earned by the Water and Power Development Authority (WAPDA) and hence nothing is payable to the province concerned.

As per the arbitration proceedings that have arisen out of an Arbitration Agreement entered into between the Government of NWFP and the WAPDA and endorsed by the Government of Pakistan with reference to the guarantee given by the President's Order No. 3 of 1991,

> "....It may also be noted that Art. 161(2) refers to "Net Profit" and not royalties. This is a fundamental difference as royalty is payment made for the

[34] Afzal A. Shigri, 'Diamer-Basha royalty issue', *The News*, July 7, 2006.

[35] "WAPDA-NWFP dispute: award of the Arbitral Tribunal: Decision of Javid Akhtar-I", *Pakistan Tribune*, October 18, 2006. See, http://paktribune.com/business/newsdetail.php?nid=1393

> exploitation of a resource and is payable whether or not any profits are made. By contrast, it may be the case that the rate determined by the CCI is so low that there are no Net Profits earned by WAPDA and hence nothing is payable to the Province concerned."

The case of the NA for royalty is based on the following points:

First, an amendment in Article 161 (2), is necessary so as to facilitate the people and the region adversely affected by the hydel project and construction of the reservoir get a due share in the hydel profits. Persistent agitation by the people continues.

Secondly, the spirit of the constitutional provision that is principally meant to recompense the area that is negatively affected by flooding of fields and villages owing to the construction of the water storage structure needs to be recognised.

Thirdly, the hydro-electric station includes the entire structures that are essential to produce electricity and not just the powerhouse which cannot operate in isolation.

Fourth, royalty needs to be paid irrespective of profits or losses and moreover the hydel profits also rightfully accrue to them.

However, the people of NA do not have any constitutional guarantees as the Constitution of Pakistan does not cover them. So their case cannot be made on this basis. This kind of lopsided, unjust applicability of the Constitution in Pakistan leaves the NA no options for constitutional remedies. The NA does not even have recourse to judicial remedy since a Supreme Judicial Council exists consisting of bureaucrats who oversee the process. There was a demand by the Balawaristan National Party (BNP) to abolish this council to ensure the independence of the judiciary which has bee ignored by Islamabad.[36] The NALC, which was initially constituted as the Northern Areas Advisory Council in 1970 was later upgraded to the NALC following the Northern Areas Council, Legal Framework Order 1994.[37] The NALC is however, controlled by the Ministry of Kashmir Affairs and Northern Areas (KANA) and has limited scope to voice grievances against Islamabad. No legislation was adopted between 1999 and 2004 but 18 Resolutions were adopted all of which were reportedly ignored by KANA.[38] In 2002, a new power-sharing formula was evolved wherein the Northern Areas affairs were delinked from the Kashmir affairs division, providing decision-making authority at the local level on all matters except for the crucial prisons, law and home affairs. Until then it had to approach the KANA for even minor issues.[39] It still does not have the right to make decisions on issues of importance as they are exempted from its purview. A Supreme Court bench headed by the then Chief Justice Ajmal Mian declared in a landmark decision that "We are of the view

---

[36] "Voices from Pakistan Occupied Balawaristan", *Tahelka,* December 6, 2001. See, http://www.tehelka.com/channels/currentaffairs/2001/dec/3/ca120301abdul1.htm

[37] On May 28, 1999, the Pakistani Supreme Court in the case *Al-Jihad Trust versus Federation of Pakistan,* directed the government to act within six months to give the Northern Areas an elected government with an independent judiciary. After the verdict, the Pakistani government announced a package that provided for an appellate court and an expanded and renamed Northern Areas Legislative Council (NALC).

[38] B.G. Verghese, "A Jammu and Kashmir Primer", Centre for Policy Research, June 2006.

[39] Safdar Khan, "Northern Areas, Kashmir division delinked: New power sharing formula", *Dawn,* October 24, 2002.

that the people of the Northern Areas are citizens of Pakistan for all intents and purposes. They have the right to invoke any fundamental rights…" which are yet to be implemented.[40] The only forum for expression dissent is to take to the streets, which the Pakistan government tries to curb with all its might, as is illustrated in the following sections.

Displacement, Compensation and Employment

The Basha-Diamer dam would displace 30,000 people and inundate 31,580 acres of barren and 1,600 acres of arable land in Diamer district.[41] Resettlement of the local people is a crucial aspect, which becomes grimmer where individual landholdings are comparatively small and the cultivable area is sparse because of the rocky terrain. The social costs are not just a matter of numbers – most of the Diamer-Basha resettled populations would have to be relocated long distances from their original homes. This would imply the scattering of the displaced people of Gilgit, who constitute a Shia minority in Pakistan, in areas of Sunni predominance. The recurrences of Shia-Sunni violence in Pakistan make this prospect extremely unsavoury to the people of NA. It also involves the dilution of their language and culture by dispersing their meagre population. The NA predicament over resettlement needs to be understood in the context of sectarian clashes in Pakistan.

Frustration over the absence of political representation has reinforced a sense of powerlessness among the people leaving protests as the only option to make their voices heard and to be taken seriously. At the same time, it has strengthened

---

[40] M. Ismail Khan, "Justice needed with or without chief", *The News,* March 20, 2007.

[41] "Protest Rallies in Diamer against Basha Dam", *The Dawn*, February 2, 2006 See, www.dawn.com/2206/02/02/nat.htm

the resolve not to let further deprivation be imposed on the region. Over 20,000 protestors took to the streets in February 2006 on the Karakoram Highway when the foundation laying ceremony was announced for March 2006. The ruling PML which comprised the majority of the NALC, the JKLF, several civil society organisations came together to protest and JKLF leader Amanullah Khan was detained for several weeks when he held a protest rally asking for proper compensation for the locals as well as the renaming of the dam.[42] Several members of the NALC such as Haji Abdul Quddus, Advocate Fidaullah, PML's provincial chief organiser Basheer Ahmed Khan, former member Haji Ameer Jan joined to voice their dissent against Islamabad.[43] Eventually the foundation laying ceremony had to be postponed to April 2006 as the government sought for time under pressure citing bad weather conditions as the reason for the postponement.[44]

The BNP had made a series of demands that were of immediate consequence to the political, economic status of the NA. Their demands included the situation of offices for power house and administration and residential quarters/ houses on Diamer, not NWFP; control of the offices equally by both the parties; handling and control of residential houses by the employees of Balwaristan; giving priority to people from Diamer for employment on the project; consideration of bills from the main meter consumption after the completion of the

---

42 "Pakistan: Medical concern/ possible prisoner of conscience: Amanullah Khan (m),aged 77", PUBLIC AI Index: ASA 33/005/2006, *Amnesty International*, February 16, 2006.

See, http://web.amnesty.org/library/Index/ENGASA330052006?open&of=ENG-376

43 "Protest rallies in Diamer against Basha dam", *The Dawn*, October 2, 2006. http://www.dawn.com/2006/02/02/nat2.htm

44 Engr Hussain Ahmad Siddiqui, "Diamer-Basha Dam project may be delayed", *The Dawn,* January 1, 2007 http://www.dawn.com/2007/01/01/ebr7.htm\

dam in the main powerhouse wherein the main meters would be handled by both Balwaristan and Pakistan equally.[45]

Environmental Issues

Like most large hydro-electric projects, the Diamer-Basha too has a number of environmental impacts. Owing to its location at a high elevation and the tough terrain, the nature of impacts becomes even more grave. Both flora and fauna, which is quite dense are bound to be affected by the project construction, taking into account the construction activities of the dam, development of roads, quarrying, etc. About 120 kms of the KKH are also expected to be submerged and the project entails improvement of the KKH in its present condition in order to transmit heavy equipment to the dam site.[46] Fluctuations based on the reservoir level could induce instability in downstream irrigation channels and vast areas of land would be ruined by soil erosion. Altered stream flow and nutrient content including sediments will cause changes in the habitat. Other downstream effects are likely to have an impact on water supply, fisheries, navigation, aesthetics and recreation.

Location of the Diamer-Basha dam is in a seismically sensitive area where a powerful earthquake in December 1974 trampled towns along the KKH and killed nearly 10,000 people. It is a matter of grave concern as there are certain researches that indicate that the impoundment of water in the vicinity of faulted area poses a potential impact towards increasing the

---

45 "Basha, why not Diamer dam?", website of Balawaristan National Front See, http://www.balawaristan.net/damCond.html

46 Report of the Government of Pakistan Planning & Development Division (Public Investment Authorisation Section) No. 23(1)PIA-I/PC/2006 Islamabad, December 19, 2006.

earth tremors.[47] In the case of a break in the dam during an earthquake, it is estimated that a 500-feet high wave would flow down from its 920-feet height and destroy downriver dams and bridges and wash riverside cities into the Arabian Sea. With complete disregard for the greater risk, the height of the planned dam was actually increased by 33 feet to give it a larger water and power capacity than KBD. The ten feet reduction in the proposed height of the dam in response to these concerns does not reduce this risk. The initial feasibility was conducted in 1984 by the Montreal Engineering Company (MONENCO).[48] This assignment was given to NEAC Consultants, a joint venture of National Engineering Services Pakistan (NESPAK) and Associated Consulting Engineers (ACE), under the technical umbrella of Binnie and Partners of the UK. The feasibility study was completed, at a cost of Rs. 350 million, in June 2004.[49] Panels of international consultants appointed by the government made an in-depth review of the feasibility study and endorsed it in August 2004. Of course this was known when the Basha project was deemed feasible, but after the October 8 earthquake, there is a renewed focus on seismic considerations which have revived doubts. The fact that the Diamer-Basha site lies precariously close to the fault line of the 2005 earthquake is not hindering Pakistan's determination to go ahead with construction.

The construction of a reservoir on Diamer-Basha Dam would inundate one of the world's greatest archaeological sites dating back to the 12th century BC. The western Himalayas

---

[47] Zulfiqar Ghuman, "Diamer-Basha Dam in a seismic zone, NA told", *Daily Times,* February 10, 2007.

[48] Pakistan Water Gateway-Key Water Information See,www.waterinfo.com.pk/fsbd.htm

[49] "NESPAK to upgrade Basha Dam feasibility study", *Daily Times,* June 4, 2002.

and Karakorum were one of the world's largest rock art regions, the discovery of over 50,000 rock carvings and 5,000 inscriptions going back to the 6th century BC has saddened archaeologists to plead for their conservation and to save the remnants of the indigenous cultures of the people of this region.[50] The Gilgit and Balti people feel strongly about the wiping out of their land and culture resulting from mass submergence and resettlement.

Government Responses

In efforts to resolve the disputes, the Government of Pakistan held four high level meetings during 1990-92 in the Ministry of KANA at Islamabad.[51] KANA constituted a Standing Committee comprising the NWFP Government and local civil administration functionaries concerned with the issue in 1995, which denied rights of royalty to NA. However, the protracted efforts of the people of NA yielded results when President Musharraf, during his visit to Gilgit in July 2006, announced that the NA would get royalty from the Diamer-Basha dam.[52] To satisfy the technical condition of the situation of the powerhouse within the region, one turbine would be built in the territorial limits of the NA and the other at Basha village, which is in NWFP. The royalties from power generation from Diamer-Basha dam would be shared by both the NA and NWFP.[53]

---

[50] "Rock Art dating to the 12th century BC: 'Basha Dam will destroy archaelogical sites', *Daily Times,* December 10, 2006.

[51] Kaleem Omar, "Basha dam: A better alternative than Kalabagh", *The News,* May 2, 2005.

[52] "NA to get dam royalty: Musharraf seeks support for PM", *The Dawn*, July 6, 2006.

[53] "Northern Areas to get dam royalty: Musharraf seeks support for PML", *Dawn*, July 6, 2006.

As for displacement and resettlement issues, the government has promised to build nine 'model villages' to resettle people displaced by the dam.[54] It has been suggested that each displaced landowner will get compensation from the government at the market rate plus 10 per cent.[55] A reduction in the height of the dam by 10 metres has been promised to prevent the submergence of Chilas city, but rejected demands of further height reduction to save the Chilas city air strip. The height of Diamer-Basha Dam is now all set to be 270 metres with the capacity to store 7.4 million acre feet (MAF) of water, with a live storage capacity of more than 6.4 MAF.

The government was pressurised into taking a conciliatory stand towards NA following such mass mobilisation, if it had to proceed with the unhindered implementation of the Project. Though not all the demands were fulfilled, the July 4 statement of the President on royalty being the just and lawful right of the people of NA showed a marked shift in Islamabad's NA policy which thus far had been one of denial. However the Speaker of NA, Malik Muhammad Maskeen, expressed his unwillingness to accept fifty per cent royalty on Diamer-Basha and has demanded the establishment of a commission under the headship of the Chief Justice of Pakistan to solve the royalty issue.[56] This demand of course remains impending and with the recent sacking of the Chief Justice of Pakistan, Iftikhar Muhammad Choudry, in March 2007, the role of the judiciary under the present military regime is going to be only perfunctory.[57]

---

[54] Ibrahim Shahid, "Musharraf opens work on Diamer-Basha Dam", *Daily Times*, April 27, 2006.

[55] "Musharraf opens work on Diamer-Basha Dam", *Daily Times*, April 7, 2004.

[56] "Fifty per cent royalty on Basha Dam not acceptable: Speaker NA", *Pakistan Tribune,* June 15, 2006.

[57] "Sacking of Pakistan Chief Justice condemned", *The Hindu,* March 14, 2007.

Project Contract in Troubled Waters

Despite technical and financial difficulties, the Diamer-Basha Dam has been chosen keeping in mind the larger political costs involved in going ahead with the Kalabagh. The estimated costs according to WAPDA is around US$200 million which is about 15 per cent of total financial costs, which comes up to US$ 7 billion. The estimated foreign exchange component (FEC) in the form of financial assistance from IFIs and donor agencies, is Rs 178 billion ($2.96 billion) for Diamer Basha.[58]

The company that has been awarded a contract for detailed design, engineering and preparation of tender documents related to the Diamer-Basha dam project in July 2005 has been recently blacklisted by the World Bank.[59] The normal practice of awarding the contract to the same consultants who carry out detailed feasibility studies are preferred for designing of the project, for practical reasons of maintaining parameters of earlier investigations was set aside and the contract was awarded to the German company Lahmeyer International. Out of the four groups of consultants who responded to WAPDA's advertisement of expression of interest (EOI), for carrying out detailed design and preparation of tender documents for the construction of the project, Lahmeyer was decided upon.

The World Bank's blacklisting of this company has serious implications for the progress of the Daimer-Basha dam project as the WB backing for the project is decisive for the progress of the project. There is no indication of the government taking any action, reportedly on the plea that the processing for project

---

[58] Fida Hussain, "$7 billion needed for dams", *Daily Times*, November 26, 2006.

[59] Engr Hussain Ahmad Siddiqui, "Diamer-Basha Dam project may be delayed", *The Dawn,* January 1, 2007. See, http://www.dawn.com/2007/01/01/ebr7.htm

financing has not yet been initiated and the World Bank loan would not necessarily be forthcoming. As instances of giant corporations resorting to large-scale corruption for securing construction contracts in developing and under-developed countries are being brought to light, would the future of the Diamer-Basha also get entangled in a tussle between IFIs and corporations is a key question. The Asian Development Bank (ADB) has made large investments for developmental projects in Pakistan and other contenders could be Overseas Economic Cooperation Fund (OECF, Japan) or Islamic Development Bank (IDB) or a consortium of these financial institutions.[60] However, it would not be too viable for the WAPDA to persist overlooking the WB observation, considering its huge dependency on the bank for financial assistance. Completion of the project within the stipulated deadline of September 2007 is fraught with uncertainty and any delay in this would exert pressure on Pakistan to commence work on one of the other mega dam projects, opening the door for rifts among its other provinces. The full implications of the blacklisting of Lahmeyer is yet to sink in wherein Pakistan would find itself torn between its inter-provincial tensions on the one hand, and financial hurdles for the Diamer-Basha on the other.

[60] "ADB to give $3 billion for power, water projects", *The Dawn,* February 16, 2007. *See,* http://www.dawn.com/2007/02/16/ebr1.htm

II

Mangla Dam

The Mangla Dam Raising Project (MDRP) is yet another controversial issue in Pakistan. It is also an offshoot of the opposition to the Kalabagh dam from the other provinces, necessitating an increase in the height of the dam to meet the pressing water requirements of water. The Mangla dam, on the Jhelum, was first constructed in 1967 in Mirpur in "AJK". At the time of its construction, the dam had a gross storage capacity of 5.88 million acre feet, and an affected area of 69,206 acres of Azad Jammu and Kashmir in addition to the area occupied by the dam.[61] After completion of the engineering plan of the MDRP in February 2004, the contract was awarded to a joint venture of one Chinese and five Pakistani contractors. The China International Water and Electric Corporation (CWE) is leading this Mangla Joint Venture (MJV) while five Pakistani contractors include DESCON Ltd, Sardar M. Ashraf D. Baluch Ltd, Interconstruct Ltd, Gammon Pakistan Ltd and Sachal Engineering Works Ltd. The construction work started on June 20, 2004 and is scheduled to end in 39 months by September 2007.[62]

The Need for Raising of the Mangla

Raising of the dam has now gained immense significance

61 "Water Economy: Running Dry", Report No. 34081-PK Pakistan Country Water Resources Assistance Strategy, Agriculture and Rural Development Unit South Asia Region, World Bank, November 14, 2005. See, www.worldbank.org.pk/

62 "Mangla Dam Raising Project", Descon Engoneering Limited Website See, www.descon.com.pk/Sectors/Infrastructure/manglaDamRaising.aspx

because of the growing shortage of irrigation owing to sedimentation of the country's two major storage reservoirs at Tarbela and Mangla. Since its completion, the gross storage capacity of Mangla reservoir has reduced by about 20 per cent due to sediments deposition.[63] In order to compensate for this lost capacity a provision for raising of the dam was kept in the original design of the dam. The project includes four earth dams with a maximum height of 454 ft. (154 metres) and total length of about 13 kilometres and the provision of, two spillways for flooding.[64] Raising of the dam by 40ft would increase the storage capacity by 2.9 million acre feet and average annual energy output is estimated to increase by 772 GWH which is 14 per cent of the present energy yields from Mangla.[65] The availability of water for irrigation purposes is expected to increase by 2.88 MAF. However, the incremental benefits of raising the dam are relatively small in contrast to the substantial cost and displacement of population.

The agreement was signed between WAPDA and the "AJK" government for raising the height of the dam in 2003[66] despite vehement opposition by the people who came out in thousands to protest the inauguration of the extension work by President Musharraf in September 2002.[67] The protests were over concerns of displacement and resettlement, compensation and deprivation of royalty and hydel profits from the Mangla, which

---

[63] "Mangla Dam work to start in May", *Daily Times*, March 22, 2004 http://www.dailytimes.com.pk/default.asp?page=story_22-3-004_pg7_35

[64] "Project Description and Financing", Pakistan Water and Power Development Authority See, www.wapda.gov.pk/pdf/PART-B.pdf

[65] Pakistan Water Gateway- Key Water Information See, www.waterinfo.net.pk/fsrj.htm

[66] Khalid Mustafa, "Mangla Dam raising pact signing today", *Daily Times*, April 17, 2003.

[67] "UA-48-2002: Pakistani police assault peaceful demonstrators in Kashmir", Asian Human Rights Commission, October 15, 2002.

are deliberated upon in the sections that follow. The opposition is now mainly expressed through the Anti-Mangla Dam Extension Committee (AMDEC).[68] Their grievance is also that the rise in silt level is a result of WAPDA's failure to clean the dam every year, which was part of the maintenance plan. They were provided with the appropriate machinery at the time of construction of the dam.[69] They also claim that the siltation problem is a result of large-scale deforestation by both the Pakistani and "AJK" governments.[70] However, the appeals of the AMDEC were overlooked and paramilitary troops were called in to curtail the protestors and tear gas and batten charge were used on the peaceful protestors.

Displacement and Resettlement

Opposition to this project comes from the people's qualms about displacement and resettlement concerns apart from the grave environmental impacts involved. MDRP would affect about 8023 households, displacing an estimated 40,000 people and submerging an area of 15,783 acres in water.[71] When the dam was first constructed, 80,000 to 85,000 people were displaced during the construction of the Mangla Dam in the 1960s and some of the affected people are still waiting payment of compensation. The package promised at the time included new colonies, appropriate compensation, relocation in new

---

68 The AMDEC campaign was formally launched in Chasawari on August 8, 2005 in the presence of the leaders of all Kashmiri political parties except the ruling Muslim Conference.

69 Shams Rehman, "Dam it? Mangla Dam Extension Project", www.chowk .com, February 7, 2003

70 Shams Rehman, "Dam it? Mangla Dam Extension Project", www.chowk .com, February 7, 2003

71 "Kashmiri group vows to stop Mangla Dam extension", *The News International,* March 11, 2005 http://jammu-kashmir.com/archives/archives2005/kashmir20050311a.html

Mirpur and inside Pakistan, visas and vouchers for England, cheap electricity and water, new roads and bridges and royalty to the "AJK" government. The whole of the Old Mirpur City, 65,000-acre surrounding land and 260 villages were drowned when water was released in 1967, but except for sending 300 people to England by the British construction company, no other promise was fulfilled.[72]

After widespread protests in Mirpur opposing the MDRP, the government came up with a compensation package in May 2005. Out of the total project cost of Rs 62.5b, Rs 36 billion will be spent on compensation and resettlement works.[73] Land for the New City near Mirpur and four small towns on the reservoir periphery have already been earmarked and a contract for the construction of primary and secondary roads at the cost of Rs 1,026.5 million has been awarded. The affected people have been promised plots of five marla[74] to one kanal[75] on payment of cost of land, while five marla plots are promised free of cost to displaced persons on the land of WAPDA and Government of Azad Jammu and Kashmir. The resettlement package includes the construction of a bridge on river Jhelum at Dhangali, establishment of a Vocational Training Institute (VTI) in New City, Vocational Training Schools in four new towns, strengthening of four existing Dastkari schools for females and vocational training from outside sources. The land compensation would be given at the market price plus 15 per

---

[72] "People's Perspective on the Mangla Dam Extension Project", Sustainable Policy Development Institute Seminar, March 11, 2004.
See, http://www.sdpi.org

[73] "Mangla Dam Raising Project", Resettlement Organisation, Website of Government of Azad Jammu and Kashmir
See, http://www."AJK"mdrp.gov.pk/

[74] A marla is equal to 25 m².

[75] A kanal is equal to 0.125 acres or 506 m² or 20 marlas.

cent compulsory acquisition charges and owners will be allowed to cultivate their land during recession. The affectees will get replacement cost of the house, which will be in addition to 10 per cent amount for the same purpose, while the owners will also be allowed to carry salvage material of their houses.[76]

The MDRP also carries compensation for the old affectees of the Mangla Dam. Moreover, the "AJK" will have hydropower projects up to 300 MW capacity. Two required dikes are going to be constructed by WAPDA in order to provide direct access to the population of the adjoining villages of Panayam and Kharak in Mirpur subdivision to the rest of the city. The dikes project will cost about Rs. 386 million – to be borne by the "AJK" government with the financial assistance of the federal government. The phased process to rehabilitate those affected is scheduled to begin later in 2007. The possibility of opening up investment avenues in Mirpur from local and foreign entrepreneurs is being projected as the positive side to the MRDP. The materialisation of this is still a long way off and to what extent the region would be allowed to benefit from these gains is a key question.

Royalty and Power Tariff

"AJK" was not paid royalty for electricity generated from the Mangla till 2003. The issue of royalty was delinked from the electricity bills that the "AJK" government had to pay to WAPDA only in 2005.[77] WAPDA released Rs. 120 million

---

76 Umer Sohail, "Mangla Dam Project to raise energy output by 12 per cent in Pakistan", *Pakistan Times,* May 2, 2005
See, http://pakistantimes.net/2005/05/02/top5.htm

77 "Mangla Dam Royalty De-linked from Power Bills Payment", *The Dawn*, April 30, 2005.

royalty to the "AJK" government, as it had been making at-source deduction earlier to set off outstanding power dues which adversely affected the "AJK" government's financial balance. However, it was agreed in 2005 that the "AJK" government will get hydel profit of Rs 0.15 per kilo watt of electricity while five additional grid stations would also be constructed in "AJK" at Chatter Pari.[78] Pakistan's attempt to ruthlessly clamp down on anti-dam protestors by use of force has created a rift of distrust and bitterness between the region and Islamabad. This has been further aggravated by unfulfilled promises that have been made to compromise with the "AJK" government. The electricity tariff in 'Azad' Kashmir was 4.25 rupees a unit and in Pakistan 2.85 rupees a unit.[79] Earlier it was set off against the other and virtually no royalty was received by "AJK" even after signing the agreement. Such discriminatory pricing policies and past experiences of the people with the promises of the federal government has disillusioned the people. The opposition for the dam continues to be as strong as before.

---

[78] Umer Sohail,"Mangla Dm Project to raise energy output", *Pakistan Times*, May 2, 2005.

[79] "Power authority asked to honour decisions", *The Dawn*, April 25, 2003.

III

Conclusion

The fore mentioned facts need to be analysed in the backdrop of the severe water stress faced by Pakistan. The issue of large dams in PoK is further exacerbated by the political status of PoK, embroiled in Indo-Pak tensions. The "development vs displacement" rigmarole makes it all the more intricate and each one of these factors and their interplay would determine the future course of events in PoK and influence the emerging conflict within the region in different ways.

Pakistan's Water Stress[80]

> "The human right to water is a prerequisite for the realisation of other human rights... State parties have to adopt effective measures to realise, without discrimination, the right to water."

The UN Committee on Economic, Social and Cultural Rights

Water stress has necessitated the Pakistani government to go ahead with at least one of the mega projects that the Musharaff's Water Vision 2025 entails. Pakistan also seems to be left with limited options, but to implement the MDRP and Diamer-Basha projects, given its water requirements for other provinces. The following table shows the existing storage reservoirs in Pakistan which have fallen short of Pakistan's increasing demands.

---

[80] According to the World Water Council, "water stress" results from an imbalance between water use and water resources.

Table Showing Pakistan's Storage Structures

Dam (Year)	River	Live Storag
Tarbela (1976)	Indus	9.69
Mangla (1966)	Jhelum	5.34
Chashma (1971)	Indus	0.61
Warsak (1960)	Kabul	0.04
Baran (1962)	Kurram	0.09
Hub (1983)	Hub	0.76
Khanpur (1984)	Haro	0.09
Tanda (1965)	Kohat Toi	0.06
Rawal (1962)	Kurang	0.04
Simly (1972)	Soan	0.02
BKD Khan (1900)	Pishin	0.04
Hamal Lake	_	0.08
Manchar Lake	Indus	0.75
Kinjhar	Indus	0.32
Chotiari Lake	Indus	0.78
Total Storage		18.71 MAF

(Source: Pakistan Development Forum, Presentation on Planning for Water Resources, by Dr. Shahid Amjad Chaudhry, Deputy Chairman, Planning Commission, Government of Pakistan, May 2003).

Pakistan's per capita availability of water has declined from 5600 cubic metres in 1947 to 1200 cubic metres in 2005, fast approaching the threshold level of 1000 cubic metres by 2007, and foreboding disaster for irrigation. Pakistan has the world's largest contiguous irrigation network with over 80 per cent of the cropland is irrigated.[81] The rivers of the Indus Basin provide 60 per cent of the water utilised for irrigation, while groundwater accounts for the rest. The inflow of water for irrigation has declined from 140 MAF in the 1980s to an average of 100 MAF in 2005. It is feared that it will decline further as the flows in the three rivers are reducing at the rate of 6.6 per cent per year. Inefficient management of irrigation networks has resulted in silting and reduction in the storage capacity of the three main dams Tarbela, Mangla and Chashma. In particular, the Tarbela dam is losing storage capacity of 100,000 cusecs each year. [82]

Intense opposition to Kalabagh by all three provinces has rendered Diamer-Basha more acceptable to them. Downstream Sindh has favoured the building of Basha Dam because it will have no irrigation canals and therefore will not divert water meant for Sindh; the NWFP has favoured it because it will not inundate any territory in that province. In order to avert an internal political crisis, Kalabagh has been shelved and Basha's superiority over the Kalabagh has been projected to avoid further delays in this critical sector. The opposition to large dams by NWFP, Balochistan and Sindh is as strong as Pakistan's

---

81 "Water Economy: Running Dry", Report No. 34081-PK, Pakistan Country Water Resources Assistance Strategy, Agriculture and Rural Development Unit, South Asia Region, World Bank, November 14, 2005.
See, http://www.worldbank.pk

82 "The Framework for Action for Achieving the Pakistan Water Vision 2025", Pakistan Water Partnership, International Water Management Institute Report.

imminent need for large dams are underscored overtime, threatening to undermine the unity of the country.

Large Dams in PoK: The Road Ahead

> "....For every high dam that is being built there is an alternative. Maybe no dam, maybe a less high dam..."[83]
>
> Arundhati Roy

Alternatives to large dams need to be explored. Better maintenance of existing utilities would increase their efficiency. Poor maintenance due to neglect and corruption have been a key factor in rendering redundant, much of the infrastructure for water distribution in Pakistan. Better management of water resources is the need of the hour. Water wastage is very rampant not only in Pakistan, but in the whole of South Asia. Pakistan's irrigation system wastes more water than it delivers – between 40 to 60 per cent. A huge quantity of water is being wasted in the tertiary watercourses as compared to rivers and canals. Farmers still prefer age-old practices like flooding; use of sprinkler and drip irrigation can irrigate twice the area irrigated through the traditional flooding method.[84] Thousands of hectares of land are lost to water logging and salinity. Better manipulation of improved watercourse is required and renovation of all remaining watercourses has been directed by the Government of Pakistan.[85] Exploring viable alternatives

---

83 "A fury building up across India", Arundhati Roy's interview by Shoma Chauduri, *The Hindu,* April 29, 2006.

84 A. Gill, M. H. Chaudhary and S.N. Afzal, "Note on: Conservation of Water Resources in Pakistan", *Pakistan Journal of Water Resources*, Vol.8(1) January-June 2004.

85 A. Gill, M. H. Chaudhary and S.N. Afzal, "Note on: Conservation of Water Resources in Pakistan", *Pakistan Journal of Water Resources*, Vol.8(1) January-June 2004.

to large dams is not an option many developing countries give serious thought to. The same applies to Pakistan. Given the volatile regional political repercussions of large dam constructions, the above mentioned methods are definitely worth employing.

The Draft National Water Policy of the Pakistan Engineering Council lays down priorities to ensure water security through integrated water management strategy that aims at maximising the sustainable economic, social and environmental returns on the water resource development, allocation among its competing demands, its use by consumers and safe disposal of post-use effluents.[86] The Pakistan Council of Research in Water Resources (PCRWR) is helping to create mass awareness on the proper use of water. It is trying to improve water quality for drinking, groundwater management, managing water pollution, increase pipe irrigation and small dams, artificial recharge and collaborative field drainage, saline agriculture and rainwater harvesting.[87]

The issue of dams in Pakistan has been a complicated one. The NA concerns over royalty, displacement, resettlement, environmental hazards and loss of the Balti heritage have thus far fallen upon deaf ears. Despite all these, the construction work on both the projects, the Diamer Basha and the MDRP have started. The government's only positive response has been the offer of a resettlement package for the displaced from both projects. However, it does not compensate for being uprooted from their homeland. Moreover the Pakistan Government's

---

[86] Draft National Policy, Pakistan Engineering Council, 2004-05. *See,* http://www.pec.org.pk/DraftNationalWaterPolicy.htm

[87] "Water Quality Report 2003-2004", Pakistan Council of Research in Water Resources. See, http://www.pcrwr.gov.pk/wq_phase3_report/chap6.htm

commitment to the timely and transparent implementation of these resettlement programmes remain doubtable, considering the track record of the government in keeping its promises to the people of PoK, as has been illustrated in the earlier sections. There is, however, a strong apprehension that efforts would be made to stop the implementation of these decisions, particularly the one on royalty being given to the people of PoK for both projects. This stems from the fact that huge financial benefits involved and sectarian vested interests are powerful and they typically attempt at balancing the myriad ethno-political considerations through their appeasement policies. The constitution of Pakistan is not applicable to the NA as it is a federally administered territory. The signing of some kind of an agreement between the elected representatives of NA and the Government of Pakistan would assuage the insecurities of the NA to some extent. President Musharraf's commitment needs to be translated into an enforceable legal document. The promises of the government need to be kept both in letter and spirit. The resonance of the same demand can be heard from many quarters in NA.

Kashmir vs Provinces

The issues of mega dam projects in PoK and people's opposition to them have caused a setback to the Kashmir issue. On the one hand, Pakistan's objection to large hydel power projects proposed by India in Jammu and Kashmir has augmented the power crisis in the state. The recent World Bank appointed neutral expert's report on the Baglihar Hydro-power Project vindicating India's stand is indicative of the futility of the former's objections. On the other hand, Pakistan is going ahead with construction of large dams in J&K on its side of the LoC, at the cost of the interests of the people. This has compromised its position of being "pro-people of J&K". While preventing the people of J&K from reaping the benefits of its own water resources, anti-people projects are being imposed on PoK in order to satiate the requirements of the rest of Pakistan's provinces. The population of J&K, particularly on the side of the LoC have taken note of this and are looking for new means to express their discontent. The overwhelming sense that Pakistan needs Kashmir to meet its water and power requirements, at the cost of political aspirations and economic, developmental needs of Kashmir seems to have set in.

The inter-provincial differences within Pakistan have delivered Diamer-Basha dam as the first of the large dams to be completed and it is clear that the NA does not have the space to assert its interest on an equal footing along with the rest of the provinces. The spillover effect of the inter-provincial politics in Pakistan is demonstrated and the political demand for a fifth province status has been impending. The strong anti-Pakistan sentiment fuelled by this matter has also now been extended into an anti-NWFP stance owing to the royalty issue. Punjab has always been resented for taking away most of the share of the benefits of development projects.

Frustration over the absence of political representation coupled with the economic and cultural dispossession is only augmenting the simmering conflict. Strong *jihadi* presence in the region coupled with constrained political space and the growing sense of alienation from Pakistan proves to be a force to reckon with for the Pakistani government, which is already troubled with violence in its other provinces.

CHAPTER 5

CHINESE STRATEGIC INTERESTS IN POK

Jabin T. Jacob[1]

When the Northern Frontier of Kashmir was partitioned in 1947, the two routes connecting India with Xinjiang in China were distributed between the successors to British India. The Ladakh route connecting Leh via the Karakoram Pass and via routes east of it to Kashgar (Kashi), Yarkand (Shache) and Khotan (Hotan) went to India, while the western route from Gilgit to Kashgar via Hunza, the Mintaka Pass and the Khunjerab Pass went to Pakistan. India's portion is now a part of its dispute with China, while the Pakistani portion is now part of a cooperative arrangement with China in the form of the Karakoram Highway (KKH). Other than the events preceding the conflict with India in 1962 and the consequent occupation of Aksai Chin, the Chinese are only in the news on the Indian side for occasional border intrusions and clashes along the LAC. In Pakistan, meanwhile the Chinese have managed to engage in a substantial military and strategic partnership as well as a small but significant economic relationship.

The Karakoram Highway (KKH) is today a strategic and commercial asset for both China and Pakistan but it has

[1] Jabin Jacob is a Research Fellow, Institute of Peace and Conflict Studies (IPCS), New Delhi.

also been responsible for transporting terrorism, drugs and disease. Indeed, for Pakistan, the resultant Chinese concerns are no small matter. Its policy towards the Northern Areas invariably invokes the link that the region provided with China and the importance of the trade with that country. Pakistani Prime Minister, Shaukat Aziz, for example, did precisely this while speaking to newly elected members of the Northern Areas Legislative Council (NALC) in late 2004 saying that their region was significant for the KKH that provided a vital link to China and asking them, therefore, to promote unity and maintain sectarian harmony to ensure the development of the area.[2] Another important detail in the Sino-Pakistan relationship that is embodied by the KKH is the fact that there have been extensive historical contacts between the Northern Areas and Xinjiang, formerly known as Eastern Turkestan and that while Xinjiang is increasingly coming into its own as a substantial economic entity, the same cannot be said of Pakistan-Occupied Kashmir (PoK).

[2] "Government paying attention to Northern Areas uplift: PM," *Business Recorder*, November 1, 2004, accessed at http://www.northernareas.org.pk/ndetail.cfm?ID=374.

I

Kashmir in China-Pakistan Relations

The ambiguous Chinese position on Hunza in the Northern Areas was an important factor in the initial stages of the China-Pakistan relationship – a factor that even led Ayub Khan to propose to India a joint defence of the subcontinent against the communist threat from across Pakistan's northern borders. Like the former Nationalist government, the Communists in China too showed Hunza as part of China on their maps, leading Ayub Khan to warn the Chinese in October 1959 that he would use force if they crossed the Karakoram and the wiser course of action would be to negotiate the border. The lack of consideration exhibited by India to his proposal had eventually led the Pakistani president to consider a change of policy with respect to China by the end of 1959.[3] China for its part had declared that it had no intention of laying claim to what Pakistan considered its territory and was only looking for a boundary settlement.

In the late 1950s, as Indian and Chinese forces began to clash along their disputed frontier, Pakistan started a dialogue with China. In 1957, Bo Yibo, chairman of the Chinese Economic Commission, had already arranged for a team of Chinese officials to visit the Hunza and Gilgit valley. Two centres were opened by Beijing in Hunza and Gilgit for promoting better relations between China and Pakistan.[4] It took

---

[3] Alastair Lamb, *Kashmir: A Disputed Legacy, 1846-1990* (Karachi: Oxford University Press, 1993), pp. 236-37.

[4] Victoria Schofield, *Kashmir in Conflict: India, Pakistan and the Unfinished War*, (London and New York: I B Tauris, 2000), p. 86.

the Chinese until January 1961, however, to respond to Ayub Khan's call for negotiations on the boundary and until February 1962 to actually begin them.[5] The Chinese response of May 31, 1962 to a protest note sent by the Indian Ministry of External Affairs on May 10, too said that, "It is entirely necessary, proper, legitimate and in accordance with international practice for the Chinese Government to agree with the Government of Pakistan to negotiate a *provisional* (emphasis added) agreement concerning this boundary pending a final settlement of the Kashmir question."[6]

Zulfikar Ali Bhutto also saw that the conflict between India and China could prove a potential diplomatic advantage for Pakistan. In 1960 as minister for Kashmiri Affairs Bhutto led the Pakistani delegation to the UN and for the first time broke ranks with the established American position on China's membership of the UN. Instead of vetoing the proposal, Pakistan abstained.[7] Still, in 1962, despite the Sino-Indian border conflict, Pakistan did not press its opportunity to attack India and perhaps seek a final solution to the Kashmir dispute.

However, just as the 1962-63 talks at Rawalpindi between Bhutto and Sardar Swaran Singh were about to begin, Pakistan announced a border agreement with China, which according to India involved ceding 5180 sq. kms. (2050 sq. miles) of Kashmir.[8] The Indian side almost called off the talks after

5 John Garver, *Protracted Contest: Sino-Indian Rivalry in the Twentieth Century* (New Delhi: Oxford University Press, 2001), p. 192.

6 "Sino-Pakistan Agreement, March 2, 1963: Some Facts," Ministry of External Affairs, New Delhi, 1963, p. 12. Quoted in Sisir Gupta, *Kashmir: A Study in India-Pakistan Relations* (New Delhi: Asia Publishing House, 1966), p. 429.

7 Victoria Schofield, *Kashmir in Conflict: India, Pakistan and the Unfinished War*, (London and New York: I B Tauris, 2000), p. 87.

8 According to Alastair Lamb, this Indian claim takes into account the area of Raskam and its surroundings. Alastair Lamb, *Kashmir: A Disputed Legacy, 1846-1990* (Karachi: Oxford University Press, 1993), p. 246, n. 30.

hearing the news of the agreement on Pakistani radio but eventually decided to continue with the talks while the government at Delhi registered its protests with Pakistan and China. The wording of the agreement between Pakistan and China did clearly state though that the agreement did not prejudice a final settlement of the Kashmir dispute between India and Pakistan.[9] The fourth round of talks between India and Pakistan was held in Calcutta from March 13-14, 1963, following the formalisation of the Sino-Pak border agreement on March 2. India protested that the agreement violated the UN resolutions of 1948 and 1949, which enjoined both parties from unilaterally altering the status quo in Kashmir.[10] The 1963 agreement between Pakistan and China aimed to settle the status of Hunza with the Chinese recognising it as Pakistani territory and Pakistan confirming that Hunza claims north of the Karakoram were withdrawn and a final alignment of the Hunza-Xinjiang border.

Following the talks with Pakistan, Nehru went to Srinagar where he noted how China's attack on India had given the Pakistanis an opportunity to revive the Kashmir issue. But he said: 'Pakistan is mistaken if it thinks it can intimidate us because we are facing this threat from the Chinese.'[11] The new relationship between China and Pakistan meant, however, that the Pakistanis also felt inclined to speak from a position of strength. 'Attack from India on Pakistan today is no longer confined to the security and territorial integrity of Pakistan,'

---

[9] *Sino-Pakistan Frontier Agreement, 1963*, http://www.ipcs.org/INDO-PAK-12-Docu.pdf.

[10] Sumit Ganguly, *The Crisis in Kashmir: Portents of War, Hopes of Peace* (New Delhi: Cambridge University Press, 1997), pp. 46-47.

[11] Jawaharlal Nehru, *Pakistan Seeks to Profit from Chinese Aggression*, New Delhi, 1963. Quoted in Sisir Gupta, *Kashmir: A Study in India-Pakistan Relations* (New Delhi: Asia Publishing House, 1966), p. 432.

said Zulfikar Ali Bhutto in Pakistan's National Assembly in July 1963. 'An attack by India on Pakistan involves the territorial integrity and security of the largest state in Asia.'[12]

In February 1964, at the conclusion of his visit to Pakistan, Zhou Enlai, in the joint statement called for a resolution of the Kashmir dispute in accordance with the wishes of the Kashmiris, thus supporting the Pakistani position.[13] Ayub Khan's visit to China in March 1965 also produced a joint statement on Kashmir and led to the President of Azad Kashmir publicly thanking Beijing for its support.[14] Thus, it was no wonder that later that year when Sheikh Abdullah while in London infuriated the Indian authorities by refusing to condemn Pakistan's relations with China. He went still further and in Algiers on the eve of the planned Afro-Asian Conference had a brief meeting with the Chinese Prime Minister Zhou Enlai that would lead to his arrest on his return to India.[15]

In August 1965, as the Indo-Pak war got underway, the Chinese intervened by protesting an apparent Indian 'aggression' in the Nathu La area on the Sikkim-Tibet border. The 'aggression' involved some structures that India had seemingly built at the mountain pass and the Indians were given a deadline of 19th September to remove the structures, subsequently extended to 22nd September.[16] The incident

---

[12] Victoria Schofield, *Kashmir in Conflict: India, Pakistan and the Unfinished War*, (London and New York: I B Tauris, 2000), p. 102.

[13] John Garver, *Protracted Contest: Sino-Indian Rivalry in the Twentieth Century* (New Delhi: Oxford University Press, 2001), p. 193.

[14] Alastair Lamb, *Kashmir: A Disputed Legacy, 1846-1990* (Karachi: Oxford University Press, 1993), p. 254.

[15] Alastair Lamb, *Kashmir: A Disputed Legacy, 1846-1990* (Karachi: Oxford University Press, 1993), p. 209.

[16] John Garver, *Protracted Contest: Sino-Indian Rivalry in the Twentieth Century* (New Delhi: Oxford University Press, 2001), p. 169.

seemed aimed at helping out the Pakistanis in their foray into Kashmir. The perceived lack of support from the West during the war would drive Pakistan more closely into the arms of the Chinese.

However, in December 1970, China concerned at the extent of Pakistan's internal problems had urged it to find a just solution to the problems of East Pakistan.[17] In fact, as 1971 progressed, China was increasingly uneasy with the Pakistani methods there. While it did accuse India of interfering in Pakistani affairs, China was privately just as critical of the Pakistani policy of repression. In April, China also stated that it would not intervene militarily in the case of any conflict. In November when Bhutto visited China to seek a repeat of Chinese diversionary moves in the Himalayas as in 1965 in the case of conflict, China refused. However, in public China continued to declare that it would 'resolutely support' Pakistan.[18]

Following the war, the Chinese had some sharp words for both India and the Soviet Union but by 1979, when Atal Behari Vajpayee visited China and called its position on Kashmir an 'unnecessary complication' for Sino-Indian relations, Beijing began to change its stance to a more neutral position. This was first evident in June 1980 when Deng Xiaoping called the Kashmir issue a bilateral dispute that had to be resolved peacefully. In December, however, the Chinese also tried to please the visiting Pakistani foreign minister by calling for a 'just settlement of the Kashmir issue in the spirit of the Simla

---

[17] John Garver, *Protracted Contest: Sino-Indian Rivalry in the Twentieth Century* (New Delhi: Oxford University Press, 2001), p. 208.

[18] John Garver, *Protracted Contest: Sino-Indian Rivalry in the Twentieth Century* (New Delhi: Oxford University Press, 2001), p. 212.

agreement and in accordance with the relevant United Nations resolutions.' China had stopped talking about the right of Kashmiri self-determination from 1980 but by referring to UN resolutions, the implication remained and by referring also to the Simla agreement, China appeared to support the Pakistani position that the two were not mutually exclusive. For these reasons, John Garver says that China's post-1980 position on Kashmir continued to be pro-Pakistan. [19]

In the 1990s, despite the Kashmir crisis in India, China's position veered much closer to that of India despite constant Pakistani demands to the contrary. In 1994, the Chinese indicated to the Pakistanis that they were firmly opposed to the emergence of an independent Kashmir, concerned that an independent Kashmir would become a breeding ground for intrigue directed at China, encourage demands for Tibetan independence as well as call into question the territory ceded by Pakistan in 1963.[20] Indeed, in 1996, on the eve of Jiang Zemin's visit to India, the Chinese ambassador to India, stated, "We do not stand for internationalisation of the Kashmir question." What is more, during Jiang's address to the Pakistani Senate later, not once did he mention Kashmir. Also, according to Garver, China had progressively toned down its level of deterrent support for Pakistan over Kashmir in the 1990s.[21]

And despite continued military exchanges and sales between China and Pakistan, this fact was further backed up

---

[19] John Garver, *Protracted Contest: Sino-Indian Rivalry in the Twentieth Century* (New Delhi: Oxford University Press, 2001), p. 228.

[20] Sumit Ganguly, *The Crisis in Kashmir: Portents of War, Hopes of Peace* (New Delhi: Cambridge University Press, 1997), p. 121 and p. 144.

[21] John Garver, *Protracted Contest: Sino-Indian Rivalry in the Twentieth Century* (New Delhi: Oxford University Press, 2001), p. 231.

by the perceived Chinese neutrality in 1999 during the Kargil conflict between India and Pakistan. The Chinese went to the extent of telling Pakistani Prime Minister Nawaz Sharif and his foreign minister, Sartaz Aziz not to expect Chinese support if they raised the Kashmir issue at the UN Security Council, stressing bilateral negotiations between India and Pakistan.[22]

Interestingly, Kashmiri voices have been heard calling for a Chinese involvement in the dispute. According to former Chief Justice of the High Court of Azad Kashmir and leader of the Jammu and Kashmir Liberation League, Abdul Majeed Mallick, the Chinese ambassador to Islamabad had promised him that China would return Aksai Chin if Kashmir were to become independent. He used this pledge as a reason for bringing China into the dialogue on Kashmir.[23] Similarly, in 2006, during the World Social Forum in Karachi, Hurriyat Chairman Mirwaiz Umer Farooq called for China to be made a party to the resolution of the Kashmir dispute saying that not only did it occupy a part of Kashmir, it was also a major player in the region. The Pakistani Foreign Office, however, ruled out any role for China saying that only India and Pakistan were parties to the dispute according to the relevant UN resolutions.[24] During his visit to Pakistan in November 2006, Chinese President Hu Jintao too refrained from committing China to a role in the resolution of the Kashmir dispute saying

---

[22] John Garver, *Protracted Contest: Sino-Indian Rivalry in the Twentieth Century* (New Delhi: Oxford University Press, 2001), p. 239.

[23] Sudeshna Sarkar, "China Will Return Akshai Chin," *The Statesman*, December 16, 2004.

http://www.jammu-kashmir.com/archives/archives2004/kashmir20041216a.html.

[24] B. Muralidhar Reddy, "No role for China in resolving Kashmir, says Islamabad," *The Hindu*, April 4, 2006.

that it supported Pakistan and India resolving the issue through dialogue.[25] However, in December 2006, Umer Farooq again raised the idea of seeking Beijing's help saying that his group was thinking of visiting China in this regard.[26]

[25] Rana Qaisar, "China not seeking 'key' role in Kashmir resolution," *Daily Times*, November 25, 2006, http://dailytimes.com.pk/default.asp?page=2006\11\25\story_25-11-2006_pg1_1.

[26] "Hurriyat Leaders May Visit China," *IRNA*, December 2, 2006, accessed at http://www.jammu-kashmir.com/archives/archives2006/kashmir20061202d.html.

II

China and PoK: Economic Linkages

Gilgit has for long provided (and controlled) access to Hunza and the passes leading to Xinjiang over which trade of some sort has existed throughout recorded history. Of the two trading routes between Xinjiang and British India – one, through Leh and the other, through Gilgit – it was the Gilgit route that the British preferred after they had acquired the Gilgit lease and decided to reorient trade from Ladakh.[27]

Following the 1965 ceasefire between India and Pakistan, China and Pakistan began to work towards improving overland links. A road was originally planned by Pakistan in 1959 to replace the Rawalpindi-Gilgit road across the Babusar Pass built originally by the British in the late 1890s with the intention still perhaps to meet a possible Chinese threat to Hunza.[28] The new road would eventually come to connect Kashgar, with Havelian in the district of Abbottabad in Pakistan with an extension to the Grand Trunk Road. But originally, the decision to connect Gilgit to Xinjiang across the Mintaka Pass was part of a secret agreement in 1964 with work beginning in 1966. In 1967, an announcement was made for a new road across the Khunjerab Pass for heavy motor traffic. It was opened to traffic in 1971, while largely unsurfaced and still suitable only for light vehicles. In 1973, with the decision to convert the road into a metalled two-lane highway, some 12,000 Chinese and

[27] Alastair Lamb, *Kashmir: A Disputed Legacy, 1846-1990* (Karachi: Oxford University Press, 1993), p. 67.

[28] Alastair Lamb, *Kashmir: A Disputed Legacy, 1846-1990* (Karachi: Oxford University Press, 1993), p. 275.

15,000 Pakistani workers were employed in completing the task. While it was formally inaugurated in 1978 as the Sino-Pakistan Friendship Highway, it was not until 1986 that the highway was fully opened to travellers.[29]

In 2003, China granted aid to Pakistan for the construction of a bypass and bridges on Karakoram Highway (KKH) near the tremor-affected areas of Diamer district of the Northern Areas. The Chinese Ambassador stressed that the bypass and bridges near the tremor-affected areas were of vital importance for the KKH. The envoy also appeared to be concerned about ensuring that the Northern Areas retain communication links with the rest of Pakistan.[30] By July 2003, Chinese firms had started arriving in the Northern Areas with engineers and equipment to undertake work on 14 bridges of reinforced cement concrete in a joint venture worth about Pakistani Rs. 3 billion.[31] The year 2003 was also the 25th anniversary of the construction of the KKH and saw the release of special postage stamps as well as the making of a Chinese television documentary. In October, the Chinese pledged a further US$6 million for repairs along the KKH.[32]

In February 2006, China and Pakistan agreed to widen KKH for heavier freight vehicles to allow China to ship its energy supplies from the Middle East through Gwadar to Xinjiang and reducing Chinese dependence on the Malacca

---

[29] Alastair Lamb, *Kashmir: A Disputed Legacy, 1846-1990* (Karachi: Oxford University Press, 1993), pp. 275-76.

[30] "China to fund construction of bypass, bridges on Karakorum Highway," *The News*, January 18, 2003, http://www.jang-group.com/thenews/jan2003-daily/18-01-2003/metro/i3.htm.

[31] "China begins building 14 bridges on Karakoram Highway," *Dawn*, July 15, 2003, http://www.dawn.com/2003/07/15/nat17.htm.

[32] "$6 million allocated for KKH repairs," *Dawn*, October 1, 2003, http://www.dawn.com/2003/10/01/nat20.htm.

Straits.[33] During President Musharraf's visit to China in March 2006, China extended soft loans of US$350 million for upgrading the 800-km length of the KKH from Hassanabdal to Sangriyal damaged in the earthquake of the previous year. The 470-km stretch from Hassanabdal to Rai Kot, was targeted for completion within the three years in order to speed up the work on Bhasha Dam.[34] It was also decided that a 140-km stretch of the Highway that was submerged due to the construction of Bhasha Dam, would be shifted higher.[35]

In June 2006, the two countries had launched their first passenger bus service on the KKH linking Gilgit with Kashgar, a 550-kilometre journey and 16 hours long. With three trips a week from each side, only a border pass was required for the locals using the bus service. Similarly, Chinese tourists and traders could come up to Gilgit on a border pass issued by the chief secretary. One of the aims of the bus service was also to increase the trade volume between the two countries. One route was Kashgar-Khunjerab-Sost-Gilgit, while the other was Tashurgan-Khunjerab-Sost.[36] Also initiated earlier in May, was a truck service between the two countries with Chinese traders allowed to bring their trucks up to port cities of Karachi and Gwadar.[37]

---

33 Tarique Niazi, "Thunder in Sino-Pakistani Relations," *China Brief*, The Jamestown Foundation, Volume 6, Issue 5, March 2, 2006, http://www.jamestown.org/publications_details.php?volume_id=415&&issue_id=3637.

34 The dam has been designed to provide water and electricity to the North-West Frontier Province (NWFP) and Punjab but has been strongly opposed by the people of the Northern Areas.

35 "Government keen on developing road network to boost trade: Shamim," *The News*, March 7, 2006, http://www.jang.com.pk/thenews/mar2006-daily/07-03-2006/metro/k7.htm.

36 "Bus services to China in June," *Dawn*, May 24, 2006, http://www.dawn.com/2006/05/24/top6.htm.

37 "Pakistan, China start first bus service," *Dawn*, June 15, 2006, http://www.dawn.com/2006/06/15/welcome.htm.

On June 30, 2006, a MoU was signed between the Pakistan Highway Administration and the State Assets Supervision and Administration Commission (SASAC) of China to rebuild and upgrade the KKH, beginning with the 335 km road between the Raikot Bridge and the Khunjerab Pass. The highway would be reconstructed by the China Road and Bridge Corporation and besides being widened from 10 metres to 30 metres would also be designed for heavy transport vehicles and for extreme weather conditions.[38] Later, in August, Pakistan won a US$1 billion loan from the Asian Development Bank in addition to the US$1.8 billion provided by the World Bank for the National Trade Corridor (NTC) project linking Karachi, Gwadar and Khunjerab. The six-year plan was intended to meet domestic transportation requirements and provide transit facilities to Central Asia, western China, Afghanistan and Iran.[39]

An agreement was signed in 1995 between Pakistan, China and Uzbekistan to establish a land route to connect the Central Asian states via Gilgit for promoting trade and tourism between the member states. The agreement was to be implemented in 1999. But in March 2003, *Dawn* reported following Uzbekistan's insistence that the link be extended to India, Islamabad had abandoned the plan.[40] Pakistan sought then to link the Northern Areas with via Ghizer to Tajikistan only 35 kms away through the Wakhan Corridor in Afghanistan, a proposal that dated to 2000, but this too was affected by continued instability in that country and the lack of any

[38] "Pakistan China Highway," *Paktribune*, July 10, 2006, http://www.paktribune.com/news/index.shtml?149389.

[39] "ADB to give $1bn for trade corridor," *Dawn*, August 19, 2006, http://www.dawn.com/2006/08/19/nat2.htm.

[40] "Plan shelved to extend Karakoram Highway to Central Asia," *Dawn*, March 23, 2003, http://www.dawn.com/2003/03/23/local30.htm.

dialogue on the issue between Islamabad and Kabul.[41]

With respect to other transport links, in April 2006, the Governor of Xinjiang, Ismail Tiliwaldi at a meeting with a visiting delegation of the Pakistan Muslim League (PML) announced that his government would undertake a study on the feasibility of a rail network through Kashgar between China and Pakistan.[42] In November 2006, Pakistan Railways short-listed two companies – one from China and another a joint German-Austrian company – for the study of the 1,000-km railway line from Havelian in Abbottabad district, up to a terminus in Xinjiang. About 750 kms of the track would pass through the Northern Areas and the remainder through the Chinese province. The entire project was estimated to cost about US$5 billion.[43]

The Chinese have invested in other projects as well in different parts of the Northern Areas, including hydro-power projects, water-diversion channels and telecommunication facilities.[44] In the power sector, Pakistan and China in 2002, had signed an agreement to set up an 18MW Hydro Electric

---

41 "Ghizer-Tajikistan road plan hits snag," *Dawn*, July 17, 2003, http://www.dawn.com/2003/07/17/nat11.htm and "Pakistan pushes for road link with Tajikistan," *Dawn*, July 18, 2003, http://www.dawn.com/2003/07/18/nat6.htm. In September 2003, Pakistan finally got a major road connecting it to Central Asia. The Horgos-Almaty-Bishkek-Kashgar-Islamabad-Karachi road running through Pakistan, China, Kazakhstan and Kyrgyzystan was expected to increase the prospects of trade between the four countries. "Road to Central Asia will be opened soon: Four countries to be linked," *Dawn*, September 30, 2003, http://www.dawn.com/2003/09/30/nat11.htm.

42 "Pakistan, China's Xinjiang region to establish rail link," *Dawn*, April 4, 2006, http://www.dawn.com/2006/04/04/welcome.htm.

43 Naqi Akbar, "Railways short lists 2 cos for China rail link study," *The Nation*, November 16, 2006, http://www.nation.com.pk/daily/nov-2006/16/bnews5.php.

44 "Diplomacy takes a high road," *The Indian Express*, March 26, 2006, http://www.indianexpress.com/story/1215.html.

Power Station on the Naltar River in Gilgit at an estimated cost of about US$20million.[45] This project would soon however, be caught up in differences between the local and federal authorities and financial problems such as the payment of the commitment and management fees to the Chinese firm responsible for the project.[46] The Chashma Power Plant supplying electricity to Dera Ismail Khan was completed by Chinese firms as also the first unit of Ghazi Brotha Hydel Power Project that became operational in 2003. Beijing is also expected to help in a major way in the construction of the Basha dam on the Indus river in the Northern Areas.[47]

Coming to bilateral trade, the agreement that was signed between China and Pakistan in 1963 lapsed in 2000 and was not revived for over three years owing to Chinese fears of Islamic fundamentalism originating in Pakistan. This brought legal trade between the two countries through the overland route almost to a standstill and in the absence of the agreement led to increased smuggling.[48] Following 9/11 tourist flow to the region had dropped markedly and so too had bilateral trade.[49] The check posts at the Pakistan-China border over the Khunjerab pass resulted in a decrease of bilateral trade of goods and services, and severely affected the livelihood of

---

45 "Pakistan, China deal to set up hydro power station in Northern Areas," *The Nation*, 24 October, 2002, http://www.nation.com.pk/daily/241002/business/bn4.htm.

46 "Naltar power project hits snags in Northern Areas," *Dawn*, July 11, 2003, http://www.dawn.com/2003/07/11/local34.htm.

47 M. Ismail Khan, "Beijing to Kashgar, Gilgit to Gwadar...," *The News*, March 1, 2006, http://www.jang.com.pk/thenews/mar2006-daily/01-03-2006/oped/o2.htm.

48 "Renewal of trade pact with China urged," *The Dawn*, January 6, 2003, http://www.dawn.com/2003/01/06/nat19.htm.

49 "Ashfak Bokhari, "Kashghar-Islamabad flights from June 8," *Dawn*, May 30, 2004, http://www.dawn.com/2004/05/30/nat13.htm.

local people engaged in small-scale border trade.[50] This was evident also from the statement of the Northern Areas Chief Executive Aftab Ahmed Khan Sherpao in 2003 when he asked the administration to be lenient in issuing border passes to China for locals.[51] Traders of the Northern Areas were later granted special permits to enter and leave Xinjiang under an agreement reached between the authorities of the Northern Areas and Xinjiang.[52] Nevertheless, Chinese officials, meanwhile, have been accused of creating problems for passengers on the bus service because of their stringent identity checks and insensitivity.[53]

In April 2003, Pakistan had finally sent a formal request to the Chinese government for revival of the land route agreement and by November the China-Pakistan Joint Declaration was signed during President Musharraf's visit to China, which promised to conclude a new border trade agreement and "strengthen transport cooperation and promote interflow of personnel and commodities through the Karakoram Highway."[54]

---

[50] Abid Qaiyum Suleri, Shfqat Munir and Syed Qasim Shah, *Impact of Trade Liberalisation on Lives and Livelihood of Mountain Communities in the Northern Areas of Pakistan* (Islamabad: Sustainable Development Policy Institute, 2002), p.18, http://www.pdg.org.pk/docs/ImpactTradeLiberlisation.pdf. See also Ghulam Amin Beg, "Understanding societal values," *Dawn Magazine*, September 5, 2004, http://www.dawn.com/weekly/dmag/archive/040905/dmag5.htm.

[51] "Restructuring plan for Northern Areas Public Works Department okayed," *Dawn*, July 12, 2003, http://www.dawn.com/2003/07/12/local25.htm.

[52] M. Ismail Khan, "Beijing to Kashgar, Gilgit to Gwadar...," *The News*, March 1, 2006, http://www.jang.com.pk/thenews/mar2006-daily/01-03-2006/oped/o2.htm.

[53] "Suspension of Sino-Pak bus service feared amid lack of facilities," *PakTribune*, June 26, 2006, http://www.paktribune.com/news/index.shtml?148004.

[54] Ziad Haider, "Clearing clouds over Karakoram," *Daily Times*, April 4, 2004, http://www.dailytimes.com.pk/default.asp?page=story_4-4-2004_pg3_3.

In between, however, the closure of the border with China at Sost in the Khunjerab valley owing to fears from SARS badly hit trade[55] and mega projects in the Northern Areas. At least three projects – the 18-MW Naltar power project, Karakoram Highway reconstruction project of over 200 kms near the border and the 4-MW Guru power project (phase II) were affected.[56] In fact, the Northern Areas home secretary admitted that despite the threat of avian flu, Pakistan was forced to reopen the Sost post in July because of increasing pressure from the traders.[57]

The Chinese have expressed their interest in investment in the Northern Areas[58] and have urged Pakistani businessmen to invest in China as well and in particular asking that they expand their focus from Urumqi, the capital of Xinjiang, to Kashgar too.[59] In 2004, a visiting trade official from Xinjiang announced that the opening of the Sost Dry Port set up by a Chinese company,[60] would be an example of friendship and promote trade among China, Pakistan, Afghanistan, and the Central Asian states.[61] In October 2004, business leaders of

---

55 "Border closure causes Rs156m loss," *Dawn*, June 7, 2003, http://www.dawn.com/2003/06/07/nat28.htm.

56 "Border closure may hit trade," *Dawn*, June 4, 2003, http://www.dawn.com/2003/06/04/nat26.htm.

57 "Pakistan-China border at Sost opens today," *Dawn*, July 1, 2003, http://www.dawn.com/2003/07/01/nat17.htm. See also Farman Ali, "Opening of Khunjerab Pass demanded," *Dawn*, May 11, 2003, http://www.dawn.com/2003/05/11/local20.htm

58 "Chinese firms ready to invest in Northern Areas," *Dawn*, October 26, 2002, http://www.dawn.com/2002/10/26/local18.htm.

59 "Traders asked to invest in Kashgar," *Dawn*, October 3, 2003, http://www.dawn.com/2003/10/03/ebr7.htm.

60 "Land route accord," *Dawn*, April 13, 2003, http://www.dawn.com/2003/04/13/ebr4.htm.

61 "Sust Dry Port to be inaugurated by June," *Business Recorder*, May 17, 2004, accessed at Northern Areas Development Gateway, http://www.northernareas.org.pk/ndetail.cfm?ID=302.

Rawalpindi and Kashgar agreed to hold exhibitions of their industrial products in the two cities to enhance bilateral trade between the two countries.[62] In November, the Kashgar administration offered "to provide all possible facilities to the Pakistani traders to undertake joint ventures for their common benefits." On the same occasion, the Pakistani ambassador, Riaz Mohammad Khan referred to the preferential trade agreement (PTA) that Pakistan and China had concluded in 2003 and noted that with China's Western Development Strategy (WDS), Sino-Pakistan trade was bound to increase, especially via Kashgar. He also said that Pakistan would allow transit trade from Xinjiang using the Karakoram Highway and the Pakistani ports of Karachi and Qasim.[63] In March 2005, the Kashgar Prefectural Administration suggested a frontier zone at Khunjerab to enhance interaction and trade between the border areas of the two countries and provide fast and convenient customs clearance and preferential policies for the traders. The Chinese side also offered to bear the entire expenditure for its construction.[64] In June, the Chinese formed the largest delegation at a trade fair in Karachi, with the contingent from the Kashgar Prefecture Administration and Xinjiang Department of Foreign Trade and Economic Cooperation forming a major section.[65]

In August 2005, the two countries held the first round of talks for a free trade agreement (FTA) at Urumqi. There was

---

[62] "Industrial products fairs," *Dawn*, October 17, 2004, http://www.dawn.com/2004/10/17/ebr7.htm.

[63] "Xinjiang region to expand trade with Pakistan," *Dawn*, November 18, 2004, http://www.dawn.com/2004/11/18/ebr2.htm.

[64] "China for frontier zone at Khunjirab," *Dawn*, March 29, 2005, http://www.dawn.com/2005/03/29/ebr10.htm.

[65] "Over 100 foreign exhibitors to attend fair: 'My Karachi'," *Dawn*, June 23, 2005, http://www.dawn.com/2005/06/23/ebr4.htm.

an expectation that Xinjiang would emerge as the hub of Sino-Pak business activities, with the implementation of a special tariff package from January 2006.[66] Habib Bank after being the first Pakistani bank to set up an office in Beijing in September 2005, also acquired 20 per cent of the stock in a major bank in Xinjiang, the Urumqi City Commercial Bank (UCCB) in February 2006.[67]

In September 2006, hosting a 50-member Chinese trade delegation from Kashgar, Punjab Governor Khalid Maqbool observed that there was much in common between the people of Xinjiang and Pakistan, and stressed the need for greater interaction and enhanced educational and cultural links. The Chinese leader of the delegation and vice-commissioner of Kashgar, pointed out that the KKH was the best way to increase bilateral trade and called on Pakistani traders to use this route, so that Kashgar would be their first stop in China.[68]

It is important to take note of one other aspect of the Pakistani trade with China through the Northern Areas, namely that of differences between the federal and local authorities. The President of the Northern Areas Chamber of Commerce and Industry (NACCI), Shahbaz Khan in 2002 called for declaring the Northern Areas as a Special Economic Zone and for an Export Processing Zone and a Dry Port in the vicinity of the city of Gilgit in order to facilitate trade and commerce with China and the Central Asian countries. The business leader

---

66 "Land route trade with China to improve," *Dawn*, September 22, 2005, http://www.dawn.com/2005/09/22/ebr15.htm.

67 "HBL to buy stake in Chinese bank," *Dawn*, February 21, 2006, http://www.dawn.com/2006/02/21/ebr11.htm.

68 "Sino-Pak relations to grow: Maqbool," *Dawn*, September 25, 2006, http://www.dawn.com/2006/09/25/nat28.htm.

also argued that a direct land access to Tajikistan be constructed by negotiating a lease out of the small corridor of Wakhan Patti with Afghanistan in exchange for giving it transit facility to China via the Karakuram Highway.[69] Also perhaps in a sign that the central government did not pay enough attention to the region, Khan asked that either the Board of Investment open an office in Gilgit or a local version of the Board of Investment be established in the Northern Areas for the promotion of investment in the country. He also called for better airport facilities in order to attract foreign as well as domestic tourists and for the promotion of tourism industry in the area.[70]

Earlier, stating that Pakistan's Central Board of Revenue (CBR) had no authority to set up any kind of customs, income tax or sales tax offices in the Northern Areas, NACCI had demanded that the government stop its collection of customs duty at the Sost check-post and remove its offices from Sost and Gilgit. Shahbaz Khan cited the decision of the Law Ministry about the Northern Areas that 'in view of the undecided constitutional status of the Northern Areas, the commissioner, income tax, Rawalpindi zone, cannot extend the jurisdiction of its subordinate office to the said Areas.' Khan also demanded that those goods imported by the local people should be allowed in duty-free and suggested that the facility be allowed only for importers, traders, unemployed youth having domiciled in the Northern Areas so as to prevent any misuse. In justifying the need for the check-post as a way of preventing smuggling, the CBR also admitted that the reason why the infraction occurred

---

[69] "NACCI for declaring Northern Areas as special economic zone," *The Nation*, November 8, 2002, http://www.nation.com.pk/daily/081102/national/oth6.htm. See also n. 38.

[70] "NACCI for declaring Northern Areas as special economic zone," *The Nation*, November 8, 2002, http://www.nation.com.pk/daily/081102/national/oth6.htm.

in the first place was because the imported goods did not really serve the Northern Areas but were meant for the markets further south.[71]

[71] "Removal of CBR offices from Northern Areas demanded," *Dawn*, October 30, 2002, http://www.dawn.com/2002/10/30/ebr5.htm.

III

Pakistan and the Unrest in Xinjiang

Part of the reasons for China's change of stance on Kashmir in the 1990s had to do with its own internal problems. Xinjiang shares religion, tradition, language and customs with parts of Pakistan and other bordering countries. Since Xinjiang last came under Chinese domination in the 1870s, it has twice had an independent existence as East Turkestan in the 1930s and 1940s. Earlier, in the late 1920s, the Chinese administration in Xinjiang had believed that the British would try and exploit Muslim unrest in the region to undermine Beijing's authority by sending its agents across the Northern Frontier of Kashmir.[72] Today, a successor to the British, namely Pakistan, continues to be watched with similar suspicion for with the fall of the Soviet Union, hopes for self-determination in Xinjiang rose anew at least with some degree of support and resources coming from Pakistan.

When the KKH opened, Uighurs greatly benefited from the freedoms afforded to them as they travelled to Pakistan for trade, or through it for the onward journey to Mecca. Uighurs also enrolled in Pakistani schools and settled and raised families in Pakistan. There have been small Uighur communities in several Pakistani cities that have assimilated with the local population.[73] In the mid-1980s, the KKH had also served as the main route through which Chinese arms were transferred

---

[72] Alastair Lamb, *Kashmir: A Disputed Legacy, 1846-1990* (Karachi: Oxford University Press, 1993), p. 53.

[73] Ashfak Bokhari, "Identity crisis in Kashgar," *Dawn Magazine*, December 12, 2004, http://www.dawn.com/weekly/dmag/archive/041212/dmag1.htm.

to Afghan mujahideen but by 1989 some quantities of these weapons were being smuggled back into Xinjiang.[74] Kashgar, a terminus of the KKH was one of the major zones of Islamic revivalism in Xinjiang and was the origin of many of the Uighurs who had joined the Afghan *jihad* in the early 1980s which was the beginning of links between Uighur and fundamentalists in Afghanistan and Pakistan.[75] In the 1990s, Uighur groups turned against the Chinese state with an often violent campaign for a separate state. In 1992, following a failed uprising near Kashgar that resulted in over twenty deaths, China closed its road links with Pakistan for several months. In 1999, China arrested 16 Uighurs who claimed to have been trained in guerrilla warfare in Pakistan and immediately lodged a protest with Pakistan.[76] The Chinese became selective in granting visas to Pakistani nationals,[77] arrested and executed several Pakistani citizens in this connection.[78] It was believed that even Pakistani nationals were involved in fundamentalist activities in Xinjiang and that the Pakistan government was turning a blind eye to such individuals and groups within Pakistan.[79] Following increasing Chinese pressure, Islamabad

---

[74] Hayder Mili, "Xinjiang: An Emerging Narco-Islamist Corridor", *Terrorism Monitor*, The Jamestown Foundation, Volume 3, Issue 8, April 21, 2005, http://jamestown.org/terrorism/news/article.php?articleid=2369633.

[75] Hayder Mili, "Xinjiang: An Emerging Narco-Islamist Corridor", *Terrorism Monitor*, The Jamestown Foundation, Volume 3, Issue 8, April 21, 2005, http://jamestown.org/terrorism/news/article.php?articleid=2369633.

[76] Ziad Haider, "Clearing clouds over Karakoram," *Daily Times*, April 4, 2004, http://www.dailytimes.com.pk/default.asp?page=story_4-4-2004_pg3_3.

[77] Ghulam Amin Beg, "Understanding societal values," *Dawn Magazine*, September 5, 2004, http://www.dawn.com/weekly/dmag/archive/040905/dmag5.htm and Ashfak Bokhari, "Identity crisis in Kashgar," *Dawn Magazine*, December 12, 2004, http://www.dawn.com/weekly/dmag/archive/041212/dmag1.htm.

[78] Hayder Mili, "Xinjiang: An Emerging Narco-Islamist Corridor," *Terrorism Monitor*, The Jamestown Foundation, Volume 3, Issue 8, April 21, 2005, http://jamestown.org/terrorism/news/article.php?articleid=2369633.

[79] Irfan Husain, "A nation of ostriches," *Dawn Magazine*, September 16, 2000, http://www.dawn.com/weekly/mazdak/20000916.htm.

acted to close Uighur settlements and markets in Pakistan, and forced Uighurs out of local madrassas.[80]

Following 9/11, the Chinese felt further emboldened to crack down hard on those they had called 'splittists,' under the guise of the war on terror. The Chinese even managed to force the international community to take action against Chinese 'terrorists.' In August 2002, following considerable Chinese pressure, the US banned the East Turkestan Islamic Movement (ETIM), calling it a terrorist group and in September the United Nations followed suit.[81] However, according to the East Turkestan Information Centre (ETIC), an umbrella organisation of the main Uighur separatist organisations, the ETIM was "an obscure group even the majority of Uighurs know nothing about."[82] In May 2002, Pakistan extradited an important leader of the ETIM, Ismail Kadir who Xinjiang's Communist Party Secretary said was arrested by Pakistan authorities as he attended a secret meeting in Pakistan Occupied Kashmir. He also said that while about 400 of the over thousand Uighurs who had fought alongside the Taliban, had been captured the rest still remained at large in Pakistan or over the border in Afghanistan.[83] Soon after the beginning of the American intervention in Afghanistan, some Pakistani mujahideen occupied the Khunjerab Pass between Pakistan and Xinjiang province of China for more than six days. Musharraf apparently

---

[80] Ziad Haider, "Clearing clouds over Karakoram," *Daily Times*, April 4, 2004, http://www.dailytimes.com.pk/default.asp?page=story_4-4-2004_pg3_3.

[81] Seva Gunitskiy, "East Turkestan Islamic Movement," *Terrorism Project*, Centre for Defence Information, December 9, 2002, http://www.cdi.org/terrorism/etim.cfm.

[82] Angela Pagano and James Conachy, "Bush's pay-off to China over Iraq: Uighur group declared 'terrorist'," World Socialist Web Site, September 20, 2002, http://www.wsws.org/articles/2002/sep2002/uigh-s20.shtml.

[83] "Separatist leader handed over to China," *Dawn*, May 28, 2002, http://www.dawn.com/2002/05/28/top10.htm.

had to send a delegation of religious leaders to negotiate their withdrawal.[84] In October 2003, Pakistani troops shot dead Hasan Mahsum, the head of the organisation, in a raid in Waziristan. Mahsum was accused of being responsible for terrorist activities, including robbery and murder, in Urumqi and in Hotan.[85]

Earlier, police officials from the Northern Areas and Xinjiang had begun meetings to review the security situation along the KKH, including security arrangements at various police check-points between Gilgit and the Khunjerab Pass along the Karakoram Highway.[86] One of the reasons behind starting weekly flights between Islamabad and Kashgar in 2004 was the fear of spreading Islamic or separatist terrorism. In May, senior Chinese officials while condemning the ETIM at a briefing of Pakistani and Afghan media delegations in Urumqi referred to the organisation as operating outside the borders of the region.[87] The killing of the three Chinese engineers in Gwadar in May 2005 was also believed to be the handiwork of Uighur separatists based in Pakistan.[88]

Traders in the Northern Areas have also expressed concern over growing cases of smuggling of narcotics to China and believed it a conspiracy against border trade with China.[89]

84 Claude Arpi, "Indo-Chinese Relations: Great Leap Forward?" *Rediff Special*, January 11, 2002, http://in.rediff.com/news/2002/jan/11spec.htm?zcc=rl.

85 Ashfak Bokhari, "Identity crisis in Kashgar," *Dawn Magazine*, December 12, 2004, http://www.dawn.com/weekly/dmag/archive/041212/dmag1.htm.

86 "Border trade with China discussed," *Dawn*, August 11, 2003, http://www.dawn.com/2003/08/11/nat16.htm.

87 "Ashfak Bokhari, "Kashghar-Islamabad flights from June 8," May 30, 2004, http://www.dawn.com/2004/05/30/nat13.htm.

88 Ashfak Bokhari, "Identity crisis in Kashgar," *Dawn Magazine*, December 12, 2004, http://www.dawn.com/weekly/dmag/archive/041212/dmag1.htm.

89 "Concern over drug smuggling to China," *Dawn*, November 5, 2006, http://www.dawn.com/2006/11/06/local26.htm.

According to authorities in Urumqi, in fact, in the first nine months of 2006, the city had 16 drug trafficking cases from Afghanistan and Pakistan, nearly double the number during the same period in 2005.[90]

[90] Zhu Zhe, "Neighbours to intensify drug crackdown," *China Daily*, November 25, 2006, http://www.chinadaily.com.cn/china/2006-11/25/content_742814.htm.

IV

China's Strategic Interests in PoK

The shift in the strategic nature of the area that the construction of a highway between China and Pakistan through the Northern Areas would entail was apparent to India which in June 1969 accused Pakistan of making it easier for Chinese troops to access occupied territory in Aksai Chin and from Tibet to the Gilgit area which lay immediately to the north of the ceasefire line in Kashmir. It stated that the road posed a threat to the peace and tranquillity in the region.[91] Years later, on the completion of the KKH, China's Deputy Premier Li Xiannian would publicly declare that the Highway "allows us to give military aid to Pakistan."[92] The KKH has also increased China and Pakistan's control over their frontiers and ability to deal with security threats emanating from India and elsewhere.

The KKH, it is believed has been used for the transfer of nuclear and missile equipment to Pakistan.[93] Meanwhile, Chinese and Pakistani plans to link the KKH to the southern port of Gwadar in Balochistan through the Chinese-aided Gwadar-Dalbandin railway, which extends up to Rawalpindi are being carried out with the intention that in the case of

---

[91] Alastair Lamb, *Kashmir: A Disputed Legacy, 1846-1990* (Karachi: Oxford University Press, 1993), p. 275 and John Garver, *Protracted Contest: Sino-Indian Rivalry in the Twentieth Century* (New Delhi: Oxford University Press, 2001), p. 207.

[92] Ziad Haider, "Clearing clouds over Karakoram," *Daily Times*, April 4, 2004, http://www.dailytimes.com.pk/default.asp?page=story_4-4-2004_pg3_3.

[93] B. Raman, "Gilgit and Baltistan, China and North Korea," *SAAG Paper*, No. 289, South Asia Analysis Group, August 7, 2001, http://www.saag.org/papers3/paper289.html.

hostilities between India and China, the PLA Navy would find Gwadar the most convenient logistic location on the Indian Ocean. Prior to hostilities actually breaking out, it would be supported by material transported over the 1300 km long highway and stockpiled at the port. Once conflict had started however, the highway would in many stretches, especially in Gilgit and Hunza be vulnerable to disruption by air attacks.[94] In addition, no traffic occurs from January to June because of the winter snowfall.

The link between the KKH and Gwadar however, has constantly been reinforced. In August 2004, a message on the renaming of a bridge on the KKH in honour of the Pakistani and Chinese workers involved in the construction of the highway, Pakistani Prime Minister Chaudhry Shujaat Hussain referred to Gwadar and in particular the killing of three Chinese engineers engaged in that project.[95]

It also needs to be noted that there were reports that China was upset with Pakistan for allowing the US to establish listening posts in Pakistan's Northern Areas and was unwilling to provide financing for the Gwadar port as a result.[96] Among China's overall strategic aims could be access to the air base in Gilgit and listening posts for itself. In a competitive game of acquiring bases and listening posts that has been underway between the major powers in Central Asia, Gilgit and Skardu

---

94 John Garver, *Protracted Contest: Sino-Indian Rivalry in the Twentieth Century* (New Delhi: Oxford University Press, 2001), pp. 289-91.

95 "Bridge on Karakoram Highway renamed," *Dawn*, August 18, 2004, http://www.dawn.com/2004/08/18/nat18.htm.

96 Tarique Niazi, "Gwadar: China's Naval Outpost on the Indian Ocean," *China Brief*, The Jamestown Foundation, Volume 5, Issue 4, February 15, 2005, http://www.jamestown.org/publications_details.php?volume_id=408&issue_id=3232&article_id=2369262.

airfields provide ideal locations for expansion and upgradation and China must fancy its chances. Indian strategic thinkers have long worried about China's string of pearls in the Indian Ocean. An arch of land bases from Pakistan through Tibet to Myanmar should be just as big a worry.

From this brief outline of Chinese strategic interests in PoK, three implications might be considered. One, while the Chinese claims to Hunza appear to have been settled by the Treaty of 1963, the region is of increasing importance to China for the reasons stated above. Here, considering the Indian experience vis-à-vis the Sino-Indian boundary dispute might be instructive. The Chinese position on the issue has changed over the years with the mid-1980s witnessing a hardening of the Chinese position on the eastern sector. The western sector is no longer considered as the main area of dispute owing perhaps to the fact that the road through Aksai Chin is no longer as critical to China as it had been in the 1950s. The eastern sector, meanwhile, with its rich natural resources is now considered too valuable to give away in addition to significant political and strategic reasons. Given, the fact that the 1963 treaty is subject to revision depending on the eventual resolution of the dispute over Kashmir and given the recent improvement in Indo-Pak relations, the possibility of the Chinese revising their position or strengthening their interests in PoK must be considered. Moreover, the current status or the lack thereof, of the Northern Areas within the Pakistani constitutional framework could complicate the situation still further.

Two, access to the Northern Areas also provides another route by which the Chinese might approach Afghanistan. Besides military goals, western intervention in Afghanistan and

Iraq also has nation-building goals military operations, and it is therefore, not unrealistic to expect that China will have an interest in getting its own say in such projects where possible. And, in the case of Afghanistan, PoK is as close as it gets. As mentioned above it has already once used the KKH to supply arms against the Soviets. Today, perhaps it is taking a longer-term perspective combining strategic aims, historical links and modern infrastructure.

Three, China is also discovering that expansion beyond its boundaries is a two-way street. China not only exports influence, but is influenced in turn and not always for the best – Islamic fundamentalism, terrorism and separatism are problems that China has begun to contend with increasingly following the opening of its overland links to Pakistan and other Central Asian countries. China will, therefore, be increasingly interested in how Pakistan and by extension, Afghanistan deal with rising Islamic sectarianism and fundamentalism, in order to safeguard its own domestic interests.

V

Conclusion

The economic linkages that China seeks to build between its various provinces and with India and other nations on India's periphery, it must be remembered come first and foremost within the context of China's development plans for its poorer interior provinces. Extending the market reach and opportunities of these provinces is crucial if China is to stem the growing regional disparities within the country. Throughout history the difficult terrains have separated China from Central and South Asia. Now, as John Garver says, with new lines of transportation being established, Chinese influence in the form of goods, businesses, investment, culture and people will be carried far across traditional dividing lines creating inter-dependencies.[97] However, with economic conditions generally being better on the Chinese side than across its borders, these new developments also carry larger implications. In the case of the PoK, Chinese activity – infrastructure building, trade and investment – needs to be viewed against this larger context. China or parts of China are increasingly becoming part of the South Asian geopolitical region. This is a development that will increasingly shape regional and global events in the future.

[97] John W. Garver, "Development of China's Overland Transportation Links with Central, Southwest and South Asia," *The China Quarterly*, Vol. 185, 2006, p. 2.

CHAPTER 6

Global Perspectives On PoK
A Critique Of Human Rights Watch And European Union Reports

Mathew Joseph C[1].

From 1947 to 2005, Pakistan succeeded substantially in creating an issue of the Indian "excesses" in Jammu and Kashmir (J&K).The insurgency started in 1989 in the Kashmir valley made it easier for Pakistan to continue and intensify its propaganda. Pakistan tried to project the insurgency as an expression of desire of the Kashmiri Muslims to liberate themselves from the yoke of "Indian occupation." The issue of Kashmir became handy for Pakistan to highlight India in a bad light in front of the international community. From 1947 to 1989, Pakistan succeeded in highlighting the "raw deal" which it received with regard to Kashmir. Pakistan could do this, due to the specific context of the Cold War. During this period, the international public opinion dominated by the Western perception always castigated India as an oppressor of the Kashmiri opinion and demands. The Cold War dynamics also made the international community to conveniently forget the non-existence of democracy and fundamental rights and the human rights violations in Pakistan-occupied Kashmir (PoK) – which includes the "Azad Jammu and Kashmir" (AJK) and the Northern Areas (NA).

[1] Dr. Mathew Joseph is a Senior Lecturer, Centre for Strategic and Regional Studies, University of Jammu, Jammu

The end of the Cold War reduced the importance of Pakistan in the international strategic chess board and consequently the West started disengaging with it in the 1990s. After 9/11, however, the Western countries had to come back to the Pakistan-Afghanistan region and West Asia to fight the "War on Terror". Even though the US and its allies were aware about the role of Pakistan in sponsoring global *Jihad* and fomenting violence in Jammu and Kashmir, in order to get the crucial Pakistani help in the War on Terror they had to allow that to continue. This was convenient for both Pakistan and the US and her allies. This scenario underwent a change in the context of the devastating earthquake on October 8, 2005 that struck both J&K and PoK, more severely in PoK.

Till the earthquake, Pakistan could keep PoK away from the gaze of the international community. Pakistan always talked about the autonomous nature of AJK in contrast to the "controlled administration" in J&K. Since the PoK was generally out of bounds for the international scrutiny, the Western media largely accepted the Pakistani propaganda over "AJK" and NA. The earthquake and its aftermath had changed everything. Within twenty-four hours after the earthquake, the representatives of the Western media and aid agencies started arriving in the affected areas of both J&K and PoK. For Pakistan, it was no longer possible to keep both AJK and NA away from the eyes of the international community. What they saw in AJK and NA was an eye opener, to the representatives of the Western media and aid agencies. For the first time, the international community could see the difference between the ground reality and propaganda. Pakistan's exaggerated claims about the autonomy of AJK and improved living conditions of the people were exposed before the international community. The literature produced on both AJK and NA after the earthquake testifies this change in perception. The reports prepared by the Human Rights Watch (HRW) in September 2006 and European Union in November 2006 are representative of the genre of writings produced on PoK after the earthquake.

The report prepared by Human Rights Watch (HRW) titled *"With Friends Like These…": Human Rights Violations in Azad Kashmir*[2] is a comprehensive review of what happened in PoK before and after the earthquake. It covers the historical background of how AJK came into being, the constitutional structure and its relationship with Pakistan, and the level of fundamental rights over there. This report exposed Pakistan's tall claims about the autonomy of PoK. It starts with a quotation which captures the essence of Pakistan's policy towards PoK from a resident of Muzaffarabad. The quotation is as follows: "Pakistan says they are our friends and India is our enemy. I agree India is our enemy, but with friends like these, who needs enemies?"[3]

To substantiate his anguish the report gives an account of the behaviour of the Pakistan Military stationed in AJK in the context of the devastating earthquake. The report observes:

> "Major cities and thousands of villages in Azad Jammu and Kashmir (AJK, Azad Kashmir), including the capital Muzaffarabad, were reduced to rubble. The devastation was immense – at least eighty-eight thousand people died, more than one hundred thousand were injured, and more than two million were left homeless… In the first seventy-two hours after the

---

2 Human Rights Watch (HRW), *"With Friends Like These…": Human Rights Violations in Azad Kashmir* (Report), Vol. 18, No. 12 (C), September 2006. URL: http://hrw.org/reports/2006/pakistan0906/pakistan0906web.pdf

3 Ibid., p. 4.

> earthquake, thousands of Pakistani troops stationed in Azad Kashmir prioritised the evacuation of their own personnel over providing relief to desperate civilians...They [the international media] filmed Pakistani troops standing by and refusing to help because they had "no orders" to do so as locals attempted to dig out those still alive, sending a chilling message of indifference from Islamabad. Having filmed the refusal, journalists switched off their cameras and joined the rescue effort themselves; in one instance they shamed the soldiers into helping." [4]

The military units stationed in AJK were always used to "ensure political compliance and control"[5] of the population. For this purpose numerous military installations were established in close proximity to the cities and towns in AJK. The myth about the Pakistan military as the only properly functioning institution in the country which would come to the help of people in situations like the devastating earthquake became exposed. The failure of the military and civil administration to cope with the aftermath of the earthquake angered the people of PoK. The apathy of the establishment towards the people of PoK calls for a review of the political and human rights conditions there by both the people of PoK and the international community.

Unlike the J&K state in India, the political status of AJK is very ambiguous. According to Pakistan, in principle, AJK is an autonomous entity having a President, Prime Minister, Parliament and Constitution. But, in practice, AJK is a province in Pakistan kept in suspended animation. The HRW Report

---

[4] Ibid., pp. 4-5.

[5] Ibid., p. 5.

unambiguously portrays this as follows:

> "Azad Kashmir is a legal anomaly. According to United Nations (UN) resolutions dating back to 1948, Azad Kashmir is neither a sovereign state nor a province of Pakistan, but rather a "local authority" with responsibility over the area assigned to it under a 1949 ceasefire agreement with India. It has remained in this state of legal limbo since that time. In practice, the Pakistani government in Islamabad, the Pakistani army and the Pakistani intelligence services (Inter-Services Intelligence, ISI) control all aspects of political life in Azad Kashmir – though "Azad" means "free," the residents of Azad Kashmir are anything but. Azad Kashmir is a land of strict curbs on political pluralism, freedom of expression, and freedom of association; a muzzled press; banned books; arbitrary arrest and detention and torture at the hands of the Pakistani military and the police; and discrimination against refugees from Jammu and Kashmir state. Singled out are Kashmiri nationalists who do not support the idea of Kashmir's accession to Pakistan. Anyone who wants to take part in public life has to sign a pledge of loyalty to Pakistan, while anyone who publicly supports or works for an independent Kashmir is persecuted.[6]

The above observation made in the report clearly exposes the duplicity in Pakistan's treatment of PoK and proves what India has been telling the international community about the political situation there. Torture and threat of torture are being widely used as tools to keep political opposition in PoK under control. Political freedom and freedom of expression are reserved only for persons and organisations who profess the

---

6 Ibid., pp. 6-7.

integration of the whole of J&K with Pakistan. This situation only allows military supported militants and militant organisations to function in the public sphere of PoK in whatever meagre form it exists. The tightly controlled public sphere and the terrified civil society of PoK are suitable to the interests of the Pakistan state and the Military.

It is interesting to note that to legitimise the militant organisations – the B-team of military in PoK – the Pakistan Military entrusted the duty of disbursing aid after the earthquake. The President of Pakistan himself praised the role of militant organisations for their services. "The Pakistani military apparently saw the earthquake as an opportunity to craft a new image for the militant groups rather than as an opportunity to disband them."[7] In its quest for rescuing its own personnel, the military allowed the militant groups like the Lashkar- e-Toiba complete autonomy in the public sphere despite the presence of the representatives of the Western media and aid agencies. This once again proves the Indian allegation of the close proximity between the Pakistan military and Islamic militant organisations.

The report outlines the history of insurgency that has taken place in the Kashmir valley since 1989 and Pakistan's involvement in it. Initially, Pakistan welcomed the Kashmiri nationalists of different hues who crossed over to PoK with great fanfare. The Pakistan establishment understood the propaganda value of the presence of Kashmiri nationalist insurgents in PoK, even though their idea of independent Kashmir was not subscribed by it. By 1994, the ISI cobbled together an umbrella organisation of militants called the United Jihad Council (UJC). The UJC included groups like the Hizbul-

[7] Ibid., p. 9.

Mujahidein, Harkat-ul-Ansar, Jamiat-ul-Mujahedin and Al-Jihad who strive for the integration of the J&K with Pakistan.[8] The Kashmiri nationalists were sidelined by the late 1990s and "…eventually began to be persecuted by the authorities and their proxies."[9]

The report gives ample evidence to the Indian allegation regarding the existence of militant training camps sponsored by the Pakistan army. The report says:

> "Through the 1990s, Azad Kashmir was increasingly dotted with militant camps operating under the supervision of the Pakistani army. Only when Pakistan began supporting the US-led "global war on terror" in 2001 did the United Jihad Council cease to operate publicly. Several groups have simply changed their names and operate independently or through clandestine underground networks. And there are many reports indicating that the Pakistani intelligence apparatus retains direct association with operations by these groups."[10]

According to the report the "post-earthquake role of militant organisations underlines the continuity of the military-militant relationship in Azad Kashmir."[11] Just after the earthquake the military used the militant groups and their frontal organisations like the Jamaat-ud-Dawa in disbursing aid to the victims. This strategy served the twin purposes of the military concentrating in the relief and rescue operations of its own personnel and legitimising the militant groups in front of the

---

[8] Ibid., p. 20.

[9] Ibid.,

[10] Ibid., p. 21.

[11] Ibid., p. 24.

people and the international community.

The report highlights the level of exploitation and resource extraction by Pakistan in PoK by giving the example of the controversies regarding the Mangala dam. "The Azad Kashmiris, particularly the Mirpuris, argue that water is a Kashmiri natural resource commandeered by the Pakistani state to the disadvantage of Kashmiris."[12] The statement of Chaudhry Arif, the convener of the Mangla Dam Action Committee, documented in the Report can be considered the representative opinion of the Mirpuris in this matter. He says:

> Water is our natural resource. Arabs have oil, the Baloch have minerals. Kashmir has water. All of Pakistan uses our water. In the process, there remain acute water shortages in Mirpur from where we can see the dam feeding the palatial homes of Islamabad. Meanwhile, water-borne diseases are on the rise in Mirpur and other parts of Kashmir due to scarce water here. We have been uprooted from our homes, not paid adequate compensation and denied royalty, while Pakistan and India steal our natural wealth. This is the worst kind of exploitation and colonisation.[13]

In principle, PoK has a constitution – the AJK Interim Constitution Act 1974, and a parliamentary form of government. But in practice under 56 of the Constitution "...the Pakistani government can dismiss any elected government in Azad Kashmir irrespective of the support it may enjoy in the AJK Legislative Assembly."[14] Moreover, of

---

[12] Ibid., p. 25.

[13] Ibid., p. 26.

[14] Ibid., p. 27.

the two executive forums – the Azad Kashmir Government in Muzaffarabad and the Azad Kashmir Council in Islamabad – the latter "…presided over by the Prime Minister of Pakistan, exercises paramount authority over the AJK Legislative Assembly, which cannot challenge decisions of the council."[15] The decisions of the Council are final and beyond judicial review. The way the administration of the AJK is being carried out exposes the myth about the sovereignty of the AJK.

The Constitution prevents political parties and groups who do not support the idea of Kashmir's accession to Pakistan from participating in the political process. According to part 7 (2) of the Constitution, "[n]o person or political party in Azad Jammu and Kashmir shall be permitted to propagate against or take part in activities prejudicial or detrimental to the ideology of the State's accession to Pakistan."[16] The 'elected' leaders of AJK never exercise political power. The real power is with the Army. The Report describes how the Army exercises power in the following words:

> Power in Azad Kashmir is exercised primarily through the Pakistani army's General Headquarters in Rawalpindi… and its corps commander based in the hill station of Murree, two hours by road from Muzaffarabad. It is widely understood in Pakistan and privately admitted by virtually all politicians from Azad Kashmir that the corps commander in Murree is known to summon the Azad Kashmir prime minister, president and other government officials regularly to outline the military's views on all political and governance issues in the territory.[17]

---

[15] Ibid.,

[16] Ibid., p. 40.

[17] Ibid., p. 29.

Despite the nature of government in Islamabad, the Army always exercised control over AJK.

The unhindered dissemination of information, print and electronic media and freedom of expression are non-existent in AJK. Newspapers and periodicals have to take permission from the Kashmir Council and Ministry of Kashmir Affairs in Islamabad. The journalists are always intimidated by the military, its intelligence agencies and militant groups. In an atmosphere of terror and fear talking about freedom of expression is meaningless. "The Azad Kashmir government regularly bans books that it considers to be prejudicial to the 'ideology of the state's accession to Pakistan.' This includes all books that propagate or discuss the Kashmiri nationalist discourse with its emphasis on independence for a united Kashmir."[18]

The report documents the various tactics followed by the government to keep the civil society in AJK under strict political control. Like in other provinces of Pakistan in PoK too "[p]olitically motivated torture is typically used to compel politicians, political activists and journalists critical of the government to change their views or at least silence them."[19] In most of the cases, ISI and other secret services are involved. Some of the accounts narrated by the victims to the HRW speak volumes about the amount of force and terror used by the authorities to control essentially a multi-vocal society.[20] The Report also gives a detailed account of the plight of post-1989 refugees who crossed over to PoK after the outbreak of insurgency in the Kashmir valley.[21]

---

[18] Ibid., p. 35.

[19] Ibid., p. 51.

[20] Ibid., pp. 51-61.

[21] Ibid., pp. 62-67.

The earthquake made it impossible for the Military to control the dissemination of information in AJK. The earthquake opened the hitherto closed territory in Pakistan-AJK to the outside world. The presence of international media persons both print and electronic in large numbers made all the more difficult for the government to curb freedom of expression and information. The Report recommends that this has to be systematised so that the right to information and freedom of expression will be protected.[22]

The second report drafted by the European Union titled *Kashmir: Present Situation and Future Prospects*[23] also highlights the lack of democracy and fundamental rights, curbs on freedom of expression and political repression in PoK. The report starts with a comparison of democracy in India and Pakistan. According to the report "…India is the world's largest democracy and has a functioning democracy at the local level, whereas Pakistan still has to show that it is respecting democratic principles in a great many areas."[24] With this observation the Report exposes the Pakistani claim of the autonomy of AJK and the role played by the Military in the context of the earthquake.

Apart from the death of 88,000 people the earthquake created three million Internally Displaced People (IDP) in PoK. Since Pakistan has not accepted the convention on the rights of the IDPs, the Report urges Pakistan to follow the UN's

---

22 Ibid., p. 37.

23 European Parliament (Committee on Foreign Affairs), *Kashmir: Present Situation and Future Prospects* (Report). URL: http://www.europarl.europa.eu/registre/commissions/afet/projet_rapport/2006/376409/AFET_PR(2006)376409_EN.doc

24 Ibid.

Guiding Principles in this regard and "…strongly recommends that the EU focus consistently on them, as well as on broader issues of democracy, justice and human rights in Pakistan."[25] The Report emphasises the absence of minimal basic rights in PoK and points out that the earthquake made the ground situation grimmer.

The report is critical of the negative attitude shown by Pakistan towards the Indian offers of helicopters, cross-LoC joint relief operations, medical relief teams and repair of telecom infrastructure and points out had it been accepted by Pakistan the casualties would have been reduced considerably. In a comparison of the way in which both India and Pakistan carry out the relief and rescue work in the aftermath of the earthquake, the Report underlines the effectiveness of the Indian response than that of Pakistan. The report observes the following in this regard:

> …Indian-administered Jammu and Kashmir was less affected by the earthquake than its neighbour and has been better able to cope; applauds the competence with which the emergency was addressed by the government, the local population and the army; notes that, as a result, of the 30,000 who lost their homes, all now have housing due in large measure to an intelligent self-help policy instituted by the government…[26]

The lack of efficiency shown by the Pakistan Military in relief and rescue operations is partly due to its apathy towards the people of PoK and its deliberate policy of non-development of structures of self-governance there.

---

[25] Ibid.

[26] Ibid.

The report highlights the relief and rescue work carried out by the militant organisations in the aftermath of the earthquake and also underlines the fact that this would legitimise their credentials and increase popularity among the people. The report blames the Pakistan military and its deliberate policy of giving space to the militant organisations in the relief and rescue work for this and warns that the increased popularity of militants would be detrimental to the growth of the structures of democracy in PoK.

The EU report brings out the level of political and constitutional restrictions on the people of PoK. It says:

> ... Pakistan has consistently failed to fulfil its obligations to introduce meaningful and representative democratic structures in AJK; notes in particular the continuing absence of Kashmiri representation in the Pakistan National Assembly, the fact that AJK is governed through the Ministry of Kashmir Affairs in Islamabad, that Pakistan officials dominate the Kashmir Council and that the Chief Secretary, the Inspector-General of Police, the Accountant-General and the Finance Secretary are all from Pakistan; abhors the provision in the 1974 Interim Constitution which forbids any political activity that is not in accordance with the doctrine of Jammu and Kashmir as part of Pakistan and obliges any candidate for a parliamentary seat in AJK to sign a declaration of loyalty to that effect; is concerned that the Gilgit-Baltistan region enjoys no form of democratic representation whatsoever.[27]

[27] Ibid.

The above description of the politico-administrative system prevailing in PoK exposes the Pakistani claim of autonomy of AJK and its propaganda of the lack of democratic rights in J&K before the international community. The Report unambiguously "[u]rges Pakistan to revisit its concept of democratic accountability, minority and women's rights in AJK..."[28]

The Pakistan establishment has successfully hidden the politico-administrative ground realities of Kashmir under its occupation from 1947 to 2005. During these years the Pakistani propaganda was harping on the lack of democratic rights and human rights violations in J&K. The Western media and the international community readily accepted this. The Western endorsement of the Pakistani propaganda was partly due to the compulsions of Cold War dynamics. Apart from that many in the West subscribed to the view that Pakistan got a raw deal with regard to Kashmir.

The earthquake on October 8, 2005 and its aftermath compelled Pakistan to open up the hitherto closed PoK to international scrutiny. After the earthquake, the representatives of the international media and aid agencies poured into the affected areas in large numbers. They could see what the ground reality in PoK was in front of their eyes. The writings on PoK appeared after the earthquake reflected the reality observed there by the members of the international civil society. The reports of HRW and EU are examples of this sort of writing.

The reports brought by the Human Rights Watch and the European Union question and demolish the Pakistani claims of autonomy of AJK and improved living conditions in both

[28] Ibid.

AJK and NA compared to what exists in J&K. These reports could do what India was not able to do for the last almost six decades. India must use these reports and similar kind of writings by credible organisations, groups and individuals to recast the political discourse on Jammu and Kashmir in the international arena.

CHAPTER 7

Northern Areas: Myths, Facts And Politics
A Critique Of The ICG Report

D. Suba Chandran[1]

In April 2007, the International Crisis Group (ICG), an independent international organisation based in Brussels published a report titled *Discord in Pakistan's Northern Areas.*[2] An analysis of this report is important, for this is perhaps the first comprehensive report on the contemporary political, legal and sectarian situation in the Northern Areas.

This essay analyses the ICG Report under three sections, followed by a conclusion. The report could be broadly classified into three parts: historical, legal and constitutional; administrative; and political.

---

1 Dr. D. Suba Chandran is Assistant Director at the Institute of Peace and Conflict Studies, New Delhi. Currently he is a Visiting Fellow at the Centre for Strategic and Regional Studies, University of Jammu.

2 See International Crisis Group Report, *Discord in Pakistan's Northern Areas*, Asia Report N°131, April 2, 2007.

I

Historical, Legal and Constitutional Issues

The ICG report commenting on the events relating to 1947-49 says: *"The maharaja's decision* (to sign the Instrument of Accession and join India) *also provoked a full-scale rebellion in Gilgit, spearheaded by the Gilgit Scouts and Muslim members of the Jammu and Kashmir state troops, with the support of the overwhelmingly Muslim local population. On 31st October, Major Brown sent a platoon of Scouts to surround the residence of the maharaja's governor of Gilgit Agency, Ghansara Singh. Other platoons took control of important locations in the city. On 1st November, Ghansara Singh surrendered, and a provisional government consisting of leaders of the victorious forces was installed and remained in place until power was transferred to the first Pakistani Political Agent in Gilgit on 16th November. Two days later, Hunza and Nagar signed instruments of accession to Pakistan."* Elsewhere, the report mentions "*on April 28, 1949, Pakistan and AJK signed the Karachi Agreement by which the latter agreed to place all affairs relating to the Northern Areas in Pakistan's hands.*"[3]

How serious was this rebellion in Gilgit? Was this rebellion limited to Gilgit town or the entire region? What was Major Brown's objectives and reasoning during this period? What support or opposition did Ghansara Singh have during this time? Why would Major Brown act against the Maharaja, if Lord Mountbatten inclined towards J&K joining India? Did he have a different set of instructions directly from London? In other words, was there a British conspiracy during this period

[3] Discord in Pakistan's Northern Areas.

on Gilgit and the region, a part of the great game?

What exactly happened during those three weeks, leading up to November 16, 1947? Who were the leaders of the provisional government? What legitimacy did they have to transfer power to the Political Agent of Pakistan on November 16, 1947? Why did Hunza and Nagar follow Gilgit? Who signed for these two? What legitimacy did they have to sign an agreement with Pakistan? Or is this union with Pakistan, as commented on by an analyst, "unconditional, the only consideration being the desire to join a Muslim state instead of linking lots with a Hindu-dominated country?"[4] Ghayoor Ahmed, a former Ambassador of Pakistan, observed in 2006 in an article, "it may also be pertinent to mention that in June 1941, the resident of Gilgit, Lt. Col. M.S. Frazer, had been informed by the British government that although Hunza and Nagar, the two major princely states and many other smaller states in Gilgit, were under the suzerainty of the State of Jammu and Kashmir they were not part of it. The British government, however, did not make their position public at that time fearing that it would be unpalatable to the ruler of Kashmir and its own war efforts in that state might also suffer a setback."[5] Another section argues that this "area was liberated by the local people who removed the Maharaja's governor on October 31, 1947 and put him under arrest. They also brought down the Jammu and Kashmir state flag from the Residency and amid great public rejoicing raised the flag of Pakistan in its place on 2nd November."[6]

---

4 See Afzal A. Shigri, "Kashmir dispute and status of Northern Areas," *The News,* December 8, 2005. Afzal Shigri, a former Inspector General of Police, is one of the few analysts who regularly comments on events relating to the Northern Areas.

5 Ghayoor Ahmed, "The Status of Northern Areas," *Dawn,* March 31, 2006.

6 This argument is highlighted in Khalid Hasan, "Northern Areas, neither fish nor fowl," *The Friday Times,* December 3-9, 2004, Vol. XVI, No. 41.

These are larger questions, which include many myths and puzzles. Facts need to be separated from them. Towards this, there is need to research these questions based on available primary documents in the National Archives in New Delhi, in the State government's archives in Jammu and Kashmir and perhaps the British Archives in UK. Today, most of the analysis and commentaries on the Northern Areas are primarily written by Pakistani scholars, who have already taken a position on the issue beginning from the question of accession. A report authored by the Institute of Policy Studies in Islamabad in fact commented on writers taking a predetermined position vis-à-vis the Northern Areas.[7] A dispassionate, but an in-depth historical research on the above questions will blow many such myths linked to the 'accession' of these regions to Pakistan and their legality. It is in India's interests, that such a research is undertaken; one only hopes that the Government of India, especially its Ministry of External Affairs approves such a study and shares the available information.

Another set of legal questions involves the linkages and relationship between the "AJK" and the Northern Areas, beginning from the Karachi agreement, 1949. What gave the "AJK" legitimacy to reach an understanding with Pakistan on Northern Areas? How can it enable Pakistan to maintain the affairs of the Northern Areas? Legally, the "AJK" had no rights whatsoever to enter or sign an agreement with Pakistan on

---

7 The report mentioned: "The hundreds of articles that appear in the newspapers generally lack objectivity even in discussing the historical position of the Northern Areas and their relations with the State of Jammu and Kashmir. Obsessed with predetermined positions, writers discuss the events and historic facts only in supporting their own stances. Barring exceptions one generally finds nothing new but a repetition of cases and arguments." See IPS Task Force Report, "Northern Areas of Pakistan: Facts, Problems and Recommendations," *Policy Perspectives,* April 2004, Vol.1, No.1, p.121.

this aspect.[8] This issue between "AJK" and Pakistan was discussed in the 1970s, as the "AJK" Legislative Assembly demanded through a resolution that the Northern Areas be 'returned'.

Later in the 1990s, thanks to three judgements, by the "AJK" High Court, the "AJK" Supreme Court and Pakistan's Supreme Court, the linkage between "AJK" and the Northern Areas was discussed again. The "AJK" High Court, in one of its verdicts, in 1995, directed the "AJK" government to "immediately assume the administrative control of the Northern Areas and to annex it with the administration of Azad Jammu and Kashmir."[9] Later, the "AJK" Supreme Court, (perhaps due to the pressure from Islamabad) gave a different verdict which said "the Northern Areas are a part of Jammu and Kashmir State, but they are not a part of Azad Jammu and Kashmir as defined in the Interim Constitution Act 1974...We have also reached the conclusion that the High Court of Azad Jammu and Kashmir did not possess the necessary jurisdiction to issue a writ against the Government of Pakistan for handing over the control of the Northern Areas to Azad Jammu and Kashmir."[10]

---

[8] Asadullah Khan, a lawyer and former President of the Northern Areas Bar Association (NABA) precisely raised this question while speaking to the ICG: "Who gave Azad Kashmir the right to determine our political destiny? The Karachi Agreement was nothing more than a sale of human beings, in which Pakistan and Azad Kashmir were customers, and we were the commodity on sale."

[9] See Khalid Hasan, "Northern Areas, neither fish nor fowl," *The Friday Times,* December 3-9, 2004, Vol. XVI, No. 41.

[10] Khalid Hasan, "Northern Areas, neither fish nor fowl," *The Friday Times,* December 3-9, 2004, Vol. XVI, No. 41. Also see IPS Task Force Report, "Northern Areas of Pakistan: Facts, Problems and Recommendations," *Policy Perspectives,* April 2004, Vol.1, No.1, p.125.

In May 1999, the Supreme Court of Pakistan passed an important judgement, in terms of the status of the Northern Areas and its people vis-à-vis Pakistan. According to the verdict, "it was not understandable on what basis the people of the Northern Areas can be denied the fundamental rights guaranteed under the Constitution. We are of the view that the people of the Northern Areas are citizens of Pakistan for all intents and purposes. They have the rights to invoke any fundamental rights... (We) direct the federation to initiate appropriate administrative/legislative measures within a period of six months from today to make necessary amendments in the Constitution...to ensure that the people in the Northern Areas enjoy their fundamental rights, namely, to be governed by their chosen representatives, and to have access to justice, *inter alia*, for the enforcement of their fundamental rights under the Constitution."[11]

This verdict by the Supreme Court, a 42-page judgement, needs separate analysis, but it is sufficient to highlight the following sections:[12]

> "...since the geographical location of the Northern Areas is very sensitive because it is bordering India, China, Tibet and USSR, and as the above areas in the past have also been treated differently, this Court cannot decide what type of government should be provided to ensure the compliance with the above mandate of the Constitution. Nor can we direct that the people of the Northern Areas should be given representation in the Parliament as, at this stage it may not be in the larger interest of the country because of

[11] See M. Ismail Khan, "The Northern Areas' dangerous limbo," *The News*, September 27, 2005.

[12] Quoted in IPS Task Force Report, "Northern Areas of Pakistan: Facts, Problems and Recommendations," *Policy Perspectives*, April 2004, Vol.1, No.1, p.131.

the fact that a plebiscite under the auspices of the United Nations is to be held. The above questions are to be decided by the Parliament and the Executive. This Court at the most can direct that the proper administrative and legislative steps should be taken to ensure that the people of the Northern Areas enjoy their above rights under the Constitution."

"...As regards the right to access to justice through an independent judiciary, it may be observed that the Northern Areas has a Chief Court, which can be equated with a High Court provided it is manned by the persons or the statute who are fit to be elevated as Judges to any High Court in Pakistan. Its jurisdiction is to be enlarged as to include jurisdiction to entertain Constitutional Petitions *inter alia* to enforce the Fundamental Rights enshrined in the Constitution..."

"...To initiate appropriate administrative/legislative measures within a period of six months from today to make necessary amendments in the Constitution/ relevant statute/statues/order/orders/rules/notification/ notifications, to ensure that the people of the Northern Areas enjoy their above fundamental rights, namely, to be governed through their chosen representatives and to have access to justice through an independent judiciary *inter alia* for enforcement of their Fundamental Rights guaranteed under the Constitution."

Despite these verdicts, the legal status of the Northern Areas remains the same. The reasons are discussed elsewhere in this essay.

II

Administrative Issues

If Pakistan has no legal claim over the Northern Areas, and if the latter has no constitutional status, how is the region being administered? According to the ICG report, "*Pakistan's rationale in linking the Northern Areas with Jammu and Kashmir and treating the region as part of the disputed territory is based on the premise that the overwhelming majority in the Northern Areas would vote in its favour if and when a plebiscite were held to determine Kashmir's future.*"[13] This argument, in fact, has become a double-edged sword, as Pakistan got trapped in its own rhetoric. While the "AJK" received an element of 'self-rule', however insufficient they have been, the Northern Areas, do not even have such an arrangement.

The history of Pakistan's administration of the Northern Areas, as subsequently explained is a history of exploitation. As has been commented, the Northern Areas have subsequently become the last living colony of the world.[14] Immediately after Gilgit 'invited' Pakistan to assume control over the region, Pakistan sent Sardar Muhammad Alam, a tehsildar with the NWFP government in 1947, to Gilgit as Pakistan's Political Agent.[15] Frontier Crimes Regulation (FCR)

---

[13] Discord in Pakistan's Northern Areas.

[14] One is not sure who attributed the phrase "the last colony" to the Northern Areas. The author has picked up the same from an article written by a former Indian bureaucrat. See Vikram Sood, "The World's Last Colony," ***Hindustan Times,*** November 8, 2005.

[15] IPS Task Force Report, "Northern Areas of Pakistan: Facts, Problems and Recommendations," *Policy Perspectives,* April 2004, Vol.1, No.1, p.121.

was imposed and the region was placed under the NWFP.[16] In 1950, this region was brought under the Ministry of Kashmir Affairs, and the Political Agent became the Resident.

In 1974, under Zulfikar Ali Bhutto, a major change in the administration was introduced. Islamabad created a Northern Areas Council (NAC), whose members were directly elected. The FCR was abolished and so was the system of considering this region as an Agency. Instead, Gilgit and Baltistan became two districts. Unfortunately, the changes were limited only to this cosmetic alteration. The NAC could neither elect its own executive nor had executive powers, except being elected by the people directly. KANA continued to control the region directly, clearly showing an understanding amongst the political elite in Pakistan – whether under military or democratic set up, Islamabad is not ready to provide any self-rule or autonomy to the Northern Areas. Not even on the patterns of the "AJK", where at least there is a Parliament, regular election, Prime Minister and a President. Even inside the KANA, unfortunately, the only elected component is that it is headed by a federal minister, who is a member of the National Parliament, though do not belong to the Northern Areas.

Zia-ul-Haq attempted to make significant changes in the status of the Northern Areas. For the first time, a major shift took place in how Pakistan perceived the Northern Areas, when Zia imposed martial rule on July 5, 1977. Northern Areas became Martial Law Zone – E, with the other four being the four provinces of Pakistan. Besides, Zia also made a startling statement vis-à-vis the Northern Areas in May 1982: "Kashmir has been a disputed issue, but so far as the Northern Areas are

---

16 IPS Task Force Report, "Northern Areas of Pakistan: Facts, Problems and Recommendations," *Policy Perspectives,* April 2004, Vol.1, No.1, p.121.

concerned, we do not accept them disputed."[17] He also nominated three individuals as observers from the Northern Areas to the Majlis-e-Shura.

In 1994, the NAC was made into the Northern Areas Legislative Council (NALC), thus giving an appearance that the body has some legislative functions, though in reality, even today all powers are exercised by the KANA and the regular activities are administered under the Legal Framework Order (LFO). The ICG report, on this LFO highlights the most important aspect of governance or lack of it, in the Northern Areas: "*Since the LFO is an administrative order, not a formal constitution, the chief executive can modify or even do away with it merely Ministry of Kashmir Affairs and Northern Areas, by issuing a notification. As a result, the legislature and judicial institutions are subservient to his will.*" As far as the day-to-day activities are concerned, the report mentions, "*non-local bureaucrats, seconded to the region, dominate the higher echelons of the bureaucracy in the Northern Areas. Since they come from outside and more often than not serve in the region for short periods, they have neither the time nor the inclination to build local government capacity.*"[18]

In 2004, General Musharraf announced a package for the Northern Areas, under which the NALC was expanded and a new district – Astore, was created.[19] This package also increased the seats for women in districts and union councils by 33 per cent, besides establishing an appellate court for the Northern Areas. However, this package did not appeal to the people of the Northern Areas, as they were expecting that Islamabad

---

[17] Quoted in IPS Task Force Report, "Northern Areas of Pakistan: Facts, Problems and Recommendations," *Policy Perspectives,* April 2004, Vol.1, No.1, p.121.

[18] Discord in Pakistan's Northern Areas.

[19] "NALC expanded, new dist created," *Dawn,* October 24, 2004.

would at least implement the judgement of the Supreme Court of Pakistan, which had earlier directed the government to provide for self-rule and fundamental rights of the people.[20]

Besides the KANA, Pakistan military's Force Command Northern Areas (FCNA) plays an important role in the local administration. According to the ICG Report, "*tasked with defending the Northern Areas' borders, the FCNA also exercises enormous influence over internal affairs, not just law enforcement but also administrative issues such as postings and transfers.*"[21]

Clearly, the Northern Areas, lack administrative structure and also local participation in whatever is available. Even the minimum local participation in the NALC is not meaningful. Commenting on this crucial aspect, a former police officer wrote: "There is an elected council and a leader of the house but the Chief Executive is the Minister for Kashmir Affairs and Northern Areas. He neither belongs to the Northern Areas nor have the people of this area elected him."[22] The NALC has remained a toothless organisation ever since it was constituted, thus being mainly an ornamental body. Two recent incidents are worth mentioning to support this case. In 2003, *Dawn,* reporting the proceedings of the NALC highlighted the discussion. The first one was a demand from one of the NALC members, that the Speaker, Deputy Chief Executives and the Advisers should resign from the NALC, as they have failed to get the medical superintendent of DHQ Hospital in Gilgit to comply with an order of the NALC health adviser regarding

---

[20] Afzal Shigri, "Reforms Package for NA," *The News,* November 12, 2004.

[21] The report also quotes a senior police official saying that the local police must seek the permission from the FCNA even for routine deployments.

[22] Afgal A. Shigri, "Status of Northern Areas," *The News*, August 30, 2004.

the transfer of a doctor.[23] The second case, which was reported at the same meeting, was on similar lines. The food department officials refused to allow the NALC Adviser of the department from visiting and inquiring into the affairs of the department.[24]

The NALC is neither taken seriously inside the Northern Areas, by the officials whose loyalty lies elsewhere nor by Islamabad. One major demand by the NALC in the recent years have been to convert the same into a Legislative Assembly, thus from NALC into NALA.[25] Given the history of Islamabad's treatment of the Northern Areas, NALA will remain a distant dream. Even if it becomes a reality, it will have only nominal powers, with Islamabad remaining the power centre.

Now the most important question: Why should Pakistan keep this region in an administrative and constitutional limbo, if it could provide some status to "AJK"? The ICG Report believes the following: "*While it* (Pakistan) *contests India's claim over AJK and the Northern Areas, it also does not claim them for fear that this could negate Kashmir's status as a disputed territory, or imply acceptance of the territorial status quo as a permanent solution.*"[26] This undoubtedly is an explanation, invariably what the government of Pakistan has also been mentioning. But how sincere and true is this argument? Afghal Shigri, a former police officer, earlier in another context, rejected this argument as "fallacious" and considers that the "real reasons are the petty, selfish and short-term gains that accrue to the bureaucracy in Islamabad and the incompetence of the Foreign Office that has failed to

---

[23] "NALC members ask cabinet to quit," *Dawn*, July 3, 2003.

[24] "NALC members ask cabinet to quit," *Dawn*, July 3, 2003.

[25] See "Assembly status for NALC demanded," *Dawn*, August 24, 2004.

[26] Discord in Pakistan's Northern Areas.

examine this vital issue in its correct perceptive."[27] If this is the reason for Pakistan's "calculated ambiguity" towards the Northern Areas, what prevents Islamabad from offering an "AJK" type arrangement to this region? In fact, a section in the Northern Areas wants such a status, while another section prefers to make this region as the fifth province of Pakistan.

Another explanation could be that Pakistan does not want to give any administrative or constitutional status to the Northern Areas, for it prefers to keep this region under its total control, for strategic and political reasons.[28] Strategically, this region is significant for two reasons – the mighty Karakoram Highway pass all through this region and Pakistan's water security is also dependent on the resources and reservoirs of this region, especially the Bhasha dam.[29]

For the above two reasons, Pakistan since 1947, has pursued different types of administration, but always making sure that this region is directly under the control of Islamabad. The Kashmir Affairs and Northern Areas (KANA) effectively

---

[27] He further says "The real reasons are the petty, selfish and short-term gains that accrue to the bureaucracy in Islamabad and the incompetence of the Foreign Office that has failed to examine this vital issue in its correct perceptive. I am witness to this drama when the officers of the Foreign Office tried to dissuade the then President General Zia-ul-Haq from allowing the representatives from the NA to sit in the assembly as observers. He however overruled them and issued instructions to allow a representative from the NA to sit as an observer in the assembly. This however did not last long." See Afzal A. Shigri, "Status of Northern Areas," *The News,* August 30, 2004.

[28] These factors have also been discussed in another essay in this work. See D. Suba Chandran, "Sectarian Violence in Northern Areas."

[29] For the importance of the Bhasha dam to Pakistan, see Ahsan Wali Khan, "The 'legitimacy' of Bhasha Dam," *The News,* January 26, 2006; Afzal A Shigri, "Bhasha Dam, the Northern Areas and Pakistan," *The News,* January 9, 2006. Shigri elsewhere also emphasises on the importance of the geo-strategic location of this region and that of water security to Pakistan. See Afzal A. Shigri, "Justice denied," *The News,* February 7, 2006.

ruled this region, initially through the Frontier Crimes Regulation (FCR) which was framed by the British to administer the Tribal regions of the North West Frontier Province.[30] The Northern Areas Advisory Council in 1969 was the first exclusive body, but without any executive powers. Reform packages of 1994 and 2004, NAC and NALC are cosmetic efforts, with clear objectives – deny any constitutional and fundamental rights; keep the local population away from any effective decision-making; provide some superficial institutions of local participation; and rule them with an iron hand.

[30] Even today, the Federally Administered Tribal Agencies (FATA) of Pakistan is governed by the FCR, which was introduced by the British in 1881.

III

Political Issues

The ICG Reports discussing the linkages between the Northern Areas and Kashmir underlines an important fact that generally gets blurred in the contemporary discourse on Kashmir. It says "*the territory that now constitutes Pakistan's Federally Administered Northern Areas, ethnically and culturally, has little in common with the Vale of Kashmir, other than the fact that the languages spoken there also belong, like Kashmiri, to the Dardic family. This lack of affinity explains in large part local rejection of any association with Kashmir today. Yet despite the region's voluntary accession to Pakistan, Islamabad policymakers still link it with Jammu and Kashmir.*"[31]

The reasons are not difficult to identify for these differences. In terms of language, culture and religious affiliation the people of the Northern Areas differ drastically from both the Kashmir Valley and "AJK". Three differences, in particular are more pronounced. In terms of language, the people of the Northern Areas do not speak Kashmiri. In fact, they speak different languages including Urdu, Shina, Balti, Wakhi, Burushaski, Khowar and Pashto. In terms of religion, they also differ from the others; the people of Northern Areas are primarily Shias and belong to different sects including the Ismailis. The Sunni population in the Northern Areas is limited more to Astore district.[32] In terms of culture and historical contacts, the people

---

[31] Discord in Pakistan's Northern Areas.

[32] Astore district has maximum Sunni population in the Northern Areas; more that 70 per cent in this district. Other districts have a Shia majoritiy.

of this region have more in common with Ladakh and Kargil, than with the Kashmir Valley and "AJK". [33]

This cultural and religious divide has an important political implication for the Northern Areas. First, unlike the leadership of "AJK", the political leadership in the Northern Areas lacks an affinity with the rest of Pakistan's political elite, especially the Punjabi elite. Since a section of the political elite in "AJK" also speak Punjabi and share cultural ties with the Punjab province of Pakistan, they have a better bargaining tool when compared to the political elite of the NA. Second, in terms of religion, the people of "AJK" are predominantly Sunnis, as in the case of Kashmir Valley. Whereas, as explained above, the people and political elite of the Northern Areas are predominantly Shias. This Shia-Sunni factor has played an important role since the 1980s, when the fault lines between the two sects became open and wide. After the first major sectarian violence in the late 1980s, the divide between the two sects widened, with the Sunnis and their radical sections having an element of official patronage of Islamabad. This not only further distanced the people of the Northern Areas from Islamabad, but also pitted the former against the latter. Since the 1990s, the politics became primarily sectarian.

Politically another important difference needs to be noted, which the ICG Report highlights. *"Since the Northern Areas have no representation in any federal, constitutional or political forum, stakeholders cannot articulate demands or grievances to a wider audience. The Northern Areas' executive serves the federal executive and has no local electoral constituency and hence no need to respond to local pressure. Absent from decision-making forums in Islamabad, the Northern Areas also have no voice on the budget. Federal allocations to the provinces are*

[33] See M. Ismail Khan, "Why not Kargil?" *The News,* September 6, 2005.

made on the basis of the National Finance Commission (NFC) Award. Since the Northern Areas are not represented, it is up to KANA to advance demands as it sees fit."[34]

Besides the above, the ICG report highlights the following four issues.[35] First, the Pakistan military has the final say on the country's Kashmir policy. The Northern Areas are directly placed under the federal control, "*for fear that even a modicum of autonomy would translate into political empowerment and demands for self-governance.*"[36] Second, the sectarian tensions and the violence in the Northern Areas are the result of Pakistan's reliance on Sunni *jihadi* groups to fight its proxy wars in Kashmir and Afghanistan.[37] Third, though yet to become a violent, the deprivation in these Areas has manifested itself *in a nationalist movement that could potentially challenge Pakistan's control over territory.*[38] Fourth, the military has made a decision to use force to suppress the discord and discontent in the Northern Areas, thereby not allowing any debate over the much delayed reforms.

Towards conclusions, the ICG report provides four options, based on perceptions of different sections of people in the Northern Areas. The first option is to make the Northern Areas into the fifth province of Pakistan. The second option is to

---

[34] Discord in Pakistan's Northern Areas.

[35] These issues and the subsequent comments are also published elsewhere. See D. Suba Chandran, "Northern Areas and the ICG Report," *Daily Excelsior,* April 2007.

[36] Discord in Pakistan's Northern Areas.

[37] Sectarian violence, though has been simmering in the 1990s, it blew up since 2004-05. In 2005 alone, more than 100 were killed due to sectarian violence in the Northern Areas. For the recent sectarian incidents and their causes see Mohammad Shehzad, "Textbook controversy in Gilgit," *The Friday Times,* July 4-10, 2003, Vol. XV, No. 19; Gulmina Bilal, "While Gilgit burns....," *The News,* November 22, 2005; Khaled Ahmed, "The trouble in Gilgit," *The Friday Times,* July 8-14, 2005, Vol. XVII, No. 20.

[38] Discord in Pakistan's Northern Areas.

merge the Northern Areas with PoK. The third option is suggested by two sections on independence – one section favouring it as a part of independent Kashmir, including PoK and J&K; and the other section favouring independence both from Pakistan and PoK. The last option is a status similar to that of the PoK.

Now an important point in the above opinions advanced by different groups is who demands what and for what reasons. The ICG report could have made an even more detailed analysis of this important aspect, though it covers them in a nut shell. The people of the Northern Areas are divided on what should be the final status of their region. A meeting in Gilgit of the NALC members with the journalists from India and Pakistan organised under the SAFMA, highlighted these differences. *Dawn* noted the following on this meeting that took place during November-December 2004:

> "The NALC legislators said they would prefer to join Pakistan if a plebiscite was held. However, another ruling PML member, Haji Abdul Quddus, said the region was part of Kashmir but before he could argue his point of view, there was a sort of pandemonium which forced the organisers to divide the NALC delegation into three groups representing the PML, the PML(N) and the PPP (Parliamentarians). PML(N) member Hafizur Rahman said there was no consensus regarding the status of the Northern Areas and called for empowering the NALC with a local chief executive and a local set-up on the lines of Azad Jammu and Kashmir Assembly. He said the NALC was devoid of any powers as claimed by PML members. PPP member Ghulam Muhammad said his party had brought about reforms in the region in 1994 and he supported the

idea of a local set-up. During the question-answer session the NALC members threw up more confusion when they kept swinging from one standpoint to another regarding the status of the region in the light of the Kashmir issue when they were approached separately. A legislator, who wished not to be named, said the PML legislators were wilfully exaggerating facts and figures about the NALC powers and development as they were eying advisers' posts which were still to be filled."[39]

A section amongst the non-Sunni community, including the Shias and the Ismailis prefer the Northern Areas to be the fifth province of Pakistan. Elsewhere, a report published by the Institute of Policy Studies mentions that the Shia groups, led by the Anjuman Ahle Tashia and Tahrik-e-Jafria-Pakistan consider that the Northern Areas historically never belonged to Kashmir and are also apprehensive that if made a part of Kashmir, "the Northern Areas will remain backward and disadvantaged, because being less developed they would never be in a position to compete with more developed Kashmiris."[40] Whereas the Sunni groups such as the Tanzeem-e-Ahle-Sunnah wal Jamaat consider that the Northern Areas should be merged with the AJK, as bringing these two will make the Sunnis a majority in the entire region.[41]

The section that demand an "AJK" type of administration for the Northern Areas include the Gilgit-Baltistan National

---

[39] "Politicians split over status of Northern Areas," *Dawn,* 1 December 2004.

[40] See IPS Task Force Report, "Northern Areas of Pakistan: Facts, Problems and Recommendations," *Policy Perspectives,* April 2004, Vol.1, No.1, pp.133-134.

[41] See IPS Task Force Report, "Northern Areas of Pakistan: Facts, Problems and Recommendations," *Policy Perspectives,* April 2004, Vol.1, No.1, pp.134.

Alliance (GBNA), an umbrella organisation which has 14 national and local political parties.[42]

Two groups have been demanding total independence from Pakistan (and also from India) including the Balawaristan National Front (BNF) and the Jammu and Kashmir Liberation Front (JKLF). According to Khan Abdul Hamid, Chairman of the BNF, "the people of Gilgit and Baltistan have been betrayed by Pakistan and made slaves in their own land. We no longer have the rights that we had been under the Dogra rule which we struggled so hard against. We do not have the political freedom people have either in Indian Kashmir or PoK. So we want the fourth option, which is to liberate our people from all foreign occupation."[43]

Elsewhere in Geneva, the BNF made similar charges against Pakistan. It has been reported that the BNF made the following observations:[44]

> "Our great nation is reeling under the stifling control of the Armed Forces of Pakistan and its security agencies like the ISI. Our innocent people are being treated as subjugated slaves. They have been deprived of all basic human, economic, cultural and political rights for the last 52 years due to the worst colonial system imposed by Pakistan in the name of religion. As a result, our simple folks are living like animals in this civilised world even at the draw of the 21st century..."

---

42 "AJK-like status for N. Areas demanded," *Dawn,* January 21, 2002.

43 See Sultan Shaheen, "Free Balawaristan movement gains momentum," http://www.jammu-kashmir.com/insights/insight20000206b.html

44 See Sultan Shaheen, "Free Balawaristan movement gains momentum," http://www.jammu-kashmir.com/insights/insight20000206b.html.

> "In the past 52 years a number of our countrymen have been brutally killed by Pakistan forces. But ours is the only part of the world where the highest court works on the basis of the contract and where no written petition is allowed against any human rights violations."
> "Pakistan intelligence agency ISI has been forcibly sending our innocent youth across the LOC to Indian - occupied Kashmir for terrorist activities. Those who refuse to work for ISI are picked up and killed. In 1999 alone Pakistani occupation forces used our innocent people as cannon fodder against India in its Kargil misadventure . More than 400 young men of our nation lost their lives, about 1,000 were wounded and approximately 40 are still missing."

The Jammu and Kashmir Liberation Front (JKLF) consider Gilgit-Baltistan as an integral part of Kashmir. Amanullah Khan, Chairman of his faction of the JKLF, has been demanding the empowerment of the NALC and that the bureaucratic machinery be made subordinate to the elected representatives.[45] According to him, unless the bureaucracy is brought under the control of the elected representatives, "the scheming bureaucrats would continue to usurp the people's rights as they have been doing since 1947." [46]

---

[45] "JKLF seeks NALC empowerment," *Dawn,* August 2, 2004.

[46] "JKLF seeks NALC empowerment," *Dawn,* August 2, 2004.

IV

Conclusions[47]

Where do the Northern Areas stand today, legally and politically? What is likely to happen? Unfortunately, the military's control over Pakistan is likely to result in the Northern Areas being perceived as a strategic and security issue. As a result, any demand for increased local participation in administration or better governance will not be seen as a natural but as a threat to the military's control, hence a security threat. As the report has stated, the military is likely to brutally suppress these demands, since it sees them not through a political, but a narrow security prism. The military is likely to use the same strategy which it is employing in Balochistan. Use brutal force, bomb them, if necessary.

As a part of this suppression, Islamabad is likely to use the sectarian card to divide and rule the Northern Areas so that there is no unified voice. In retrospect, it appears now, that the sectarian violence in the Northern Areas is not a collateral damage or a negative fall out of Pakistan's *jihadi* policy elsewhere. Rather, it is a deliberate policy to keep the Northern Areas divided and under control. As mentioned above, the Northern Areas is strategically important for Islamabad for two reasons – the Karakoram Highway and Pakistan's water security. Precisely for these reasons, Pakistan has kept the Northern Areas behind an iron curtain, with neither the local media being allowed to flourish nor the national and international media permitted to cover events inside. In an

---

[47] The conclusions are the author's.

interview, Abdul Hamid Khan, chairperson of the Balawaristan National Front, said, "foreign journalists and human rights activists are not allowed to enter Balawaristan. If at all anybody does risk entering Balawaristan, the ISI and other agencies monitor the activities of that person very closely. All copies of a local magazine, *Balawaristan Times*, were confiscated and banned in 1994; the *Gilgit Digest* was banned in 1998; *Weekly K2* was banned and its editor, Raja Hussain Khan Maqpoon, was kidnapped by the ISI from his Rawalpindi office twice, and sent to prison. Dozens of fake cases were registered against him in different courts in Balawaristan."[48]

In the long run, the divide between Islamabad and the Northern Areas are likely to increase further. There have been rumblings of separatist movements, which the report has also touched upon. How serious is this nationalist discourse in the Northern Areas? Will this finally challenge Pakistan's control over territory? Is the Northern Areas ready for such a nationalist movement? These are larger questions that need to be understood from an Indian perspective. Opening of the Kargil-Skardu Road, will give India an opportunity to understand what exactly is happening inside the Northern Areas.[49]

---

[48] See "'If we had a choice between India and Pakistan, we would not be part of Pakistan'"http://www.tehelka.com/channels/currentaffairs/2001/dec/3/ca120301abdul2.htm.

[49] Besides there are other reasons why India should insist on opening the Kargil-Skardu Road. See D. Suba Chandran, "Moving on the Kargil-Skardu Road," *The Indian Express,* April 25, 2007.

CHAPTER 8

Political/Constitutional Developments In Pok
A Chronology Since October 2005

Priyashree Andley[1]

October 4, 2005

Justice Reaz Akhtar Chaudhry, AJK Chief Election Commissioner announced that the elections for four seats of the Azad Jammu and Kashmir Council (AJKC) would be in Muzaffarabad on 27th October. The AJK Council consists of six members who are elected by the AJK Legislative Assembly members through the proportional representation by means of a single transferable vote. The tenure of the elected AJKC members is five years.[2] The term of four members, three belonging to the People's Party and one to the ruling Muslim Conference expired on 2nd October, necessitating the election within 30 days of the vacancy.

October 8, 2005

More than 50,000 deaths resulted from a devastating earthquake, which hit parts of Pakistan and Azad Kashmir severely. A vast majority of Azad Kashmiris either died or left for their

---

[1] Priyashree Andley is a Research Officer at the Institute of Peace and Conflict Studies, New Delhi.

[2] "AJKC election on 27th," *Dawn,* October 5, 2005.

rural damaged homes, causing all relief work to come to a standstill.[3]

October 22, 2005

India and Pakistan agreed to open at least three sectors along the LoC for relief operations. The sectors included Kaman near Aman Setu in Uri, Tithwal in Tangdhar and Chakan Da Bagh in Poonch.

November 7, 2005

India and Pakistan opened five crossing points along the LoC after officials from both countries reached an agreement in Islamabad. The agreed crossing points included Nauseri-Tithwal; Chakoti-Uri; Hajipur-Uri; Rawalakot-Poonch and Tattapani-Mendhar. Musharraf observed that the earthquake had provided an opportunity for both sides to move forward on Kashmir.[4]

December 27, 2005

All Jammu and Kashmir Muslim Conference issued a ticket to Shama Malik for contesting by-elections for the seat of the AJK legislative assembly. The seat in the AJK assembly was left vacant after the death of Shireen Waheed, AJK minister, in the October earthquake.[5] MC members welcomed the issuing of a ticket to Shama Malik for contesting by-polls for the assembly seat.

---

[3] "40,000 feared dead in parts of AJK," *Paktribune,* October 10, 2005.

[4] "Fifth relief point opened along LoC," *Paktribune,* November 17, 2005.

[5] "MC issues ticket to Shama Malik for by-polls," *Paktribune,* December 27, 2005.

December 27, 2005

Mufti Mansoor ur Rehman, AJK Minister for Tourism and Environment, announced that 64,000 shelters were provided to Azad Kashmir quake survivors. He said coordinated efforts were underway to provide more shelters to the survivors in an effective manner.

January 3, 2006

Sahibzada Ishaq Zaffar, Central President Pakistan People's Party (PPP), Azad Kashmir assured that PPP would get a clear-cut victory in the upcoming general elections in Azad Kashmir, i.e. two-thirds majority in the upcoming polls in Azad Kashmir. He noted that PPP, Azad Kashmir was only bound to the directions of Benazir Bhutto. Bhutto had selected the applications of four PPP candidates to the contest forthcoming elections of the Azad Kashmir Council.[6] He directed four candidates Sales Kyani, Irshad Burki, Chaudhry Mazhar and Hameed Potho to submit their documents to the Election Commission by 5th January.

January 7, 2006

Raja Najabat Hussain, the central leader of All Jammu and Kashmir Muslim Conference (AJKMC) welcomed the fielding of party workers for the Kashmir Council tickets and said that keeping in view the situation, the party leadership decided to give tickets to its three representatives.[7]

---

6 "AJK PPP will get 2/3rds majority in the upcoming elections: Ishaq," *Paktribune*, January 3, 2006.

7 "AJKMC field its three contestants for KC," *Paktribune*, January 7, 2006.

However, there was selection for only three seats, so the party leadership decided to field its three contestants according to the demands and situation. He said that by accepting the decision the workers of the Muslim Conference (MC) had to prepare themselves for the upcoming elections.

Sardar Atiq Ahmed Khan, President Muslim Conference (MC) said that the movement regarding increase in seats of the Kashmir Council would be tabled in the Assembly. He noted that all decisions in politics were not taken in line with justice; however some of the decisions had to be taken instantly keeping in view democratic stability, parties' interest and ground realities.[8] He said that he was fully confident that the decisions of the parliamentary board would be in the larger interests of the country and parties.

January 27, 2006

Barrister Sultan Mehmood Chaudhry and twelve other members of the Pakistan People's Party Azad Kashmir tendered their resignations expressing their dissent to AJK party leaders. The rebel group expressed its confidence on the leadership of Barrister Sultan Mahmood Chaudhry and nine members of the group dispatched their resignations to party chairperson Benazir Bhutto demanding an immediate change in party leadership. The decision to this extent was taken in the parliamentary party meeting held at the residence of Barrister Sultan Mahmood Chaudhry which was attended by Haji Javed Akhtar, Sardar Mohammad Hussain, Dewan Ghulam Mohiuddin, Sardar Ghulam Sadiq Khan, whereas newly elected member legislative assembly Chaudhry Hameed Pothi also at-

[8] "Proposal for increase in Kashmir council seats to be tabled in Assembly: MC," *Paktribune,* January 7, 2006.

tended the meeting.[9] The PPP leaders urged party chairperson Benazir Bhutto to change the party leadership because it was imperative for the success of the party in Azad Kashmir. The PPP leaders maintained on the occasion that nobody violated party discipline in the Kashmir Council's elections but it was the inability of party leadership, which created misunderstandings.

January 31, 2006

Sardar Sikandar claimed that the Muslim Conference (MC) would gain victory in the upcoming general elections. The Parliamentary Board of the Muslim Conference issued a ticket to his son for contesting the Kashmir Council elections on merit base, he maintained.[10]

Muhammad Anwar Mir of Mantrigram Bandipora was nominated as party representative in AJK and Pakistan. This was decided at an extra meeting of Jammu and Kashmir Mass Movement (JKMM) in Srinagar under the Chairmanship of JKMM Farida Behanjee.

February 28, 2006

Sardar Attiq Ahmed Khan, President All Jammu and Kashmir Muslim Conference announced in Muzaffarabad that the upcoming general elections in Azad Kashmir should be held in three phases. He noted that in view of administrative difficulties, polls should be held in Muzaffarabad Division in the

[9] "12 members of PPP AJK chapter repose confidence in Barrister Sultan," *Paktribune,* January 27, 2006.

[10] "MC to win upcoming general elections: Sardar Sikandar," *Paktribune,* January 31, 2006.

first phase and in Mirpur Division in the second phase. While elections should be held for Kashmiri refugees in Pakistan during the third phase, he maintained. He said that there was great need of political stability presently in the Azad region of Kashmir.[11] The MC president said that the Pakistan Muslim League (PML) wing would not be established in Azad Kashmir, as the talks between the MC and PML leadership had already been held in this regard. He went on to say that the Muslim Conference gives priority to Pakistan's interests and Tehrik-e-Hurriyat.

March 1, 2006

Maulana Abdul Hai, Secretary General All Jammu and Kashmir Jamiat ul Ulema Islam (JUI) announced that the Muttahida Majlis-e-Amal (MMA) wing would be established in Azad Kashmir within a few days. He noted that the masses of Azad Kashmir were fed up with the two-party system in the Azad region of Kashmir. The Secretary General said that those who support the program me for the establishment of MMA in Azad Kashmir would be welcomed.[12] The new government in Azad Kashmir will have to get the support of MMA, otherwise it will not succeed in establishing its government, he said.

March 3, 2006

Pir Attiq ur Rehman, Patron-in-Chief Jamiat Ulema Islam Jammu and Kashmir and member AJK Legislative Assembly clarified that the Central Executive Committee (CEC) of Jamiat

[11] "Sardar Attiq suggests elections in three phases in AJK," *Paktribune,* February 28, 2006.

[12] "MMA wing to be established in AJK soon: Maulana Hai," *Paktribune,* March 1, 2006.

Ulema Islam had power to take decisions regarding the establishment of Muttahida Majlis-e-Amal (MMA) chapter in Azad Kashmir. Pir Attiq stated that the Central Working Committee of Jamiat Ulema, Jammu and Kashmir would meet in Mirpur on 6th March to take a decision on whether the MMA chapter should be set in Azad Kashmir or not.[13] He said that if leaders of other religious parties announced MMA establishment in the Azad region of Kashmir, then the Central Executive Committee of the Jamiat Ulema would decide either to join MMA or not.

March 24, 2006

Basharat Afzal, Secretary General of All Jammu and Kashmir Muslim Conference, District Muzaffarabad, resigned from the slot of Secretary General of the Union Council No. 4 Khawara.

Basharat Afzal said until the matters of the constituency was in the hands of senior minister, Raja Muhammad Abdul Qayum things were running smoothly.[14] He, however, stated that now the relatives of Raja Muhammad Abdul Qayum were dealing with all the important matters of the constituency and it was not possible to work with them. Basharat Afzal said that that he was still Secretary General of District Muzaffarabad and would continue to perform his political activities.

---

13 "JUI has power to decide MMA establishment in AJK: Pir Attiq," *Paktribune*, March 3, 2006.

14 "Basharat resigns from slot of Secretary General of Union Council 4, Khawara," *Paktribune*, March 24, 2006.

March 25, 2006

Sardar Sikandar Hayat Khan, PM AJK, praised the role of AJK Ombudsman adding that the credit of the establishment of AJK Ombudsman goes to the Government of Muslim Conference. Justice Raja Ashraf Kiani was sworn in as the new ombudsman. Sardar Sikandar Hayat affirmed that AJK ombudsman played a significant role to mitigate the sufferings of people. He praised the valuable services of Justice Ashraf Kiani and observed that the government would pay attention to any proposals and suggestions to improve the work of this organisation.[15] He confirmed that the government respected the decisions made by the ombudsman, adding that the government directed the administration to ensure the implementation of orders and decisions by ombudsman.

March 27, 2006

Sahibzada Muhammad Ishaq Zafar, President PPP AJK, announced submission of a formal application to Chief Election Commissioner regarding registration of PPP Azad Kashmir for the elections and list of central representatives under the political parties act.[16]

April 1, 2006

Barrister Sultan, former PM AJK, warned that no outsider had the right to contest elections in Khoirata. He commented on the decision of Matlob Inqalabi to contest elections from Khoirata, and said that he should contest elections from his own constituency No. 4 not from Khoirata. He said that those

---

15 "Sikandar praises role of AJK Ombudsman," *Paktribune,* March 25, 2006.

16 "Application of registration of PPP AJK filed with CEC," *Paktribune,* March 27, 2006.

who would test the dignity of the people of Khoirata would face serious consequences.[17] Barrister Sultan further said that their candidate from Khoirata was Rafique Nayyar and expressed his confidence that he would be successful with a heavy majority.

April 21, 2006

The differences between disgruntled groups of Pakistan People's Party in AJK finally closed down as Barrister Sultan Mahmood Chaudhry announced the formation of his own new party People's Muslim League in Islamabad. He also formed a nine-member parliamentary board and sought applications from aspirants for issuing party tickets before 30th April and set 2nd May to launch the election campaign.[18] He said people in AJK were fed up of the two-party system in the valley and his party would uproot the elements that had been playing with the people of the valley. He added that this decision would prove to be a milestone in the history of AJK.

April 22, 2006

Amanullah Khan, Chairman and M. Sagheer Khan, Advocate Secretary General of JKLF announced that its Policy and Planning Committee (PPC) meeting discussed a ten-point agenda to consider whether or not JKLF should contest the forthcoming elections to the Azad Jammu Kashmir Legislative Assembly. The Committee discussed the issue in the light of the current state of affairs regarding Kashmiris' freedom movement, the Kashmir issue, the JKLF ideology, the condition of taking the

---

17 "No outsider has right to contest election in Khoirata: Sultan," *Paktribune*, April 1, 2006.

18 "Barrister Sultan forms new party 'People's Muslim League," *Paktribune*, April 21, 2006.

oath in favour of states' accession to Pakistan and of other related matters and came to the conclusion that JKLF should participate in the election but under the manifesto of working for independence of the entire Jammu Kashmir State instead of its accession to any other country.[19] The PPC sent its advice to the Central Executive Committee (CEC) which met on April 23, 2006 and discussed the issue in the light of the advice from PPC as also on merit and came to the conclusion that JKLF should contest the forthcoming election on the manifesto of independent Jammu and Kashmir.

April 26, 2006

Jammu Kashmir Liberation Front (JKLF) announced that it would contest the forthcoming elections to AJK Legislative Assembly on the manifesto of independent Jammu and Kashmir. It has called upon the governments of Pakistan and Azad Kashmir to remove the provision from nomination papers of taking oath of being a supporter of Kashmir's accession to Pakistan.

JKLF also put an end to efforts for re-unification with Yaseen Malik group calling it an exercise in futility in the light of retraction of the Yaseen group from the agreed formula.[20] These announcements were made at a press conference in Islamabad chaired by Amanullah Khan Chairman and M. Sagheer Khan Advocate Secretary General of JKLF.

---

19 See "JKLF to contest AJK elections on manifesto of independent Kashmir," *Paktribune,* April 26, 2006.

20 "JKLF to contest AJK elections on manifesto of independent Kashmir," *Paktribune,* April 26, 2006.

April 26, 2006

The establishment of subordinate organisations of Jammu and Kashmir People's Muslim League (PML) was taken in principle. Barrister Sultan, the PML Quaid and former PM AJK, approved the names of Student Wing and Youth Wing. In this context, a meeting was held under the chairmanship of Raja Faisal Azad Khan.[21] Barrister Sultan, the chief guest on the occasion said that after coming into power, we would lift the ban on Student Unions and will hold the Union Elections, which are vital not only to safeguard their democratic rights but also bring the true leadership of students.

May 8, 2006

The All Pakistan Minorities Alliance (APMA) demanded to allocate minorities' seats in the Legislative Assembly of AJK ahead of the general election. Shahbaz Bhatti, President APMA, said minorities living in Kashmir and non-Muslim nationalists played a sincere pivotal role for the development and prosperity of the country but were deprived of the representation in the AJK Legislative Assembly.[22]

He added that the President AJK and Chief Justice of the Supreme Court should take notice in this regard and should issue orders to allocate minorities seats in the AJK Legislative Assembly ahead of the next general election. Shahbaz Bhatti noted that allocation of minorities' seats in AJK Legislative Assembly was in accordance with the principle of democracy.

---

21 "Decision to establish subordinate organisation of Kashmir PML taken," *Paktribune,* April 26, 2006.

22 "APMA demands more seats in AJK Legislative Assembly," *Paktribune,* May 8, 2006.

May 16, 2006

Sardar Anwar Khan, President AJK, withdrew his decision to tender resignation from the slot of President as he failed to find any proper position in any main party in AJK. The decision shattered rumours about his inclusion in the People's Muslim League and also removed chances of any significant breakthrough in AJK elections to be held on 11th July.[23] After the decision of AJK President, the demands of the Muslim Conference for the existence of the two-party system in AJK has been fulfilled and now only PPP-AJK and the Muslim Conference are the main parties participating in the election.

May 19, 2006

Major (Retd) Tahir Iqbal, State Minister for Kashmir and Northern Areas, promised that the July elections in AJK would be held in a free, fair and transparent manner.He dispelled the impression that government machinery would be used for the victory of the Pakistan Muslim League (PML) in the coming election. Referring to the recently inked deal between PPP and PML-(N), he said that the Charter of Democracy was a mockery with the nation and people were aware of previous governments who tried to implement dictatorship in the name of democracy.[24] He affirmed that the election would be held in 2007 and the assembly would complete its tenure.

May 20, 2006

Election Commission Azad Jammu and Kashmir issued notice to three officers including Sardar Amer Akbar, Minister

---

[23] "President PPP-AJK withdraws resignation decision," *Paktribune,* May 16, 2006.

[24] "Minister promises fair, transparent election in AJK," *Paktribune,* May 19, 2006.

for Power, for violating the code of conduct. There was always an allegation directed at Sardar Amer Akbar from the opponent candidate Assembly that he was involved in installation of new poles and lying new wires of electricity.[25] Election Commission AJK issued transfer notices to Sardar Amer Akbar, Chairman Education Board Mirpur and In-charge Electricity Department of Bagh and also sought explanation in this regard.

May 30, 2006

The Jammu and Kashmir People's Muslim League (PML) issued party tickets to 39 candidates for the forthcoming Legislative Assembly election to be held on 11th July. Tickets to the remaining two candidates would be issued in the next two days. The tickets were issued to the candidates on the basis of merit.[26] All the candidates who were issued tickets were interviewed. Sardar Muhammad Hussain, chairman parliamentary board PML stated this during a press conference at the residence of Barrister Sultan Mehmood Chaudhry.

May 31, 2006

Hundreds of workers of the Muslim Conference in protest decided to resign from the party owing to the continuing differences among the MC leadership. These were intensified over the decision of its leadership not issuing ticket to Dr. Mustafa Bashir for the July AJK election. The leadership of MC issued ticket to Dewan Chughtai for Constituency No. 6 Muzaffarabad but the political campaign of Dr. Mustafa Bashir was started by some influential political and social personalities

---

25 "EC AJK issues notice to three officers for violating code of conduct," *Paktribune,* May 20, 2006.

26 "J&K PML issues party tickets to 39 candidates," *Paktribune,* May 30, 2006.

of the constituency.[27] Sardar Muhammad Abdul Qayum, Supreme Head of MC, and Sardar Sikandar Hayat, PM AJK, had pledged to issue a ticket to Dr. Mustafa Bashir over his decision to withdraw in favour of Dewan Chughtai in the 2003 by-polls. However, the MC leadership did not issue a ticket to Dr. Mustafa Bashir for the July 2006 election.

June 6, 2006

Sardar Sikandar Hayat Khan, PM AJK, demanded that restrictions of keeping ID Cards in the upcoming AJK elections, be abolished. He expressed these views while addressing the elected office bearers of Jammu Kashmir Union of Journalists. He informed that 40 per cent of AJK people did not have their ID cards. AJK PM while expressing his disappointment over the behaviour of the Chief Election Commission said that unnecessary restrictions were being imposed in the name of code of conduct.[28] He said that unfair election would defame Pakistan and impact negatively on the freedom movement in Indian Kashmir.

June 12, 2006

Barrister Sultan Mehmood Chaudhary, JKPML President, announced that after winning the election his party would raise the Kashmir dispute effectively on the international level. He said that the international media and observers were invited to monitor themselves the AJK election and compare them with rigged elections of Indian Kashmir.[29] Barrister Sultan

---

[27] "MC workers decide to resign from party," *Paktribune,* May 31, 2006.

[28] "Sikandar demands to abolish restrictions of ID card in election," *Paktribune,* June 6, 2006.

[29] "International media invited to observe AJK election : Sultan," *Paktribune,* June 12, 2006.

Mehmood Chaudhary said that JKPML had emerged as a big political power in AJK and had its roots in the masses, adding that after the formal restructuring of the party, the names of office bearers would be announced.

June 16, 2006

Sardar Attiq Khan, President Azad Jammu and Kashmir Muslim Conference, appointed Sardar Tariq as coordinator of the election campaign of district Poonch. He was directed to make prompt coordination with all the four candidates of MC in the district, Sardar Abdul Qayyum Niazi from Abbas Pur, Sardar Bhadar Khan from Hijera, Sardar Tahir Anwar from Rawalakot and Sardar Syab Khalid from Panewala.[30] All political activities in the area remained in contact with the central control room.

June 20, 2006

Jammu and Kashmir People's Muslim League (JKMPL) and Awami Tehrik formally announced an electoral coalition in the upcoming elections. Barrister Sultan Mehmood and Sardar Mansoor Khan announced this in a joint press conference. Barrister Sultan Mehmood informed that both parties decided to launch a worldwide campaign for self-determination of Kashmiris and as a party in the dispute.[31] He declared that JKPML the only party to play a vital role to forge unity among nations over the issues of sectarianism and protection of sanctity of Holy Prophets. He pledged to construct the devastated earthquake area on a scientific basis, eradication of corruption, inflation, and unemployment.

---

[30] "Tariq appointed as election campaign coordinator MC," *Paktribune,* June 16, 2006.

[31] "JKPML, Awami Tehrik form coalition for AJK elections," *Paktribune,* June 20, 2006.

June 20, 2006

Sardar Sikandar Hayat Khan, PM AJK, withdrew his nomination papers. Two days earlier, he announced to take part in the electoral process with great enthusiasm but after the inauguration of Rawlakot-Poonch bus service, and after a press conference in Muzaffarabad he announced withdrawal of his nomination paper. Scores of MC supporters showed their annoyance over the decision of the AJK PM.[32]

June 26, 2006

Justice Muhammad Riaz Akhtar Chaudhry, Chief Election Commissioner AJK, approved declaring offices of Returning Officers at polling stations for casting votes by those government employees who would be on duty on 11th July. Returning Officers also told the Election Commission that concerned candidates tried to get postal ballot papers, which were given to on-duty employees due to which they could not freely use their right to cast their vote.[33] In the wake of this, Chief Election Commissioner declared Returning Officers offices as polling stations so that on-duty employees could freely caste their vote. He said that on-duty employees would be given ballot papers that he would take behind the scenes to cast votes and put this ballot paper in the box in front of the Returning Officer or Assistant Director.

[32] "AJK PM withdraws nomination paper," *Paktribune,* June 20, 2006.

[33] "AJK CEC declares ROs offices as polling stations for on duty employees," *Paktribune,* June 26, 2006.

June 30, 2006

AJK Muslim League formally announced its manifesto for the AJK Legislative Assembly elections. Barrister Sultan Mehmood, former AJK prime minister and AJK ML convener announced the manifesto. The manifesto included increase in the seats of AJK Legislative Assembly and Kashmir Council, highlighting the Kashmir freedom movement at the international level, establishment of senior ministry, independent judiciary, independent accountability commission, reconstruction and rehabilitation of quake victims, establishment of independent public service commission, restructuring of all departments, administrative reforms, equitable and just distribution of financial resources among the administrative units and amendment in rules of business to improve the performance and efficiency of the government.[34] Barrister Sultan Mehmood alleged that the incumbent government of the Muslim Conference failed in the rehabilitation of 8th October quake survivors. He offered that an electoral alliance could be forged with all leaders barring Sardar Attiq Ahmad Khan.

July 1, 2006

Sardar Sikandar Hayat Khan, former PM AJK, affirmed that although he was not contesting in the July election, he was still active in politics. Addressing the inauguration of Election Office of Malik Muhammad Nawaz Khan, nominated candidate of Muslim Conference from Constituency No. 1, Kotli, he said that his supporting candidate for the slot of Prime Minister would succeed.[35] He also said that MC would

[34] "Provision of annexation to Pakistan may be scrapped from interim act: Barrister Sultan," *Paktribune,* June 30, 2006.

[35] "I have not left politics: Sikandar," *Paktribune,* July 1, 2006.

win the AJK election to be held on 11th July with a majority and form the government because people had expressed satisfaction over the work done by it in the five-year tenure.

July 2, 2006

Maulana Fazlur Rehman, opposition leader in the lower house, claimed that the Muttahida Majlis-e-Amal (MMA) was emerging as a political force in AJK, and called on Kashmiri masses to get rid of Sardars and cast their votes in favour of the religious alliance backed contenders. Maulana Fazl expressed these views while addressing a gathering in Ringla locality. Hafiz Hussain Ahmad, Maulana Nazir Farooqi, Abdul Rashid Turabi, Maulana Salim Ijaz, Amin-ul-Haq, Maulana Imtiaz Ahmad Abbasi, Maulana Mufti Mussarat Iqbal Abbasi, Qari Altaf Abbasi, Maulana Nadeem Ahmad Azad, Maulana Qazi Shahid Hameed, Khan Abdul Ghafar Khan and others also spoke on the occasion.[36] Hundreds of people on the occasion joined MMA. He added that the establishment of MMA as a powerful political party was the long-standing demand, which was now fulfilled by the people of Azad Kashmir.

July 5, 2006

Barrister Sultan Mehmood, former Prime Minister of AJK and head of Jammu Kashmir People's Muslim League (JKPML) began his visit to Azad Kashmir for his election campaign. He invited international observers and media to monitor the AJK elections to prove the existence of democracy in AJK without intervention of foreign elements. He alleged that India was engaged in negative propaganda against the AJK election but

---

[36] "Fazl urges AJK people to vote MMA-backed contenders, get rid of Sardars," *Paktribune,* July 2, 2006.

the world community would keenly watch the situation in AJK before the election.[37] Barrister Sultan assured that after the 11th July election, a free immigration process would start aiming to provide jobs opportunities to AJK youths in Canada, Britain and other countries.

July 7, 2006

Nearly 172 Independent candidates were taking part in 11th July elections. Out of the 41 seats for the Legislative Assembly, 40 were for Muslim Conference (MC), 36 for PPP AJK, 37 for People's Muslim League, 33 of MMA, 23 seats for Muthahida Qaumi Movement, whereas four each candidates of Jammu and Kashmir People's Party, Awami Tehreek, Sunni Tehreek, Pakistan JUI Jammu and Kashmir, Muthahida Kashmir People's National Party, All Jammu and Kashmir Awami Conference, Kashmir Freedom Movement while one each of Mahaz Rai Shumar, PPP Shaheed Bhutto Group, Kashmir Labour Party and Liberation Front respectively.[38] The AJK Election Commission under the instructions of the Chief Election Commissioner (CEC) promised to hold free, fair and transparent elections by implementing the code of conduct and election rules applicable to all the contesting candidates and their supporters. Muslim Conference, Pakistan People's Party Azad Kashmir and People's Muslim League were expected to have a major competition in the elections.

July 8, 2006

Shaukat Aziz, Pakistan PM, in consultation with Sardar Attiq Ahmed Khan, President Muslim Conference, decided to

---

[37] "AJK election to be free and fair: Sultan," *Paktribune,* July 5, 2006.

[38] "172 Independent candidates contesting in AJK polls," *Paktribune,* July 7, 2006.

assign three Members of AJK Legislative Assembly as PM's advisers. Raja Iftikhar Ayub, Syed Ghulam Murtaza and Sardar Naseem Sarfraz, members AJK Legislative Assembly were likely to be the advisers of the Prime Minister on matters related to the Kashmir issue. The notification in this regard was to be issued in two days.[39]

July 11, 2006

Polling for the Azad Kashmir Legislative Assembly elections were held. About 24, 20,396 registered voters cast their votes in 29 constituencies of Azad Kashmir and in 12 constituencies of Kashmiri refugees in Pakistan. Besides local police, over 90,000 army contingents and a great number of para military troops were deployed in different constituencies to prevent rigging incidents. Army, police and para military forces were deputed at all polling stations. The polling was held from 8 am-5 pm. Of the 41 seats in the AJK Legislative Assembly, members elected from the Kashmiri community in Pakistan occupied 12 seats.[40] Two of these were won by the MQM that contested 26 seats.

July 14, 2006

Sardar Attiq informed government officials that the Parliamentary Party of Muslim Conference would take the decision about premiership and presidentship. He noted that formation of 15 to 20 members AJK cabinet was likely. He added that it would be the priority of the Muslim Conference government to take steps for the welfare of people,

---

39 "PM to appoint 3 members of AJK legislative assembly as his advisors," *Paktribune,* July 8, 2006.

40 "Azad Kashmir poll results," (Editorial) *Dawn,* July 14, 2006.

reconstruction and rehabilitation of quake-affected victims besides resolving the refugees' problem.[41] Sardar Attiq responded to questions on 'self-governance,' maintaining the stand that the Parliamentary system existed in Azad Kashmir since 1947 and the democratic system was completing five years. He expressed concern over increasing human rights violation in Kashmir and asked India to withdraw its troops from the Valley. AJKMC president said that like Azad Kashmir, transparent elections must also be held in Indian Kashmir.

July 18, 2006

Sardar Attiq Ahmed Khan promised that the Muslim Conference would cooperate with the opposition to run the government in Azad Kashmir. He said that all the phases of the formation of government in Azad Kashmir would be covered with consensus. Sardar Attiq said that the members who violated the Party's decisions would be fired and new nominations would replace them.[42] He observed that the the Muslim Conference was united and free to take decisions. He said that Muslim Conference would bring the revolution of development and progress in Azad Kashmir.

July 22, 2006

Syed Mujahid Hussain Naqvi, Central Leader of Muslim League (ML) and Advocate Supreme Court, claimed that Sardar Sikandar Hayat Khan, AJK PM, was not eligible to

---

[41] See "Muslim Conference has gained simple majority to form government in AJK: Attiq," *Paktribune*, July 14, 2006.

[42] "MC to run governmentt in AJK with opposition's consultation: Attiq," *Paktribune,* July 18, 2006.

contest the Presidential election. He said that according to AJK Interim Constitutional Act 1974, the person to contest the Presidential election should fulfil requirements of being a Muslim, at least 35 years of age and his name should be enlisted in the electoral list.

He said that Sardar Sikandar Hayat Khan did not fulfil the legal requirements of Elections Ordinance 1970, and was involved in accumulating property by the use of unlawful means.[43]

Syed Mujahid Hussain said Sikandar Hayat had hidden property related to him and his family when he submitted his returns at the time of the July elections. A formal case was filed to the Chief Election Commissioner AJK to take action against him.

July 24, 2006

Sardar Attique Ahmad Khan, President Muslim Conference was sworn in as Azad Jammu and Kashmir Prime Minister. Sardar Mohammad Anwar Khan, AJK President, administered the oath of office to Sardar Attique at a ceremony attended by AJK assembly and council members, civil and military officials, and members of the superior judiciary. Sardar Sikandar Hayat Khan, outgoing AJK premier, also attended the ceremony in the premises of the Legislative Assembly.

Sardar Attique became the seventh prime minister of Azad Kashmir after the parliamentary form of government was introduced in the region in 1975.[44] After the swearing-in

---

43 "Sikandar not eligible to contest Presidential Election: ML Leader," *Paktribune,* July 22, 2006.

44 "Sardar Attique sworn in as AKJ premier," *Dawn,* July 25, 2006.

ceremony, the new premier was presented a guard of honour by contingents of the AJK police. He said the Kashmir freedom movement and reconstruction of the quake-hit region were his priorities.

July 27, 2006

Raja Zulqarnain Khan of the ruling Muslim Conference won the presidential election and defeated his rival Sardar Qamaruz Zaman of the People's Party by 32 votes.[45] Justice Reaz Akhtar Chaudhry, AJK Chief Election Commissioner, announced the result in the AJK Legislative Assembly building. Raja Zulqarnain Khan secured 40 votes against 8 bagged by his rival.

August 4, 2006

Zakat Riaz Zargar, Central Leader Azad Jammu Kashmir Muslim Conference and Chairman District, addressed a meeting of MC workers, presided over by Sajjad Mughal in Constituency No 6, and said that Barrister Sultan Mehmood Chaudhry should admit defeat instead of criticising elections. There was no reality in allegations of Muttahida Majlis-e-Amal (MMA) and the Pakistan Army played a vital role during the destructive earthquake.[46] He confirmed that Sardar Attiq had complete support of the party as well as AJK masses. Central Leader of Azad Jammu Kashmir Muslim Conference asserted that the Opposition should respect the mandate of the AJK people.

---

[45] "Zulqarnain elected AJK president," *Dawn,* July 28, 2006.

[46] "AJK election held in fair, transparent manner: Riaz Zargar," *Paktribune*, August 4, 2006.

August 7, 2006

A 16-member Azad Kashmir Cabinet formally took oath at a ceremony at Kashmir House, in Islamabad. The ceremony was attended by Sardar Attiq Ahmed Khan, AJK PM, Major General retired Muhammad Anwar Khan, President AJK, Raja Zulqanain, elected President, Shah Ghulam Qadir, Speaker and others. The oath-taking ceremony started with the recitation of the Holy Quran. As soon as President AJK came on the rostrum, he was given a warm welcome. President AJK Major General retired Muhammad Anwar Khan administered the oath to Malik Muhammad Nawaz Khan, Minister for Power, Chaudhry Muhammad Yousaf, Minister for Trade and Industry, Raja Naseer Ahmed Khan, Minister for Local Bodies and Rural Development, Raja Nasir Ahmed Khan, Finance Minister, Abdul Rashid Abbasi, Law Minister, Hafiz Hamid Raza, Minister for Zakat, Auqaf and Usher, Sanalluah Qadiri, Minister for Restoration, Sardar Muhammad Naeem Khan, Revenue Minister, Dr. Muhammad Najeeb Khan, Health Minister, Syed Ghulam Murtaza Gillani, Forest Minister, Shama Malik, Minister for Social Welfare, Colonel retired Raja Muhammad Naseem Khan, Minister for Construction, Mirza Muhammad Shafiq Jharal, Agriculture Minister, Chaudhry Muhammad Akbar Ibrahim, Tourism Minister, Sardar Abdul Qayuum Niazi, Minister for Food, Relief and Ali Shan Chaudhry, Minister for Sports & Culture.[47]

August 9, 2006

AJK cabinet ministers, after being sworn in, started their formal duties. Workers and supporters of MC congratulated them and distributed sweets. The ministers were in pressing

---

[47] "16-member AJK Cabinet sworn in," *Paktribune,* August 7, 2006.

engagement with workers during their first day in office.[48] The ministers assured to fulfil right demands of workers and protect their rights.

August 10, 2006

Sardar Attiq addressed a ceremony held in connection with the oath-taking ceremony of Naheed Tariq, adviser to the AJK government. He noted that culture of change had began in Azad Kashmir and the steps were being taken for the welfare of the common man. He said that a cordial atmosphere was created after the victory of the Muslim Conference.[49] Sardar Attiq said that workers of the Muslim Conference and the activists of its coalition parties would participate in the decision making process and the approval of projects. He observed that AJK administration comprised competent people and had the cooperation of the bureaucracy. He said that the central government fully supported the democratic system of the state government.

August 11, 2006

Raja Muhammad Yasin Khan, Minister for Information, Interior and Hydral Power AJK, claimed that Attique Khan empowered all the ministers by handing them their designated powers. He said that the PM was also seeking responsible members to appoint them in different portfolios.[50] He said that a cell would be set up in all the national construction departments including the Construction Department to monitor developmental projects in AJK.

---

48 "Kashmiri ministers assume duties," *Paktribune,* August 9, 2006.

49 "Democratic process is moving forward in Azad Kashmir: Sardar Attiq," *Paktribune,* August 10, 2006.

50 "AJK PM has empowered all ministers: Raja Mohd," *Paktribune,* August 11, 2006.

September 1, 2006

The Election Commission of Pakistan issued directions to enrol all AJK refugees in the country in the voters' lists for the upcoming general polls. Under the Pakistan Citizen Act 1951 Article 14-B the Election Commission issued written directives to the Provincial Election Commissions of Karachi, Quetta, Lahore and Peshawar that all inhabitants of AJK who fully comply with the Electoral Rolls Act 1974 were citizens of Pakistan. He also issued directives to the Registration Officers, Assistant Registration Officers in this regard.[51] The Election Commission of Pakistan took the decision in response to a letter in which Syed Muhammad Ikram Shah, President Pakistan People's Party AJK, that the Registration Officers were preventing the AJK refugees from registering their names. The name of Kashmiris', photocopy of National Identity card, Pakistan Passport and domicile of AJK refugees had to be presented.

September 7, 2006

The Central Working Committee of Jamaat-e-Islami Azad Kashmir formally cancelled the membership of those who violated the decisions of the MMA during the recent AJK LA elections. A Central Working Committee was held under the chairmanship of Amir Jamaat-e-Islami Sardar Ejaz Afzal in which a host of issues were discussed concerning Kashmir movement, Organisation affairs of JI and last but not the least violation of discipline of some of the party members during the recent elections of AJK LA.[52] It was decided at the meeting

---

[51] "ECP issues directives for enrolment of AJK refugees in voter lists," *Paktribune*, September 1, 2006.

[52] "Membership of 3 JI AJK members cancelled due to party violation," *Paktribune*, September 7, 2006.

to cancel the membership of three members for not supporting the candidates of MMA in the elections as they were supporting an Independent Candidate in Muzaffarabad.

September 18, 2006

Justice Muhammad Riaz Akhtar Chaudhary, Chief Election Commissioner AJK, directed the authorities to take necessary measures to maintain law and order ahead of by-poll election of LA 28 Muzaffarabad 5.The Election Commission clarified all the parties to follow the code of conduct issued during the previous general elections and directions were given to Deputy Commissioner and SP Muzaffarabad too. According to the code of conduct, the very political party allowed to conduct only one public gathering while 200 people were allowed to attend corner meetings. Political parties were directed to obtain copies of code of conduct from the office of the Election Commission located in Muzaffarabad.[53] All the directions with complete details are mentioned in the copies of the code of conduct to ensure a transparent, free and impartial election.

September 22, 2006

Jahangir Badar, Central Secretary of Pakistan People's Party, stressed for free, fair and transparent by-election in constituency No. 5, Muzaffarabad. The seat fell vacant after the death of Sahibzada Ishaq. Jahangir Badar urged participants to cast their vote in favour of Ashfaq Zafar PPP candidate for the by-election to be held on 28th October.[54] He said that PPP did not believe in nepotism as it had the representation of all

[53] "CEC-AJK for all measures to ensure peaceful by-poll election," *Paktribune*, September 18, 2006.

[54] "PPP for fair by-election in Muzaffarabad," *Paktribune*, September 22, 2006.

segments of society. Other speakers were Ch. Muhammad Yasin, Central Vice President PPP-AJK, Ch. Latif Akbar, Secretary General and Pervaiz Ashraf, Chief Organiser.

September 25, 2006

Chaudhry Muhammad Akbar Ibrahim, Azad Jammu Kashmir Tourism, Wild Life Environment Minister contradicted the report of Human Rights that the Chief Secretary has the authority to dissolve the AJK Legislative Assembly. He said that some Human Rights Organisations favoured negative propaganda to get popularity by taking bribes from Indian intelligence agencies. He added that no member of AJK Legislative Assembly or representatives of the Federation had power to dissolve the assembly. The Minister noted that under the AJK constitution and United Nations resolutions there is no option of sovereign Kashmir.[55] He reiterated that Sardar Attique Ahmad Khan is a self-directed Prime Minister of AJK and IG Finance and Chief Secretary were bound to follow instructions of federations according to provinces.

September 30, 2006

Jammu and Kashmir Mass Movement nominated Abdul Majeed (Ishfaq Majeed) as its new representative for the All Parties Hurriyat Conference Azad Kashmir and Pakistan branch.[56] Farida Bahan Jee, head of the organisation, chaired the meeting of the Mass Movement in Srinagar. Abdul Majeed would represent the Mass Movement in the Hurriyat

---

[55] "Autonomous Kashmir not part of AJK constitutions, says Akbar," *Paktribune*, September 25, 2006.

[56] "Abdul Majeed nominated APHC representative," *Paktribune*, September 30, 2006.

Conference in Pakistan and Azad Jammu and Kashmir. A letter in this regard was formally issued to Muhammad Farooq Rehmani, Convener of APHC.

October 3, 2006

Raja Farooq Haider was selected to contest by-election on constituency No-LA 28 Muzaffarabad 5 Haitian Bala. This was decided during the meeting of All Jammu and Kashmir Muslim Conference (MC) Parliamentary board after the consideration, consultations and hearing of the candidates. Raja Muhammad Yasin Khan, Chairman Parliamentary Board All Jammu and Kashmir Muslim Conference, chaired the meeting.[57] Raja Muhammad Yasin hoped that MC workers while observing the party's responsibility would make Raja Farooq successful to prove their political attachment.

October 4, 2006

Iftikhar Naveed, Secretary Chief Election Commission AJK announced that fair and transparent election would be held on constituency No-LA 28 Muzaffarabad 5 Haitian Bala. The Legislative Assembly seat was vacant owing to the death of Sahibzada Ishaq Zafar, former Pakistan People's Party President.[58] Strict action was to be taken against those found guilty of rigging during election. Iftikhar Naveed added that elections of July 11 in AJK were held in a transparent manner and opposition parties needed to admit defeat.

---

57 "MC nominates Raja Farooq to contest by-election," *Paktribune*, October 3, 2006.

58 "Fair election to be held on vacant Hattian Bala seat: Secretary EC AJK," *Paktribune*, October 4, 2006.

October 6, 2006

Protest demonstrations were observed in Azad Kashmir against the death sentence of Muhammad Afzal Guru and demanded the withdrawal of the death warrant against him. All Parties Hurriyat Conference (AJK) members staged a peaceful sit-in in front of the UN Observer Office in Muzaffarabad. Muhammad Farooq Rehmani Convener APHC AJK chapter handed over a memorandum to the UN officials appealing to Kofi Annan, UN Secretary General, to use his good offices to prevent execution of Afzal Guru.[59] The memorandum said that the police unjustly implicated Afzal Guru in the parliament attack case.

November 1, 2006

Farooq Sikandar, son of Sardar Sikandar Hayat, former AJK Prime Minister, said that one person should not hold the post of Prime Minister and Party President. According to him, the Muslim Conference (S) was not consulted in the appointment of members of the Central Executive Body of Muslim Conference like in the issuance of party tickets in 2001.[60] He concluded that the party president had the authority to appoint members of the Executive Body, adding that now the tradition should stop as unsuitable people were selected in important posts.

---

[59] "Protest demonstrations observed against death sentence of Afzal Guru along both sides of LoC," *Paktribune*, October 6, 2006.

[60] "Post of AJK PM, Party President should not be held by one person: Farooq," *Paktribune*, November 1, 2006.

November 4, 2006

Political differences widened the rift between the Qayyum group and Sikandar Group of the All Jammu-Kashmir Muslim Conference. The Sikandar "S" group advised its member to avoid any participation in the meetings of the Central Executive Committee. This doubt has been reinforced after the directives were given by the former PM, and the supreme leader of "S" faction, Sardar Sikandar Hayat. The Qayyum group tried its level best to win the consent of "S" dissidents for their participation in the meeting but to no avail.[61] Sardar Sikandar Hayat decided upon a new strategy after the elections.

November 9, 2006

Sardar Qamar Zaman of Pakistan People's Party of the AJK chapter became the opposition leader of the Legislative Assembly. There were severe differences between Sardar Qamar Zaman and Chaudhry Latif Akbar over the nomination of opposition leader.[62] Chairperson Benazir Bhutto with the consultation of Asif Ali Zardari appointed Sardar Qamar Zaman as opposition leader by issuing a notification. The Secretary of the Legislative Assembly issued an official notice of appointment to the opposition leader.

November 15, 2006

Chaudhry Muhammad Yasin, Senior Vice-President of Pakistan People's Party (PPP) Azad Jammu and Kashmir (AJK) and Former Communication and Construction Minister

---

[61] "Rift between Sikandar, Qayyum group in MC widens," *Paktribune,* November 4, 2006.

[62] "Qamar Zaman new opposition leader of AJK assembly," *Paktribune,* November 9, 2006.

announced that appointment of Riaz Akhtar Chaudhry as Chief Justice (CJ) of AJK Supreme Court was based on the constitution and merit.[63] According to him, the citizens of AJK had appreciated the steps of the Chief Justice in the judiciary and the crime rate had declined with the help of reforms in the judiciary. However, he expressed disappointment over the statements against Chaudhry Riaz Akhtar and hoped it would stop.

November 15, 2006

The AJK government in Muzaffarabad, decided to postpone the Local Body election for one year. The election will be held in March 2008. Chief Election Commission directed to prepare computerised voting list for the upcoming election.[64] The government decided to appoint political workers to execute the affairs of the local body government. The government decided that after one year, new elections will be held according to the Local Body election of Pakistan. Sardar Attiq Ahmad Khan asserted that introduction of political workers in the Local Body government would ensure efficiency.

November 21, 2006

Barrister Sultan Mehmood Ch, President Jammu and Kashmir People's Muslim League (JKPML), Sardar Khalid Ibrahim, President Jammu and Kashmir Pakistan People's Party (JK-PPP), and Abdul Majid President Pakistan People's Party Azad Kashmir, boycotted the Pakistani government's hearing on Kashmir, protesting against the unilateral steps taken by

---

[63] "Appointment of Riaz as CJ in AJK SC according to constitution: Yasin," *Paktribune,* November 15, 2006.

[64] "AJK Local Body polls postponed for one year," *Paktribune,* November 15, 2006.

the Federal Government in Azad Kashmir. Sardar Ibrahim said that the Federal Government brought corrupt and dishonest people to the Azad Kashmir government.[65] Also, the federation intended to take decisions against the aspirations of Kashmiri people. Barrister Sultan said that a decision regarding the formation of the grand alliance against the AJK government would be announced. Criticising the government's policies regarding the Kashmir issue, Barrister Sultan said that opposition parties were not taken into confidence on the Kashmir dispute.

November 28, 2006

Shaukat Javed Mir, former Prime Minister AJK, announced that all opposition parties from Pakistan and AJK would be invited to the historic party convention to be held in London on 10th December. For him, the People's Muslim League was the single National Party in the territory. Mir was sure that that there was complete planning to rig the AJK election before the finalising the election schedule. He said that the Muslim Conference despite all out support from President Musharraf was able to get only about 0.4 million votes in the AJK election.[66] Commenting on the differences that emerged in the ranks of the opposition; Javed Mir said that it allowed the rulers to take decisions against the interest of the masses freely.

November 29, 2006

Sardar Sikandar Hayat, former Prime Minister of AJK announced that Sardar Muhammad Abdul Qayum Khan

---

65 "3 AJK Parties boycotts briefing on Kashmir issue," *Paktribune*, November 21, 2006.

66 "Party convention to prove turning point for restoration of true democracy: Shaukat Javed," *Paktribune*, November 28, 2006.

allowed for the return of real workers of the Muslim Conference. Sardar Muhammad Abdul Qayum Khan also held talks with Sardar Attique Ahmad Khan in this respect.[67] Former AJK Prime Minister further said that the disciplinary committee of the Muslim Conference should remove elected members of AJK Legislative Assembly from the party. However, Sardar Sikandar warned that the disciplinary committee of MC would face severe consequences in case of taking wrong decisions. He maintained that no disciplinary committee of MC could remove ideological MC workers from the party.

December 6, 2006

The elections of Azad Jammu and Kashmir Union of Journalists District Bhamber for the year 2007 were completed successfully in Samahani. Dr. Tariq Mehmood Shakir was nominated as President and Muhammad Ishaq Chaudhry was nominated as General Secretary. Sarfraz Kazmi was performing the duties of Election Commissioner, while the coordinators include Shahid Mehmood Mirza and Raja Ghulam Mohiuddin.[68]

December 13, 2006

All Parties Hurriyat Conference (APHC) Azad Jammu and Kashmir (AJK) Chapter and All Jammu Kashmir Muslim Conference Islamabad held protest demonstrations, rejecting the report of Member European Parliament (EP) on Kashmir.[69] The protest demonstration was held on the embassy road at

---

[67] "Sardar Qayyum has given green signal for return of real MC workers: Sikandar," *Paktribune,* November 29, 2006.

[68] "Election of AJK Union of Journalists completed," *Paktribune,* December 7, 2006.

[69] See "APHC AJK, MC to hold demo against current report of EP member," *Paktribune*, December 11, 2006.

10:00 am under the aegis of APHC AJK and MC Islamabad. Leaders of APHC and Raja Muhammad Yasin Khan, Adviser to Prime Minister AJK on Information and Political Affairs, took part in the protest demonstration. They presented a protest memorandum in the consulate of the European Union.

December 20, 2006

Demanding the National Accountability Bureau (NAB) to reopen cases of corrupt Kashmiri leaders, Parliamentary Leader of Mutahida Qaumi Movement (MQM) in the AJK Legislative Assembly, Tahir Khokar said that disqualification reference would be filed against the government. Tahir Khokar said that cases against 40 corrupt personalities of AJK who incurred loss worth of millions of rupees to the national exchequer, should be reopened.[70] Reference would be filed against AJK government for including corrupt elements in the cabinet and in the bureaucracy. It was hoped that Major General (retd) Tariq Shabbir, Chairman NAB, would take effective action against those who were involved in the corruption.

December 20, 2006

Sardar Attique Ahmad Khan, AJK Prime Minister, announced that the AJK government strove hard to strengthen its institutions. He said that the two-party system was running successfully in Azad Kashmir and opposition was being consulted in the reconstruction process in areas affected by the earthquake in October 2005.[71] His government was against the past traditions and gave due status to the opposition. He

---

[70] "AJK MQM demands reopening of cases against corrupt Kashmiri personalities," *Paktribune,* December 20, 2006.

[71] "AJK government for strengthening institutions: Attique," *Paktribune,* December 20, 2006.

clarified that in the first stage of the review sessions, the Muslim Conference would be included, while the opposition would be included in the second stage.

December 30, 2006

Ulema in Muzaffarabad protested over the demolition of a mosque as a result of the approved master plan for the reconstruction of AJK Capital. In a resolution passed in several capitals' mosques it was demanded from the AJK government to immediately rebuild all the demolished mosques at the same location.[72] Moulana Fazal Karim, Moulana Mufti Mehmood-ul-Hassan Mahsoodi and other ulema maintained that when some part of land had been allocated for the mosque then no kind of construction could be carried out at that place.

The AJK government finalised a plan to observe right of self-determination day on January 5, 2007. The United Nations Security Council had adopted a resolution on January 5, 1949 urging India to give right of self-determination to the Kashmiri people. On that day, the AJK government would arrange ceremonies in all the eight districts of Azad Kashmir, that would be addressed by Members' Legislative Assembly.[73] In Muzaffarabad, the President and Prime Minister of AJK would address the seminars.

---

72 "Ulema in Muzaffarabad protest over demolition of mosque," *Paktribune*, December 31, 2006.

73 "AJK government all set to observe right of self-determination day," *Paktribune*, December 31, 2006.

INDEX

Abbas Pur, 217
Abbasi, Altaf, 220
Abbasi, Mufti Mussarat Iqbal, 220
Abdullah, Sheikh, 130
Abbottabad, District, 139
Act of Parliament, 7
Afghanistan, 13, 29, 65, 77, 78, 138, 145, 150, 155
    American Intervention, 149
    Chinese approach, 145
    Proxy war, 193
    Western Intervention, 154
    US-led coalition forces air strikes, 66
    Western countries role, 154, 160
Afghan Mujahideen
    Chinese arms, 147,148
Afghan refugees, 13
Afro – Asian Conference, Algiers, 130
Agency system
    Abolition, 70
Afzal, Basharat, 209
Ahmed, Hafiz Hussain, 220
Ahmed, Mukhtar, 82
Ahmed, E, 46
Ahmed, Ghayoor, 179
Ahmed, Maulana Qazi Nisar, 68
Ahmed, Khaled, 75, 81, 83
Airport Facilities, 145
Akbar, Ch. Latif, 230, 233
Akbar, Sardar Amar, 214
Akhori, 91, 93
Akhtar, Haji Javed, 206
Aksai Chin, 125, 133, 152, 154
Alam, Sardar Muhammad, 184
Al-Badr, 42, 47
Al-Fiqh Al-Abwat, 17
Al-Hussaini, Agha Rahat, 68
Al-Jihad, 165
Al-Mansooran, 41
Al-Musawi, Syyid Abbas, 17, 22
Al-Rashid Trust (ART), 43, 44
Ali, Didar, 64
Ali, Hazrat, 63
Ali-Lt. Col.-Ehsan, 22
Ali, Manzoon, 76
Ali, Maulwi Hamza, 19
Ali in Abu Talib, 15
All Jammu and Kashmir Awami Conference, 221
All Jammu and Kashmir Muslim Conference, 204, 236
All Pakistan Minorities Alliance (APMA)
    Demands, 213
All Parties Hurriyat Conference Azad Kashmir and Pakistan Branch (APHC), 230-236
Aman Setu, Uri, 204
    CIA, 58
Amir of Tanzeem Ahle Sunnah Wal Jama'at, 68
Anchan, Ali Sher Khan, 17, 22, 25
Anjuman Ahle Tashia, 195
Anjuman Sipah Sahaba (ASSP) , 10.
Annan, Kofi, 87, 232
Anwar, Sardar Tahir, 217
Aparytae of Herodotus, 21
Appellate Court this is my Computer no Network Establishment, 186
Arabian Sea, 104
Arabs, 21

Argon, 35
Arif, Chaudhry, 166
Army Contingents
    Deployment during elections, 222
Arun III hydropower project, 89, 89n
Ashraf, Perviaz, 230
Asian Development Bank, 108, 138
Assassination, 10, 41
Assistant Registration Officer, 228
Astor, 5, 30, 66, 76, 77, 82, 186, 191
Astor Wazarat, 3
Atrocities, 7
Attiq, Pir, 209
Avian flu
    Threat, 142
Awami Tehrik, 217, 221
Ayub, Raja Iftikhar, 222
Azad Jammu and Kashmir (AJK) Cabinet, 222
    Ministers, 226-227
    Oath-taking ceremony, 226
    Prime Minister address, 227
    Portfolios, 226
    16- members, 226
AJK Constitution, 69, 167, 182-183, 230
AJK Interim Constitution Act 1974, 4, 166, 171, 224
Azad Jammu Kashmir Assembly, 166, 167
    Federation Power To Dissolve, 230
    Pakistan's exaggerated claims, 160, 161
    Resolution on Northern Areas, 181
    Self-rule, 184
    Sign the Karachi Agreement of 1949, 178
Azad Jammu and Kashmir Legislative Assembly elections, 220, 221
Allocation of minorities' seats, 213
    Breakthrough, 214
    By – Election, 204, 216, 229, 231
    Code of conduct, 215
    Constituencies, 219, 231
    Date, 220
    Independent Candidates, 221
    ID Cards, 216
    JKLF, 212
    PML candidates, 215
    PPP-AJK and Muslim Conference, 214
    PPP and PML (N) deal, 214
    Polling Stations, 222
    Results, 225
    Sardar Sikandar Hayat Khan withdrawal of his nomination papers, 218, 219
    Rules, 221
Azad Jammu & Kashmir Council (AJKC)
    Composition, 203
    Election, 167, 205, 207
    Tickets for candidates, 204, 205, 207
    Tenure, 203
AJK Muslim League
    Election manifesto, 219
AJK Ombudsman
    Role, 210
AJK Refugees
    Enrolment, 228
    Identity card, 228
Azad Jammu and Kashmir Union of Journalists District Bhamber election 2007, 236
Azar, 62
Aziz, Sartaz, 133
Aziz, Shaukat, 45, 126, 221

Babusar Pass, 135
Badakhshan, 15
Badar, Jahangir, 229
Baglihar Hydro Power Project, 120
Balhara, M.S, 42
Balochistan, 5, 6, 7, 8, 10, 32, 70, 91, 117, 152, 166, 198
Baltistan
- Anchan role, 22
- Black Day Celebration, 13
- Buddhism, 21
- Character, 13
- Conversion into, 17-20, 22, 125
- Cultural and political purges, 23, 24
- Cultural renaissance, 26
- Cultural ties, 14
- Rich Regacy, 14
- Demands, 11
- Denouncing Nur-Bakshia practice, 18
- Development funds, 14
- Dialect, 24
- Ehsan Ali Conquering, 22
- Exploitation mineral and forest resources, 13
- Foreign tourists visits, 13
- History, 21
- Identity erosion, 25
- Independence demand, 23
- Insufficient funds for the development, 13
- Islam influence, 24
- Isolation, 24
- Kashmiri influence, 24
- Language, 24, 26, 28
- Liberation, 12
- Links with Tibetan, 26
- Mullah Peshawar arrival, 18
- Muslim ruler invasion, 21-22
- Nur – Bakshia reassertion, 19-20
- Nur-Bakshia Sufi Order, 16, 21
- Origin, 22, 24, 25
- Pak annexalion, 19, 22, 23
- Pak betrayal, 196
- Persian influence, 24
- Persian Twelver Shia Cleric inroads, 21
- Population, 24, 34
- Protection Tibetan languages, 24
- Relationship with Ladakh, 23, 26
- Relationship between Little Tibets, 22
- Religious education in Iran & Iraq, 18
- River waters, 13
- Sectarian movement, 9
- Sectarian violence, 55
- Self rule & civil rights demands, 23
- Settlement Pathan problems, 13
- Tehrik-I-Jaffaria Pakistan (TJP), 25
- Tibetans rule, 21, 22
- Tibetan Script reivival, 25
- Villages, 24

Baltis' Buddhist, 17
Baltistan Students Federation (BSK), 11, 26
Balwaristan , 82, 103
- Concept, 11
- Ideology, 12

Balwaristan National Front (BNF), 11-13, 23, 100, 102,196
Balwaristan Times, the,
- Confiscation, 199

Bandipora, Muhammed Anwar Mir, 207
Bandits, 66
Bara Parang, 90
Baramulla, 41, 48
Barclays Plc, 47
Basantgarh, 41
Bashir, Mustafa, 215, 216
Batalik, 31
Behanjee, Farida, 207
Beijing, 6, 127, 130, 134, 140, 147
    Habib Bank, 144
Bema, 31
Bhatti, Shahbaz, 213
Basha Village, 105
Bhutto, Benazir, 30, 70, 205, 206, 207, 233
Bhutto, Zulfikar Ali, 5, 6, 70, 128, 130, 131, 185
Black Day in Gilgit & Baltistan, 13
Bo Yibo, 127
Board of investment, 145
Bokha's, Makpon, 21
Baloristan, 21
    Creation, 12
Boloristan Democratic Front (BDF), 12, 23
Bon religion, 28
Bonji, 58
Boundary Treaty, 4
Brelvi ideology, 78
Bridges
    Chinese Assistants to Pak for construction, 136
    Cost, 136
    Joint Venture, 136
Britain, 221
British Archives, 180
British India, 125, 135
Brokpa, 29, 31
Brown, Major, 178
Buddhism, 16, 17, 28, 32
    Tibetan, 31
    Brokpa, 31
    Shinas, 32
    Stupas & Monuments, 17
    Tantric, 17
Budshah Chowk
    Gun-battle, 41, 42
Bureaucracy, 72, 188, 197
Burki, Irshad, 205
Burushaski, 32, 33
    Shina Lingua Franca, 27
Bypass construction
    Chinese aid to Pakistan, 136

Canada, 221
Carius, Alexander, 87
Caste
    Affinities, 14
    Social division, 14
Ceas-fire line, 22, 23, 135
Central Asia, 8, 138, 153, 155
    Plan shelved to extend Karakoram Highway, 138
Central Asian States, 79
    Pak-China-Uzbekistan Agreement, 138
    Sunni tradition instruction, 15
Chak dynasty, 16
Chakan, 204
Chakma, 90
    Language, 90
Chakoti-Uri, 204
Chang-Pas, 135
Charter of Democracy, 214
Chaqchan of shrine, 17, 20
Chashma
    Dam, 117
    Power plant, 140
    Right Bank Canal Project, 91

Chatter Pari, 114
Chaudhry, Ali Shan, 226
Chaudhry, Iftikhar Muhammad, 107
Chaudhry, Justice Muhammad Rees Akhtar, 203, 218, 225, 229, 234
Chaudhry, Brrister Sultan Mahmood, 210, 211, 213, 215, 216, 217, 219-221, 225, 234
Chalungkha, 24
Chibhalis, 28
Chief Election Commissioner (CEC), 210, 216, 218, 221, 224
  Direction, 229, 234
  Notification, 221, 222
Chilas, 5, 8, 33, 65, 66, 76, 77, 82, 97, 106
  Darrel dialect, 29
  Shina dialect, 27
China, 23, 25, 28, 78, 79, 81, 94, 182
  Development plans, 156
  Engineers Killing, 150, 153
  Naval outpost, 153
  Nuclear and missile equipment, KKH base for the transfer to Pakistan, 152
  Regional Disparities, 156
  SARA threat, 79
  Transportation links with Central South West & South Asia, 156
China international water & Electric Corporation (CWE), 109
China Western Development Strategy (WDS), 143
China-Pak road links
  Closure, 148
Chinese terrorist
  Action, 149
Chitral, 11,15, 22, 23, 28, 29,30.
  Khowar mother tongue, 27
Chitral Scouts
  Unrest over recruitment, 13
Chuchot, 24, 34
Chughtai, Dewan, 215, 216
Chiktan. 17
Chulichen, 31
Civil rights
  Demand, 11, 23
Civil Society Movement South Asia, 89
Code of conduct, 215, 229
Code of laws, 4
Cold War, 159, 160, 172
Colombia, 94
Communication Centers for HM
  Damage, 43
Compensation, 101-103, 106, 111, 112, 119
Conference in Islamabad (1993)
  Ladakh Scholars Participation, 26
Constituencies of Azad Kashmir
  Numbers, 222
Constitutional Amendments, 7
Constitutional Petitions, 183
Conversion, 19, 20, 22, 25
  Factors, 17-20
Corporations, 108
Corruption, 108, 237
Court
  AJK High Court, 8, 9, 13, 23, 181
  Pak Supreme Court, 69, 71, 181-183, 187
Custom Duty
  Stop its collection, 145
Custom revenue collection,
  Decline, 79
Curriculum Controversy, 55-56, 61-68, 83
Da Bagh, Poonch, 204

Dabelko, Geoffrey D, 87
Daily times, the, 46-47
Dar, Ghulam Nabi, 41
Dardic, 27, 28
Dards, 21-22, 33
Dialect, 28-32
Dardistan, 28
Darel, 5, 30
Dartsik, 31
Darot, 58
Dasu-Sazin, 94
Dawn, the, 72, 138, 187, 194.
DESCON Ltd., 109
Dera Ismail Khan, 140
Dha, 31
Dhangali Bridge, 112
Diamer District, 5, 8, 76, 83, 136
Diamer - Basha Dam, 84, 91-108, 115, 117, 119, 137, 140, 189
    Anti-NWFP, 121
    Blacklisting, 107, 108
    Breadth and length, 96
    Construction, 104-105
    Contract, 107-108
    Controversy, 94-95
    Corruption, 108
    Displacement, compensation and employment, 89
    Donor agencies, 107
    Environment impacts, 103-104
    Estimated cost, 107
    Financial assistance, 107
    Government responses, 106
    Height, 94
    Inter-provincial tensions, 108, 121
    Location, 94-97
    Mega reservoir store (MAF), 94, 106
    Power generation capacity, 94
    Profits, 98-99
    Reduction in height, 106
    Reservoir area, 94
    Royalty, 97-101
    Studies, 107
    Technical difficulties, 94-96, 107
    Tender documents, 107
    Tussle between IFI's and Corporations, 108
    Vision 2025, 115
    World Bank loan, 108
Dihang, 227
Disease, 126
Displacement, 101-102, 106, 111-113, 119
Divine Love
    Nur Bakshia emphases, 17
Doda district, 41
Dogras, 5, 8, 10, 28
Dom, 10, 14
Domas, 33
Dras, 32, 35
Drugs trafficking, 126, 151
Dry port, 144
Duber Valley, 29
Dughlat, Maja Haider, 16, 21

EarthQuake (1974), 103-104
    Jammu & Kashmir, 160
    Pakistan (2005), 40,203
    POK (2005), 66, 137, 160, 169, 172, 217, 237
    Cross-Loc Joint relief Operation, 170
    Deaths, 40, 169, 203-204
    Incidents, 40-42
    Jehadi group presence in rescue operations, 43, 46
    Men and material loss, 40
    Pak Army role, 225

Relief operation, 39-40, 204
Security arrangement, 40
Shelters to the survivors, 205
Terrorist crusade, 40
Terrorist training camps damages, 42-43
East Pakistan problem, 131
East Turkestan, 147
East Turkestan Information Center (ETIC), 149
East Turkestan Islamic Movement (ETIM),
Ban, 149
Election Campaign, 211, 217, 220
Election Commission Azad Jammu and Kashmir, 205, 218, 221, 229, 236
Notification, 214, 215
Election Commission of Pakistan
Directives, 228
Election manifesto, 212, 219
Election Ordinance 1970, 224
Election rigging, 216-217, 222, 235
Electoral Alliance, 219
Electoral Coalition, 217
Electoral list, 224
Electoral Rolls Act 1974, 228
Employment, 102-103
Energy output, 110
England, 112
Environment hazards, 96
Issues, 103-105
Etikaaf, 20
Etikess, 19
Ethnic group, 10, 14, 27
European Parliament (EP) Report on Kashmir, 236-237
European Union, 237
Report, 161, 169-173
Export Processing Zone, 144
Farooq, Hazrat Umar, 62
Farooq, Mirwaiz Umar, 133, 134
Federally Administered Northern Areas (FANA), 5
Federally Administered Tribal Agencies (FATA) of Pakistan, 4, 60, 82
Federation Dissolution power of AJK legislative Assembly, 230
Farooqi, Maulana Nazir, 220
Fidayeen, 41
Fiqh, 17
Flooding method, 118
Foreign office (FO's), 80, 188
Foreign policy, 87
Foreign policy Pakistan, 77
Frazer, Lt. Col. M.S., 179
Free Trade Agreement (FTA) Urumqi, 2005, 143
Freedom Day, 13
Friday Times, The 57
Frontier Constabulary (FC), 58
Frontier Crimes Regulation (FCR), 4, 190
Abolition, 5, 70, 185
Imposition, 184
Fundamental rights, 70, 183
Denial, 69, 182, 187
Protection, 71-72
Supreme Court, 69
Violation, 159

Gabur– Doro– Yudai, 30
Gahkuch, 8
Gammon Pakistan ltd., 109
Gandhara, 21
Civilization, 28
Garver, John, 132, 156
Gas pipeline
Chinese investment, 80
General Election in Azad Kashmir,

207-208 See also AJK Assembly Elections
Geneva, 196
German-Austrian Company, 139
Ghanche, 8
Creation, 6
Ghazi Brotha Hydel Power Project
Chinese assistance, 140
Ghizr, 6, 8, 15, 138
Gilgit, 4, 5, 7, 8, 22, 23, 30, 33, 34, 58, 62, 65, 70, 78, 82, 83, 97, 101, 105, 125, 135, 137, 144, 145, 152, 153, 179, 184, 185
Black Day Celebration, 13
British conspiracy, 178
Chinas strategic aims to air base, 153
Chinese official visit, 127-128
Chinese tourists and traders, 137
Cultural ties, 114
Dards speaking, 28
Demands, 11
Development funds, 14
Division, 5
DHQ Hospital in, 72, 187
Geo-strategic location, 77
Invasion, 15
Liberation, 12
Pak betrayal, 196
Rebellion, 178
Rich historical legacy, 14
Sectarian population, 76
Sectarian violence, 55, 66, 84
Security arrangement at police checkpoints, 150
Sinha Language, 27, 29
Separation from NEFA, 4
Settlement Pathans problem, 13
Shina language, 27, 29
Separated from NEFA, 4
Gilgit Agency, 3, 4, 5, 178
Gilgit Meeting of NALC members with journalists from India and Pakistan, 194-195
Gilgit Scout (later converted to the Northern light infantry), 4, 178
GilgitWazarat, 3
Gilgit Baltistan demands, 14
Gilgit Baltistan National Alliance (GBNA), 195-196
Gilgit Baltistan National conference (GBNC), 12, 23
Gillani Syed, Ghulam Murtaza, 226
Global Water Partnership, (GWP), 93
Gomal Zam, 93
Grand Trunk Road, 135
Groundwater, 117, 119
Guerrilla warfare, 148
Gujar, 28
Gultari, 24, 34
Gupis, 77
Guru, Mohammad Afzal
Demonstration against the death sentence Parliament attack, Memorandum to UN observer office, 232
Guru Power Project, 142
Gwadar, 80, 137, 138, 152, 153
Gwadar Dalbandin railway
Chinese aid, 152
Gwadar port, 153

Habib Bank, 47, 144
Hai, Maulana Abdul, 208
Haider, Raja Farooq, 231
Haider, Iqbal, 67
Hajipur-Uri, 204

Hajong tribes, 90
Hamdani Amir Kabir Syed Ali, 15, 16
Hameed, Maulana Qazi Shahid, 220
Hamid, Khan Abdul, 196
Hanu, 31
Hara, 30
Haramosh, 29
Harkat - ul - Ansar, 165
Harkat–ul–Jihadi–al–Islami (HUJI-BD), 48
Harkat-ul-Mujahideen (HUM), training centers, 42
Hasnain, Mohammad, 25-26
Hassanabdal, 137
Havelian, 139
Herald Report, 68
Hizbul Mujahideen (HM) 42, 48, 164-165
HM recruitment camp at Jungle-Mangal (POK) damage, 42
Himalayas, 16, 22, 24, 104, 131
Hindu revivalism, 16
Hindustan, 15, 16
Hotan, 150
Hu Jintao, 133
Human Rights, 51, 230
    Activities, 199
    Organisation, 230
    Violation, 159, 197, 222
Human Rights Watch (HRW) 2006, 161-169
    European union report, 161, 169-173
Hunza, 5, 15, 29, 30, 77, 135, 153
    Burushaski and Domaaki language, 27
    Chinese claim, 154
    Chinese position, 127
    Chinese threat, 135
    China-Pak against, 129
    Dardic speaking people in, 28
    Forceful abolition, 6
    Sign instrument of Accession to Pakistan, 178-179
    Valley, 28, 33
Hunza - Xinjiang border, 129
Hussain, Chaudhary Shujaat, 153
Hussain, Raja Najabat, 205
Hussain, Sardar Mohammad, 206, 215
Hussain, Syed Mujahid, 224
Hyat, Sardar Sikandar, 207, 216, 218, 223, 224, 232, 235

Ibex, 11
Ibn-e-Ziyad, 63
Ibrahim, Chaudhry Muhammad Akbar, 226, 230
Ibrahim, Sardar Khalid, 234-235
Ahl-I-Hadith Sect of Sunni, 18
Imamas, 25
Imam, Husain, 18
Imanbargabs construction, 20
Imported goods, 145
Importers facilities, 145
Independent Jammu & Kashmir Elections, 212, 216
India, 12, 23, 34, 78, 89, 120, 125, 152, 182,
Indian intelligence Agencies, 230
Indian Ministry of External Affairs, 128
Indian Ocean, 153-154
Indo-Aryan, 27, 28,
Race, 32
Indo-Bangladesh relation Gange Rivers, 90
Indo-Nepal Mahakali River Treaty, 90

Indo-Pak relations
Bilateral negotiations, 133
Composite Dialogue, 50
Confidence building measures, 48, 50-51
Relation improvement, 154
Relation Loc official's agreements, 204
Peace process, 50-57
Simla Agreement, 131-132
Relation Rawalpindi talks, 128
Indo-Pak wars, 24, 130
Ceasefire, 135
Indus Basin, 117
Indus –Kohistan dardic dialect, 29
Indus-River, 27, 29, 140
Indus-Water, 13
Indus Valley, 29, 94, 95
Inscriptions
Discovery, 105
Institute of Policy Studies Islamabad, 73, 180, 195
Instrument of Accession,
Maharaja's decision to sign, 178
Instrument of Accession to Pak Nagar Hunza signed, 178, 179
Insurgency, 159, 168
Intelligence Agencies, 44
Inter marriages, 23
ID Cards, 216
Internally Displaced People (IDP), 169
International Association for Ladakh Studies (IALS), 127
International Crisis Group Report, 75-76, 178-179
IFIS, 107
International Islamic terrorist groups
Network, 43
International Islamic terroristsm
Major act, 46,47
Iqbal, Tahir, 214
Iqbal, Zafar, 45
Iran, 15, 18, 138
Revolution, 25
Iraq, 18, 155
Irrigation, 118-119
Inflow of water, 1117
Ishkoman, 5
Dilect, 27
Valley, 29
Islam, 10, 14, 15, 34
Islamiat, 62-65
Islamic Development Bank (IDB), 108
Islamic front, 41
Islamic fundamentalism, 155
Chinese fears, 140
Islamic militancy, 39
Islamic Organsations or sectarian organisations
Zia regine, 10
Islamic sectarianism, 155
Ismailia
Faith, 15
Population, 14
Ismali, 76, 191, 195
Israel, 89
Ishaq, sahibzada, 229

Jagirdari system
Pak government abolition, 5
Jaglot, 58
Jaish-e-Mohammed (JEM), 42, 43, 47, 77
Jamaat-e-Islam Azad Kashmir, 43
Central working committee, 228-229
Jamaat-ul-Dawa, 44, 165
Jamiat-ul-Muhahedin, 165

Jamiat ulema Islam
  Central committee, 208-209
Jammu and Kashmir
  Insurgency, 159
Jammu & Kashmir Jamiat ul ulema Islam (JuI), 208
Jammu & Kashmir Liberation Front (JKLF) 102, 196-197
  efforts for re-unification with Yaseen Malik group, 212
  election manifesto, 212
  Ideology, 211-212
  Policy and Planning Committee (PPC), ten-point agenda, 211
Jammu and Kashmir Mass movement, 230
  Srinagar meeting, 207
Jammu and Kashmir Peoples Party, 221
Jammu and Kashmir Peoples Muslim League, 217
Japan, 94
JD
  Adoption of quake-hit children, 45
  Relief operation efforts during earthquake, 44
Jee, Farida Bahan, 230
Jharal Mirza Muhammad Shafiq, 226
Jhelum River, 109, 112
Jiang Zemin, 132
Jihad or Jihadi, 40, 46, 77, 121
  Ban, 81
  Campaign in J & K, 40
  Earthquake relief efforts, 44
  Fomenting violence in J & K, 160
  Growing power, 44
  Infrastructure damage reconstruction, 43, 46
  Organization, 77
  Pak Policy, 198
Jirgas, 5, 68
Joint Secretary of Kashmir Affairs Division, 5
Joint ventures, 136, 139
Jordan River conflicts, 89
Judiciary
  Independence, 71
  role, 107
Justice Ministry, 60

Kabul, 139
Kadir, Ismail, 149
Kafiristan , 28
Kalabagh Dam, 84, 91, 93, 109, 117
Kandia, 29
Kaptai Dam, 90, 90n
Karachi, 60, 133, 138, 228
  Bombing, 83
Karachi Agreement of 1949, 4, 180
  Pakistan and AJK signing, 178
Karachi Port, 137, 143
Karachi Trade Fair, 143
Karakoram Highway (KKH), 23, 24, 28, 66, 78-79, 82, 96, 102, 103, 105, 125, 129, 136, 141-143, 147, 155, 198
  ADB loan, 138
  Chinese aid for repairing, 136
  China and Pak role, 152
  Chinese engineers killing, 153
  Chinese interests, 152-153
  Chinese soft loans, 137
  Chinese television documentary, 136
  Cost, 96
  Economic significance, 79-80
  First passenger bus service linking Gilgit with Kashgar, 137

Link between Gwadar and, 153
Major zones of Islamic revivalism in Xiniang, 148
Mou between Pakistan China for up grading, 138
Review of security arrangement, 150
Special postal stamps release, 136
Strategic importance, 125-126
Threat to India, 152
Transit facility, 145
Truck service, 137
25th Anniversary, 136
Karakoram nation, 12
Karakoram National Movement (KNM), 12, 23
Karakoram Pass, 125
Karakoram Students Organization (KSO), 11
Karbala, 63
Kargil, 17, 22, 23, 25, 26, 31, 32, 192
Population, 34-35
Kargil conflict of 1999, 80, 133, 197
Kargil-Skardu Road
Opening, 199
Kashgar (Kashi), 78, 125, 135, 137, 139
Kashgar Prefectural Administration, 143
Kashgar-Islamabad flights, 150
Kashgar-Khunjerab-Sost-Gilgit, 137
Kashmir
Influence, 168
Nur-Baksh Order, 16
Proxy war, 193
Terrorist activities, 197
Valley, 16, 191, 192
KANA – Kashmir Affairs and Northern areas, 72, 100, 105, 168, 185-186, 189-190, 193
Kashmir dispute, 4, 51, 58, 80, 95, 100, 120, 128, 129, 154, 188, 195, 222, 235
Chinese Policy, 131-134, 147
International Public Opinion, 159
Pakistan final say, 193
Self-determination, 132, 238
Kashmiri
Commonalities among, 10
Refugees, 208, 222
Kashmir's Freedom Movement, 211, 219, 221, 225
Kashmir Labour Party and Liberation Front, 221
Kathmandu, 26
Kazmi, Sarfraz, 236
Kazmi, Syed Abbas, 26
Kesar, King, 21
Kesar epic, 26
Khirghiz, 28
Khalid bin Walid, 63
Khaplu, 8, 24
Khan, Abdul Hamid, 199
Khan, Khan Abdul Ghafar, 220
Khan, Agha, 15
Kiani, Justice Raja Ashraf, 210
Khan, Ayub 127, 128, 130
Khan, Raja Faisal Azad, 213
Khan, Muhammad Anwar, 214, 224, 226
Khan, Amanullah, 102, 197, 211, 212
Kan, Sardar Atiq Ahmed, 206-207, 217, 219, 221-224, 226, 227, 230, 234, 236, 237
Khan, Sardar Bahadar, 217
Khan, Basheer Ahmed, 102
Khan, E-M, 75
Khan, Sardar Ghulam Sadiq, 206

Khan, Ismail, 84
Khan, Sardar Mansoor, 217
Khan, Riaz Mohammed, 143
Kasim, Moulana Fazal, 238
Khan, Sardar Muhammed Abdul Qayum, 235, 236
Khan, Shahbaz, 144, 145
Khan, Dr. Muhammed Najeeb, 226
Khan, Raja Muhammed Nassem 226
Khan, Malik Muhammed Nawaz, 219, 226
Khan, Raja Naseer Ahmed, 226
Khan, Sagheer, 211, 212
Khan, Sardar Sikandar, 210
Khalid, Sardar Syab, 217
Khan, Raja Muhammed Yasin, 227, 231, 237
Khan, Raja Zulqarnain, 225
Khandaq, 62
Khanqabs, 16, 19-20
Khaplu, 16, 19
Khapulu, 34
Kharak, 113
Kharmang, 18, 24, 34
Khateeb of the Imamia Mosque, 61
Khatoon, Gyal, 22
Khawara, 209
Khoirata, 68, 210, 211
Khoja Community, 15
Khokar, Tahir, 237
Khotan (Hotan), 125
Khulfa-e-Rashideen, 62
Kunjerab, 138, 142, 143
  Pass, 125, 135, 140, 149, 150
Khurmang, 29
Khurram Valley, 60
Kidnapping, 199
Kiris, 16
Koh-I-Ghizer, 5
Kohistan, 83
Kotli Constituency, 219
Kremin, 10, 14
Kubrawiya Sufi order, 15
Kuh, 15
Kulgam shrine attack, 41
Kulhand, 41
Kaman, 204
Kunar Valley, 29
Kupwara sector, 42
Kuran Tangi, 93
Kyani, Sales, 205
Kyirs, 32

Ladakh, 11, 14, 16, 21, 23, 24, 25, 28, 29, 31, 32, 34, 125, 142
  Scouts, 24
  Wazarat, 22
Ladakhis, 23, 24, 31, 32, 35
Lahmeyer International, 107-108
Lahore, 26
Languages, 111
  Arabic, 25, 62
  Balti, 28, 1
  Burushaski, 19, 27, 33
  Domaaki, 27, 33
  Gujari, 28
  Islamiat, 62, 63
  Kashmiri, 28, 32
  Kohistan, 27
  Khowar, 27, 29, 197
  Ladakhis, 26
  Non-Dardic (Indo-Aryan), 33
  Persian, 24
  Punjabi, 25, 27, 28, 192
  Pushto, 19, 27, 28,
  Shina, 19, 27, 29, 33
  Tibetan, 25, 26, 34
  Turkish, 24
  Urdu, 25, 27, 28, 32, 33, 62, 63, 91

Wakhi, 191
Lalon Galla, 41
Lalung, 31
People's opposition, 120-121
Pak vision, 91
Lashkar-e-Jhangvi, 77
Lashkar-e-toiba (LeT), 41, 42, 43, 47, 58, 77, 164
Law Ministry, 145
Legal Framework Order (LFO), 100, 186
Leh, 25, 26, 34, 35, 95
Population, 24
Lha (Protector of God), 17
Li Xiannian, 152
Line of Control (LOC) 12, 39-40, 42, 48, 121, 125, 197, 204
Little Tibets, 21, 22
Local Body Election postpone, 234
Local Police
Deployment during elections, 222
Local Rajas control of the people, 5
London , 178
Lone, Dr. Ghulam, 41
Love
Nur-Bakshia emphasis, 117

Madad, Sultan, 97
Madrassas, 149
Cause of Sectarian violence, 75
Damage, 45
Maharaja of Jammu and Kashmir, 178
Mahmud, Ershad, 73
Mahsoodi, Moulana Mufti Mehmood-ul-Hussan, 238
Mahsum, Hassan, 150
Majeed, Abdul, 230, 234
Majlis-e-Shura, 59, 186
Makpon, 22
Dynasty, 21
Malacca Strarts,136-137
Malik, Shama, 204, 226
Mallick, Abdul Majeed, 133
Manus or Desi – Si - Manus, 32
Manawar, 58
Mangla Dam Raising Project (MDRP)91, 117, 119, 166
Agreement, 110
Annual energy output, 110
Anti-Mangla Dam Extension committee (AMDEC), 111, 116
Availability for Water Irrigation, 110
Compensation, 111-112
Construction, 108
Cost, 111
Displacement and Resettlement, 111, 113
Height, 109-111
hydel profits, 110
Joint Ventures, 109
Resettlement, 111-113
Royalty, 111-114
Storage, 107, 110
Mansehra, 58
Maqbool, Khalid, 144
Maqpoon, Raja Hussain Khan
Kidnapping, 199
Martial Law Zone, 185
Martial rule, 10, 185
Maskeen, Malik Muhammad, 107
Mazhar, chaudhry, 205
Me-Phang, 25
Meditation
Nur-Bakshia emphasis, 17
Mega Dam Project Opposition, 189
Mega Water Project
Controversal, 91

Opposition, 89
Mian, Ajmal, 100
Middle East, 137
Ministry of Kashmir Affairs, 4,9,71,171,180,185-187
Mintaka Pass, 125,135
Mir, Ghazi, 17
Mir, Ghulam Hassain, 41
Mir, Shaukat Javed, 235
Mir of Hunja, 5-6
Mirpure, 112,113,165
Division, 208
Mirja, Shahid Mehmood, 236
Miskeen, Malik Muhammad, 68
Model village building, 106
Mohiuddein, Dewan Ghulam, 206,237
Molai, 10,15
Molagi, 10
Molasim, 10
Monineed, Farooq-wa-Amiral, 62
Mons (Indo-Aryan Group) 21, 32
Montreal Enginering Company Consultants, 104
Mosque
Cause of sectarian violence, 75
Ulema protest against demolition, 238
Mountbatten, Lord, 178
Mughal, 21
Mughal, Sajjad, 225
Mughli or Maulai sect, 15
Muhammad, Ghulam, 194
Muharram, 18
Mujlahids, 18
Munda, 93
Murree, 167
Murtaja, Syed Ghulam, 222
Musharraf, Pervej, 43, 44, 46, 50, 58-60, 71, 79, 83, 84, 93, 105, 110, 120, 132, 149, 161, 186, 204
Mughni or Islamic Charity Organization remittance
Muslim Conference, 203, 206, 207, 219, 221, 223, 225, 235, 236, 238,
Demands, 214
Differences, 215,236
Parliamentary Board, 207,231,
Victory in the elections, 227
Muslim Conference (S), 232
ML, 208
Muslim Sects, 18
Muthahida Kashmir Peoples National Party, 221
Majlis-e-Amal (MMA), 208-209, 220,225,229
Mutahida Qaumi Party of Gilget and Baltistan, 12,222
Myanmar, 151
Nadwat-1 Islamiya, Nur-Bakshia, 19
Nagar, 5, 29, 30, 33, 76, 77, 179
Signing instruction of accession to Pakistan, 178, 179
Naji, Nawaz Khan, 23
Naltar Power Project, 142
Naltar River Hydro Power Station, Gilgit.
Simo–Pak Agreement, 139-140
Namgyal Gyalpojamyang, 22
Naqvi, Syed Mujahid Hussain, 223
Narmada Valley Development Project,
Agitations, 89
Nathu La
Chinese attack, 130
National Accountability Bureau (NAB), 237
National Archives, New Delhi, 180
National Assembly, 60
National Finance Commission, (NFC), 193

National Highway Authority of India (NHAI), 96
National Trade Corridor (NTC) Project
World Bank aid, 138
National Water Development Agency, 398
Nauseri-Tithwal, 204
Naveed, Iftikhar, 231
Nawa-I-Sufiya, 19
Nayyar, Rafique, 211
Nehru, Jawaharlal, 129
Nepal, 89
Niazi, Sardar Abdul Qayyum, 217, 226
Nisar, Qazi, 68
NATO, 83
NGO
Threat, 47
North West Frontier Province (NWFP),9, 13, 42, 43, 58, 60, 66, 74, 83, 84, 91, 97, 98, 102, 105, 117, 184, 185
Separation from Gilgit Agency, 4
Textbook Board, 65
Northern Areas (NA)
Administrative issues, 184-190
Analysis, 198- 199
And AJK relations, 180-181
Appellate Court, 186
Area, 3
Atrocities, 7
AJK High Court Ruling, 8, 13
AJKS Objection, 7
AJK Supreme Court, 181
AJK talk of sharing commonalities with the people, 110
Changes in the Status, 185-186
Chinese investment, 80, 142
Chinese Policy, 126
Commentaries, 180
Debate in Pakistan becoming fifth province of the Federation,7
Demand an "AJK" type of administration, 195-196
Demographic profile, 75-78
Dialects, 27
Differ from both the Kashmir Valley and AJK, 191-192
District and Capital, 7
Dogra Maharaja deal, 8
Enthusiasm about absorption, 8
Failure of the Governance, 73-75
Federal control, 193
Frontier Crimes Regulation (FCR), 184-185
NCNA Role, 187
Fundamental rights denied, 182, 187
Geo-strategic importance, 78-82
Historial Issues, 178-183
Languages spoken, 27-28
Legal issues, 7, 180-183
Linkage between Kashmir and, 191
KANA Control, 185, 186, 189-190
Ministry of Kashmir Affairs interest 9
Options, 9, 193-194
Pak double talk over the status, 9
Pakistan exaggerated claims, 160-161
Pak government administration, 4

Pakistan's Jihadi policy fall out, 198
Pakistan Occupation, 3
Pak Supreme Court verdict, 180-183
Plebiscite, 3, 4
Political issues, 191-197
Political Leadership, 192
Political turmoil, 3, 8-9
Prefer to Join AJK, 7
Population, 3
Reforms packages, 6, 14, 186-187, 190
Sectarian Violence, 8-9, 55-58, 192
Self-rule, 187
Separatist movements, 199
Separation from AJK, 4, 8
Sunni and Shia Population, 191-192
Total Independence from Pakistan, 196
US deal, 8

Northern Areas Council (NAC), 9, 70, 185, 190
See also NALC

Northern Area Advisory Council, 100, 145, 190

NALA, 126, 188

Northern Areas Legislative Council, (NALC) 44, 71, 97, 100, 102, 186, 187, 190, 194-195, 197
Adviser, 186-187
Demands, 187-188
Election, 74-75
Expansion, 186
Highest decision making body, 72
Power, 72
Powerless, 74
Proceedings, 187

Northern Areas syllabus Issue Committee, 65

Northern Areas Transport Corporation (NATCO) 79-80
Bus traveling, 65

Northern Areas United Front (NAUF), 23
Conference, 12

Northern Frontier of Kashmir Partion
Routes, 125

Nowgam, 41

Nuclear explosion of 1998, 73

Nur-Baksh,
Syed Muhammed founder of Nur-Bakshia
Baltis denouncing, 18
Doctrines sources, 17
Pioneering work, 19
Sufi Order, 14, 16, 21
Syed Muhammed, 15-16
Syed Muhammed, 19
Founder of the Nur-Bakshia, 15
Syed purge and exile, 16
Population, 19
Teachings, 19
Dar Ul-Ulema, 19
Educated Baltis rejection, 19
Religions Schools, 19
Faith, 35
Sect of Shiasm, 35

Nurbakshi, 76

Operation sledge, 22

Overseas Economic Cooperation Fund (OECF, Japan), 108

Paharis, 28

Pakistan Army, 43-49, 51, 63, 165

Firing Shias, 10
Role in earthquake, 225
Pakistani Army General Headquarters, Rawalpindi, 167
Pakistan Citizen Act 1951, 228
Pakistan Constitution, 7, 98-99
Pakistan Council of Research in Water Resources (PCRWR), 119
Pakistan Intelligence Agency, 47, 151, 163, 164, 197, 199
Pakistan JUI Jammu and Kashmir, 221
Pakistan Muslim League (PML) 102, 139, 194, 208, 214
PML (N), 194
PML-Q, 71, 74
Pak National Assembly, 171
Pakistani Mujahideen, 149
Pakistani Senate
Jiangs address, 132
Pakistani Military's Force Command Northern Areas (FCNA), 187
Pakistan People Party (PPP), 194, 205, 206, 221
PPP and PML (N) deal, 214
Member resignations, 206
Discipline, 207
Change in leadership, 206
PPP Azad Kashmir for Elections
Submission of application to Chief Election Commission regards registration, 210
Pakistani Political Agent in Gilgit, 178
Pakistan Central Board of Revenue (CBR), 145
Pakistani Water Security, 198
Pakistani Water Vision, 93
Pakistan – Occupied Kashmir (POK or Azad Jammu and Kashmir (AJK) 194, 196
Chinese Interests, 153, 154
Implication, 154-155
Political/Constitutional developments a Chronology, 203-238
Seminar for integration with, 15
Palolo, 21, 34
Pamirian, 33
Panchayats, 5
Para Military forces
Deployment during the election, 222
Pari, 58
Partition of India, 23
Pathans settlement, 13
PLA Navy, 153
Peoples Party (PP), 203, 211
PPC
Advice to the Central Executive Committee (CEC), 212
Persia, 16
Peshawar, 228
Phalura, 29
Pharol, 24
Plebiscite, 3, 4, 9
Political Parties Obtain
Copies of Code of Conduct, 229
Pollution
Water, 119
Postal Ballot Papers, 218
Pothi, Chaudhry Hameed, 205, 206
Power
Generation Capacity, 94-95, 98, 104-105
Grid Stations, 114
Projects, 120, 139
Simo-Pak Agreement of Power

Station, 139-140
Royalty, 105
Station, 99
Tariff, 113-114
Transmission, 95
Pre-Buddhistic Bon Customs, 26
President, 5, 222, 226
Presidential Election, 224
Presidential Order No. 3 of 1991, 98
Prime Minister, 222, 236
Address to The Azad Kashmir Cabinet, 227
Prime Minister Advisers, 222
Prophets, Holy, 62, 63, 217
Provincial Election Commissioners of directions, 228
Proxy war, 193
Ptolemy's Byaltae, 21, 34
Punial, 5, 15, 30, 76, 77
Punjab, 13, 58
Textbook Board, 65
Punjabi Youth movement agent, 11
Punjabi's 22, 25
Purigs , 24, 28, 34
Purig-Pass, 22, 26, 35
Qadir, Shah Ghulam, 226
Qadir, Sanalluah, 226
Qasim Port, 143
Qayum, Sardar Muhammed Abdul, 209, 216
Quaid, 213
Quake-hit Childern
Colonies setting up, 45
Government ban adoption, 45
JD and other groups adoption, 45
Qayum group and Sikandar group rift, 232
Quddus, Haji Addul, 102, 194
Quetta, 59, 228
Quran, 226
Rahman , Hafizur, 194
Rail Network, 139
Chinese investment, 80
Rain water harvesting , 119
Rajajas, 5
Rakhiot Bridge, 94
Rana, Muhammed Amir, 45
Rawalakot-Poonch, 204
Bus service inauguration, 218
Rawalpindi, 13, 65, 68, 128, 143, 152, 167, 199
Rawalpindi-Gilgit road, 135
Reform Package, 6, 14, 70-72
Refugee Problem, 168, 223
Registration Officers, 228
Rehman, Pir Attiq ur, 208
Rehman, Maulana Fazlur, 220
Rehman, Mufti ur, 205
Rehmani, Muhammed Farooq, 23, 232
Relay, Muzaffar, 97
Religions Group
ban, 46
Resettlement or replacement, 96, 106, 119
RAW, 58
Residency, 179
Resident, 185
Creation, 5
Political agents, 5
Power, 5
Resident Commissioner, 7
Returning Officers at polling Station, 218
Revenue Commissioner, 5
Right of Self-determination Day on January 5, 2007, 238
Right to Vote, 11
Rizvi, Agha Ziauddin, 61, 64, 65
Rizvi, Allama, 81
Ringla, 220

Robbery, 66, 150
Rock Carvings
  Discovery, 105
  Protection, 25

Rom, 30
Rongdu, 24. 29, 34
Ronu, 10, 14
  Caste, 30
Roy, Arundhati, 118
Royalty, 13, 84, 97-101, 105, 107, 110-114

SARS, 79, 142
Sectarian Violence, 9-10, 20, 55-68, 101, 192
  Assassination of leaders, 10
  Controversy over textbooks, 55, 61-68, 83
  Demographic profile, 75-78
  Factors, 55- 56, 69-75
  Failure of the Government, 73-75
  ICG Report, 58
  Jirga role in peace process, 67-68
  Member of killings, 57-58, 61, 66
  Madrassa factor, 75
  Mosque factor, 75
  Pakistani firing, 10
  Pakistani burning, 10
Sighting of Moon controversy, 57, 61
Sachal Engineering Works Ltd, 109
Saeed, Hafiz Muhammed, 44
Safavid dynasty, 16
Sandra Postel of the Global Water Policy Project, 87
Sangriyal, 137
Sardar M. Ashraf D Baluch Ltd, 109
Sardar Sarover Project, 89
Sarfraz, Sardar Naseem, 222
Saudi Pak Bank, 47
Sayeed, Mufti Mohammed, 41
Schools destruction, 45
  See also Earthquake
Sekhon, Lt. Gen. A.S., 48
Self-determination of Kashmiris, 132, 147, 217
Separatism, 155
Shabbir, Tariq, 237
Shah, Ibrahim, 21
Shah, Syed Attaullah, 147
Shah, Syed Muhammed Ikram, 228
Shaheed Bhutto group, 221
Shakar, 17
Shakir, Dr Tariq Mehmood, 236
Shamsuddin- Iraqi, Nur, 16, 21
Shariat Law, 10
Shariff, Nawaz, 133
Sharshing, 30
Sherpao, Aftab Khan, 46, 141
  Shias, 192
  Holding regional Identity, 11
  Brokpa, 31
  Doctrine of Taqqiab, 15
  Groups, 195
  Islam, 17
  Law, 17
  Population, 14
  Sects, 10, 15, 18, 19
Shigar, 16, 18, 24, 34
  Valley, 17
Shigri, Afzal, 71, 80, 188
Shi'ism, 31, 35
  Baltis Conversion, 17-18
  Nur-Bakshi Part, 18
Shin, 10, 14
Woman
  Yashkin marriage, 30

Shiasim, 31, 35
Shinas, 22
Shumar, Mahaz Rai, 221
Siddique, Abu Baker, 62
Siddique-Wa-Amirul Momineen, 62
Sikandar, Farooq, 232
Sikandar Group and Qyyum group rift, 233
Sikkim Tibet Border, 130
Silmo, 31
Sind, 13, 117
Singh, Ghansara, 178
Singh, Sardar Swaran, 128
Singh, Zorawar, 22
Sino_Indian Border dispute, 154
Sino-Indian Conflict (1962), 125, 128, 132, 152-153
Sino-Pak relations, 130
  Business activities, 144
  Border agreement, 129
  China selective in Granting Visa to Pak National, 148
  Bus Service Suspense, 141n
  Economic, 125
  Land route Agreement, 141
  Military exchanges and sales, 131-133
  Trade Agreement, 140-144
Sino-Pakistan Friendship Highway (1978), 136
Sino-Pakistan Frontier Agreement of 1963, 4, 6
Sino-Pak Military strategic Partnership, 125
Sino-Pak- Afghanistan and Central Asia Trade, 142-143
Sipah-e-Muhammed Pakistan (SMP), 60, 61
Sipah-e- Sahaba, (SSP), 44, 60, 77
Sistani, Ayatollah, 83
Skardu, 3, 8, 13, 17, 21, 22, 24, 26, 29, 34, 64, 76, 153
  Buddhist movement protection, 25
  Dam, 91
Small Dams, 119
Smuggling, 140, 145, 150
  Weapons, 148
Sost Dry Port, 79, 142
Sost-Post, 145
  Clourse, 142
  Reopeing, 142
SAFMA, 194
Soviet Union, 131, 147, 155, 182
  Jihad Against, 61
Special Economic Zone, 144
Spiti, 32
Sri Lanka, 89
Standard Chartered Bank, 47
State Assets Supervision and Administration Commission (SASAC) of China, 138
State governments Archives in Jammu & Kashmir, 180
State Paper on Internal Security Situation, 47
Students Union, 213
  Elections, 213
Student Wing, 213
Subcontinent
  Communist Threat, 127
  Joint defence, 127
Submergence, 137
Sufi meditation discourage, 17
Sub ethmic communities, 10
Sufi Order, 16
Sunni, 192
  Islam, 15, 18
  Jihadi group, 193
  groups, 195

Ideology, 77
- Population, 14
- Schools, 18
- Sect, 18, 19
- Tenets, 18
- Tehreek, 221
- Wahabism , 31

Supreme Judial Council, 100
Suru, 35
Swat,
- Dardic Speaking people in, 28

Swat-Gilgit region, 32
Tahrik-e-Jafria-Pakistan (TJP) 25,195
Tajikistan, 138,145
Taliban, 65,82,149
Tangdhar, 204
Tangir, 5, 29
Tanjeem-e-Ahle-Sunnah wal Jammaat, 195
Tangmarg Explosion, 41
Tarhela, 110
- Dam, 117

Tareen, Sakhiullah, 65
Tarigami, Mohammed Yousef, 41
Tariq, Naheed, 227
Tariq, Sardal, 217
Tashergan-Khunjerab Cost, 137
Tattaapni-Mendhar, 204
Tehrik-e-Hurriyat, 208
Tehreek-e-Nafaz-e-Fiquah-e-Jafria (TNFJ), 10,71
Tehreek-ul-Mujahideen (TuM), 42-43
TeleCommunication lines
- ban, 81
- Chinese assistance, 139

Terrorism, 40, 126,155
- Glohal war, 165
- Casualities, 40-41,48-50
- Incidents, 41-42
- Post-earthquake hole, 51

Terrorist Training Camps, 42,46,48,165
Text books Controversy, 55
Thakot Bridge, 96
Thang, 24
Tharva, 41
Thikse, 24, 34
Tibet, 26, 35, 152, 154,182
Tibetan, 21, 22,25,26,28,32
- Dilect, 35
- Independence Demand, 132
- Languages, 27
- Spript, 24,25,34

Tiliwaldi, Ismail, 139
Titbwal, 204
Tolerance
- Nur-Bakshna Emphasis, 17

Tourism Promotion, 145
- Decline in tourist flow, 140

Tirakhan dynasty, 15
Transmission Costs, 95
Treaty of 1963, 154
Tribal Regions of the North West Frontier Province, 190
Tulsibagh, 41
Turahi, Ahdel Imtiaj, 220
Turfan Schools, 21
Thirtuk, 24,34
Turuk, 132
Twelver Shism, 14,15,16,1721
Tyakshi, 24
Udhampur district, 4
Uighurs
- Chinese arrest, 148
- Chinese Engineers Killings, 150
- Enrolment in Pak Schools, 147
- Gherrilla warfare in Pakistan, 148
- Pak Close Settlements and markets, 149
- Violent against Chinese, 148

Ulema

Protest against Mosque demolition, 238
Ullah, Saif, 63
Unemployed Youth, 145
Unemployment Action Committee in Gilgit, 11
United Jihad Council (UJC), 164-165
United Nations, 48, 149,183
American Position on Chinese membership, 128
UN Committee on Economic, Social and Cultural Reports, 115
UN Global Security Report on Water Conflict and Cooperation, 87
UN's Guiding Principles, 169-170
Upper Kotmale Hydropower Project, Sri Lanka, 89-90
UN Observer Office, 232
UN Negotiations, 4
United Nation Resolutions, 11, 132, 163, 230
UN Security Council, 133
Resolutions, 238
United National World Water Development Report, 88
Upper Hunza Valley, 33
Upper Yarkun Valley, 33
Upper Valley of Ishkoman, 33
Urumqi, 142,150,151
Urumqi City Commercial Bank (UCCB), 2006,144
USA, 80,83
State Department, 43
Uzbekestan, 138
Vajpayee, Atal Bihari, 131
Violence, 20,40,50,193
Vocational Training Institute (VTI), New City, 112
Voters Registered, 222
Wahabi, 23
Missionaries, 25
Wahabism, 18
Waheed, Shreen, 204
Wakhan Corridor, 33, 138
Wakhan Patti, 145
Wakhi, 28, 33
Water
Agreements, 88
Availability, 110
Chinese Aid, 139
Conflictive events, 88
Course, 118
Fight, 88
Global FFA, 94
Involved Violence, 88
Issues, 90
Long Term Vision, 93
Mega Reservoir (MAF), 94
Musharraf Vision 2025, 115
Military acts, 88
Per Capita Availability, 117
Policy, 119
Pollution, 119
Potential source of conflict, 87
Preventive steps, 88
Quality, 119
Regional Framework for Action (RFA),93-94
Resources, 90, 118-119
Security, 119
Sharing Tension Between Countries, 90
Storage, 115-116
Stress, 92, 115
Supply, 94
Turbine, 105
UN Report, 88
Vision in 2005, 94
Wars Prophecy, 88
Wastage, 118

World Water Vision, 93
Water and Power Development Authority (WAPDA), 98, 94, 107-108, 110-111, 113
Washington Report on Middle East Affairs, 89
Wazeristan, 150
Weekly K2, the
  Ban, 199
West Asia
  Western Countries role, 160
Wolf, Aaron T, 87
Women Seats in Union Councils, 186
World Bank, 89, 107, 108, 120, 138
World Social Forum Karachi, 133
World Water Council, 115n
World Water Vision of the World Water Council (WWC), 93
Xinjiang, 125, 135, 137, 140, 143, 144
and Pakistan, 144
  Chinese domination, 147
  Contact between Northern Area and, 126
  Department of Foreign Trade and Economic Cooperation, 143
  Major Bank, 144
  Muslim Unrest, 147
  Pak fundamental activities, 148
  Self-determination hopes, 147
Yaseen Malik Group, 212
Yashkun, 10,14
  Caste, 30
  Woman Shin Marriage with, 30
Yasin, 5, 15, 29, 30, 33, 77
  Different dialects, 27
Yasin, Gohar Aman, 12
Yasin, Ch. Muhammad, 230, 233
Yazid, 63
Youth organization, 11
Youth wing, 213
Zaffar, Shibazada 1shaq, 205, 210, 229, 231
Zaman, Sardar Qamaunz, 225, 233
Zandre, 30
Zanskar, 32
Zardari, Asif Ali, 233
Zen zam, 32
Zhou Enlai, 130
Zia-ul-Haq, 10, 11, 57, 58, 59, 60, 70, 185-186
Zulquanin, Raja, 226
Zun zan, 32